Gravitas for Leaders

# Gravitas for Leadership

*How to Make an Impact and
Be Taken Seriously*

ANDREW J. DUBRIN

Toplight

*Jefferson, North Carolina*

ISBN (print) 978-1-4766-9919-6
ISBN (ebook) 978-1-4766-5765-3

LIBRARY OF CONGRESS CATALOGING-IN-PUBLICATION DATA

Library of Congress Control Number 2025041699

Front cover photograph © Shutterstock

Printed in the United States of America

Toplight is an imprint of McFarland & Company, Inc., Publishers

Toplight

*Box 611, Jefferson, North Carolina 28640
www.toplightbooks.com*

# Table of Contents

# Table of Contents

## Table of Contents

# Acknowledgments

Thank you to Layla Milholen and other members of the editorial team at McFarland and Toplight Books for accepting *Gravitas* for publication. Thanks also to the production team getting the manuscript into print, and for the marketing team making the book available to the public. Appreciated also are the people with gravitas whom I have met in person or through the media over the years who have given me insights into the nature of being taken seriously.

Writing without loved ones would be a lonely task. My thanks therefore go to my family: Drew, Heidi, Douglas, Gizella, Melanie, Justin, Rosie, Clare, Michael, Camila, Sofia, Eliana, Julian, Carson, Owen, and Drake. Thanks also to another part of my family, Stefanie, the woman in my life, and her daughter Sofie.

# Preface

*Gravitas for Leadership* deals in depth with the need for present and aspiring leaders to be taken seriously by other people—often referred to as having *gravitas*. *Gravitas* has many meanings, as will be described in Chapter 1, but as a starting point the following definition will point in the direction of the key topic of this book: Gravitas refers to seriousness, dignity, a certain depth of personality, and authority. The purpose of this book is to help the reader understand in depth the nature of gravitas and how it can be developed to enhance leadership and professional effectiveness.

This book describes opinion and research about the most relevant aspects of gravitas as it applies to leadership and professional effectiveness, yet the emphasis is on leadership. Equally important, each chapter contains suggestions for making better use gravitas. Some of the suggestions are listed at the end of each chapter, labeled "Guidelines for Action." A self-quiz is provided in nine of the chapters to help the reader personalize the major idea under consideration. Among the self-quizzes are those related to value clarification, big picture thinking, making others feel important, imagination, propensity for risk-taking, and blunder committing. Most key points throughout the book are illustrated with examples, both made-up and real-life. Case histories of business leaders who demonstrate gravitas, including Walmart CEO Doug McMillon, are included.

Gravitas as it relates to leadership effectiveness is covered from many angles. Among these topics are the nature and career impact of gravitas, components of gravitas relating to the self, and those relating to others. We also describe key leadership gravitas actions and behaviors, key leadership skills for gravitas, charisma and gravitas, and executive presence and gravitas. A description is provided about developing the internal and interpersonal attributes of gravitas, and actions and attitudes that detract from gravitas.

# 1

# The Nature and Career Impact of Gravitas

A fundamental need for present and aspiring leaders is to be taken seriously by other people. If a person is not taken seriously by superiors and coworkers, that person might not be chosen for a leadership position. After being placed in a leadership role, the need for being taken seriously intensifies. By definition, a leader is supposed to influence people toward attaining worthwhile goals. Without being taken seriously, influencing others is close to impossible.

The word *gravitas* is now used frequently in reference to a person who is taken seriously. *Gravitas* is the Latin word meaning dignity, weight, or seriousness. In modern use the term refers to seriousness of demeanor, as well as having real substance.[1] Gravitas is part of what gets leaders listened to, respected, promoted, and assigned choice opportunities. Having effective communication skills may contribute to being perceived as having gravitas, but gravitas reflects the total person including actions and accomplishments.

The purpose of this book is to help the reader understand in depth the nature of gravitas and how it can be developed to enhance leadership and professional effectiveness. To begin, we take a deeper look at some of the many meanings of gravitas.

To get started thinking about how the subject of gravitas applies to you, you are invited to take the accompanying self-quiz.

## The Gravitas Checklist

To reflect on your present level of gravitas, respond "Yes" or "No" to the statements on the checklist below. We understand that this checklist relies on subjective perceptions and is therefore not considered to be a valid psychological test of gravitas. Instead, it is an instrument for self-reflection that might provide clues for personal development.

| Statement about Gravitas | Yes | No |
|---|---|---|
| 1. People come to me for advice frequently. | | |
| 2. I am often asked my opinion on work-related topics. | | |
| 3. When I am in a meeting, people tend to listen to what I have to say. | | |
| 4. I have a lot of high-quality contacts and followers on social media. | | |
| 5. I have received many compliments for the quality of my work. | | |
| 6. At least once in my life I have been described as a "go-to" person. | | |
| 7. I would rate my ability to accomplish goals as well above average. | | |
| 8. My ability to concentrate on my work is better than most people I have observed. | | |
| 9. I attempt to help people rather than laugh at their mistakes. | | |
| 10. I accomplish something worthwhile almost every day, whether on the job or in my personal life. | | |

**Scoring and Interpretation:** The more times you checked "Yes," the stronger your gravitas tendencies. It might be helpful to have one or two people who know you well answer the questions about you to help verify the objectivity of your answers.

## A Variety of Definitions and Meanings of Gravitas

A challenge in having or developing gravitas is that the attribute is more complicated and nuanced than most people think. Carefully examining a variety of definitions of gravitas as it applies to the workplace will help clarify what being taken seriously means in practice.

1. Gravitas was one of the four Roman virtues. It indicates seriousness, dignity, a certain depth of personality, and authority.[2] This definition is presented first because it is consistent with the meaning of gravitas used throughout this book.

2. According to Manfred Kets de Vries, a psychoanalyst and professor of leadership development at INSEAD, it is difficult to pin down exactly what people mean when they use the word "gravitas."

Yet he writes that gravitas connotes seriousness of purpose, solemn and dignified behavior. The person is also perceived as important and compelling while combining style and substance.[3]

3. Gravitas is the extent of your seriousness, and the authority with which you conduct yourself and communicate. A good level of gravitas, when required, can encourage feelings of trust and respect in others.[4]

4. In reference to today's business world, gravitas is an elusive quality that incorporates confidence, authority, and presence. Gravitas helps you become an influential, respected figure who commands attention and achieves success.[5]

5. In the modern era, gravitas is weight, seriousness, or importance. During Roman Imperialism about 2,300 years ago, gravitas was associated with military and civic deeds.[6]

6. Gravitas refers to having expertise in a relevant topic and the ability to speak confidently about your expertise in a way that others notice and are influenced by. A person with gravitas is self-assured, relaxed, approachable, and highly informed about his or her subject.[7]

7. Gravitas refers to a depth of personality, reliability, respect, and trust that draw people to the person.[8]

8. Possessing gravitas at work means that a person is taken seriously, the person's contributions are considered important, and the person is trusted and respected.

9. Gravitas is the combined effect of factors that tell the world you are the real deal, a heavyweight in your field and in the organization. As a result, you are someone worthy of being heard and followed.[9] (This definition makes the important point that gravitas is not a single trait but a combination of attributes.)

An underlying theme to these related definitions of gravitas is that a person with these qualities is taken seriously. As a result, the person with gravitas is listened to carefully and influences others—an essential attribute for a leader.

Our first example of a leader with gravitas is Andy Jassy, who succeeded Jeff Bezos as the president and chief executive officer of Amazon.com. Jassy joined Amazon in 1997, and before founding Amazon Web Services he held a series of leadership positions in the company, including those involved with business-to-business and direct sales to consumers. All these positions presumably required heavy thinking and determination. The choice of Jassy to succeed Bezos surprised many business analysts. Jassy was a technologist rather than a person with deep retail experience. Yet with the future of retail being so tied to artificial intelligence, Bezos thought that Jassy would be a good CEO fit for the future of the company.

An early-career indicator of Jassy's seriousness of purpose is his formal education. Jassy obtained an AB from Harvard University and an MBA from Harvard Business School. Later in his career Jassy founded and was the head of Amazon Web Services (AWS) from its inception. He served as CEO of AWS from 2016 until 2021.

A major demonstration of Jassy's seriousness of purpose was when he focused Amazon on becoming a profitable company. The vision of Bezos was to build an enormous customer-centric company, and the profits would ultimately follow. Jassy felt more pressured by investors to bring about profitability more quickly. In 2022 and 2023 Jassy spearheaded slashing expenses through layoffs and eliminating unproven ventures. He pared back underperforming projects in health care and grocery stores, placed a freeze on corporate hiring, and eliminated 27,000 positions. Under Jassy's leadership, Amazon changed into a leaner version of itself. In July 2023, Amazon posted earnings that almost doubled the projection of analysts, a surprise that had not happened since the fourth quarter of 2020.

Although it may appear that Jassy's gravitas is focused on cost cutting, he also takes a lofty view of the future. In reference to how artificial intelligence (AI) can bolster the sales of AWS, Jassy said to investors, "I would like to have the challenge of having to spend a lot more capital on generative AI because it will mean that customers are having success, and they're having success on top of our services."[10]

## *What Gravitas Is Not*

A complete understanding of what gravitas is includes recognizing what it is not. Above all, gravitas is not fake seriousness to enhance your image or distance yourself from other people by acting superior to them.[11] Faking gravitas is much like an emotionally immature person who is usually disruptive during meetings. He or she decides to act seriously in one meeting because a high-level executive will be attending.

Organizational psychologist Rebecca Newton explains that displaying gravitas does not mean putting up a front that masks your true personality. You do not have to compromise your values and preferred working style to be taken seriously and respected. Newton describes this type of gravitas as *surface gravitas*. The term refers to such behaviors as posturing, dominance, or self-importance designed to charm or subdue people. In extreme form, these behaviors can be counterproductive, eroding your relationships and diminishing your influence. In contrast, *authentic gravitas* aligns with who we really are.

Building surface gravitas focuses exclusively on outward appearance, typically diminishing a person's authenticity. Newton believes that most leaders and professionals recognize intuitively the hazards of surface gravitas. These people want to be respected and valued, but not if it means hiding their real selves.

Building gravitas by simply putting on an outward appearance can be dysfunctional. Research suggests that authenticity contributes to personal well-being. Authenticity in this context refers to understanding and acting as your real self and includes deep-level and conscious thoughts, emotions, beliefs, and values.[12]

## *The Positive Impact of Gravitas on Your Career*

A major justification for reading about and studying gravitas is that the right amount of this attribute can help a person carry out leadership and professional roles. One of dozens of possible examples is that the advice of a wealth advisor with gravitas will be taken more seriously than if the wealth advisor is perceived as immature and flippant. In this section we focus on how gravitas can improve leadership and professional effectiveness. Other advantages of gravitas, however, will be apparent through the book.

*Leaders with Gravitas Are in Demand.* Many hiring managers are eager to hire individuals who possess self-confidence, dignity, and the ability to connect with other people. Executive coach Lida Citroën explains why. She notes that team members often want to be led by people who possess gravitas. A leader with gravitas can articulate a vision and explain how it will work. Furthermore, such a leader is open to input from others and will help align people to attain team goals. Gravitas gives a leader the credibility to have his or her direction accepted and often has the calm demeanor that contributes to a comfortable working environment.[13]

*Gravitas Contributes to Upward Mobility.* Gravitas is an additional quality that helps talented employees advance in their careers and maintain key positions. People with gravitas are typically more effective in leadership roles, communicate more effectively, and build stronger networks. It has been observed that leaders who possess gravitas build stronger relationships, win more business for their employers, and get promoted more quickly.

An underlying factor contributing to upward mobility is that people who are perceived to have gravitas are more likely to receive highly positive performance evaluations, including favorable ratings on leadership potential. The opposite is also true in the sense that many people are told during a performance appraisal that they "need more gravitas" to receive a promotion to a major leadership role.[14]

An exceptional example of a business leader whose gravitas facilitated her career mobility is Angela Ahrendts. Her latest position is a senior operating advisor at SKKY Partners, a private equity firm. SKKY was started by the reality star and entrepreneur Kim Kardashian, along with the longtime Carlyle Group consumer head, Jay Sammons. SKKY focuses on making investments in consumer products, e-commerce, media, and entertainment. At SKKY, Ahrendts focuses on identifying and assessing brands and calculating the firm's ability to add value to the brand. She also coaches and mentors executives that SKKY has in its portfolio.

Ahrendts held the position of Apple's head of online retail and physical stores from 2014 until 2019. She left that position amid a slowing of iPhone sales in 2019, a slowdown that proved to be temporary. Ahrendts was one of the most influential and highest paid executives during her tenure at Apple. During her five years with Apple, she integrated the company's physical and digital business to help create a smooth journey for more than one billion visitors a year.

Ahrendts built a strong reputation as CEO of the old-line British clothing company Burberry from 2006 to 2014. During her tenure, company sales tripled, and the stock price quadrupled. Prior to her time at Burberry, Ahrendts acquired intensive experience in women's fashion, with roles as executive vice president at Liz Claiborne and president at Donna Karan. She served as executive vice president of LCI Inc., where she oversaw the acquisition and integration of 25 brands. Ahrendts is a board member of Ralph Lauren, Airbnb, and advertising holding company WPP. She is also chair of the board of Save the Children International.

When Ahrendts joined SKKY Partners, a statement by Kardashian alluded to her gravitas: "Angela's wealth of leadership experience and deep understanding of building brands and influencing culture makes her a perfect fit for the firm." Ahrendts made the following public statement about joining SKKY: "I look forward to bringing my expertise to the team, along with my experience working with creative business leaders, as we invest in great consumer companies and continue to build a great firm."

Another indication of her gravitas is that Ahrendts has been frequently recognized by *Forbes, Fortune,* and the BBC as a Top 100 Global Executive. She received a bachelor's degree in marketing and merchandising from Ball State University in 1981 and has been honored with an Indiana Living Legends award.[15]

*Gravitas Helps a Leader Provide Stability to Group Members.* A group of executive coaches observes that a leader with gravitas can provide group members with a feeling of stability even in a rapidly changing environment. The coaches note that in an uncertain world, it is important to have leaders who steer the ship safely, thereby instilling feelings of stability. Leaders who lack gravitas tend to become over-authoritarian during periods of turbulence, such as a recession.

Andy Jassy at Amazon was able to provide a sense of stability to employees during a period when online retailing became much more competitive. For example, the online retailer Shein was offering clothing similar or identical to Amazon offerings at one-fourth the price. Jassy emphasized how Amazon was adapting to changes and remained strong in providing other companies with information technology services.

*Gravitas Helps Leaders and Professionals Build Relationships.* Gravitas is a subtle attribute that can set successful leaders apart from their less successful counterparts. A major reason is that gravitas contributes to building relationships. An executive with gravitas has the ability to connect with others on a more personal level. Leaders with gravitas are respected by their colleagues, group members, superiors, and clients or customers. The respect helps build relationships, based on behaviors such as the following:

- being empathetic and understanding toward all work associates
- actively listening to others even when they offer opinions that contradict the leader
- encouraging open communication and feedback
- demonstrating a willingness to help and support others[16]

*Gravitas Helps Leaders and Professionals Command Attention.* Leaders and professionals cannot carry out their mission unless they capture other people's attention and prompt them to listen. If you have gravitas, work associates are much less likely to ignore you. Leaders and professionals with gravitas command attention through several techniques, including the following aspects of interpersonal communication:

- speaking clearly and effectively
- maintaining eye contact
- using appropriate body language such as making welcoming hand gestures
- delivering a message with conviction, particularly saying something the leader truly believes[17]

*Gravitas Helps Leaders Display Authority.* Having an impressive job title such as chief information officer helps a leader display authority, but personal attributes also contribute. Executives with gravitas have a way of inspiring trust and making it clear they are in charge. Among the ways leaders with gravitas demonstrate their authority are as follows:

- making tough decisions such as dropping a product that was a longtime sentimental favorite, such as ending production of the Cadillac Sedan DeVille
- delegating tasks effectively, such as assigning the tasks to the people with the talent and experience to accomplish them
- keeping cool under pressure, such as when a labor union is making wage and retirement demands the company cannot afford
- setting high standards and expectations, such as demanding a 10 percent productivity increase from remote workers[18]

*People with Gravitas Are Frequently Asked for Their Opinion on Important Issues.* Legendary tennis player, and now TV tennis commentator and coach, John McEnroe was well known for his frequent bursts of the expression, "Are you serious?" If you have gravitas, people will think that you are serious and have mental stature. As a result, work associates will often ask your opinion on important job-related issues. In addition to enjoying the recognition and flattery, it is inherently enjoyable for many people to share their expertise with superiors, subordinates, and coworkers. Being asked your opinion gives you the opportunity to clarify your thinking on a given issue and receive input from the other person. Here is an example of this frequent type of interchange, with the setting being a retailer of household appliances:

# 1. The Nature and Career Impact of Gravitas

*STORE ASSOCIATE DEREK:* I've been reading a lot lately about credit card debt piling up. One news story said that Americans have accumulated about one trillion dollars in credit card debt. How do you think this piling up of debt might affect our store?

*STORE MANAGER CRYSTAL:* Derek, you are on to something important because most of our customers pay for appliances with a credit card. But when credit card debt gets too difficult for most people to manage monthly, they look for ways to cut back on spending. And for sure, they might be hesitant to add any more charges to their credit card. I could see that many potential customers would hold off on buying a new appliance until they lowered their existing credit-card balance. Have you noticed this tendency?

*DEREK:* Yes, I have, and that's part of the reason I wanted your opinion. A pickle ball buddy of mine said that he and his wife are starting to worry about their credit-card balance. They might not make any more big-ticket purchases until their card payments are less than $200 per month.

*CRYSTAL:* Thanks for the case history that supports my overall observation.

Being asked for advice frequently has another potential advantage. A person who is known to be frequently sought for advice is perceived to be an influencer, and therefore an effective leader or a person with leadership potential. *Social network analysis* is a formal technique to map the relationships and links between and among people. A person who is linked to many other people is considered important and influential. People with gravitas are the individuals who will most likely surface as having many links, and therefore as being influential.

A research study conducted with 56 work teams bears on how leadership stature is related to both giving and receiving advice. The key leadership attribute studied was charisma, which is related to gravitas. As will be explained in detail in Chapter 6, leaders with gravitas are often seen as charismatic, and charismatic leaders are perceived to have gravitas. One major finding in the study was that when a leader is charismatic, the person tends to be a key figure in an informal advice network. Another major finding was leaders who are socially active in giving and receiving advice tended to be perceived as charismatic. The study therefore gives some support to the idea that if you are perceived to be charismatic—perceived as having gravitas—you will be asked of your advice.

Another finding of the study also supports the relevance of charisma, and therefore gravitas to some extent. When leaders occupy a central position in the advice network, team performance tends to be higher.[19]

*Gravitas Helps a Person Receive a Job Offer for a Key Position.* When a person is a candidate for a high-level position, the interviewer often ponders, "Does this person have enough gravitas to carry out the role?" The interviewer asking this question might be the hiring executive, a human resources management specialist, or an industrial psychologist. It is also possible that one, two, or three of these people might be evaluating the same candidate and ponder the same question. The interviewer or interviewers often have in mind such issues as the following:

- Does the candidate seem like somebody group members will respect?
- Is the candidate enough of a heavyweight to carry out this role successfully?
- Does the candidate impress me as somebody I would go to for guidance and direction?
- As an outsider coming into the company, can this person quickly gain the respect of company insiders?
- Has this candidate shown me the type of deep thinking the position requires?
- Does this candidate have the physical appearance of a high-level leader?

You guessed correctly. A person with gravitas has the best chance of being perceived positively with respect to the issues on the mind of the interviewer. In contrast, a candidate for the high-level leadership position who provides superficial and stereotyped answers to the interviewer's questions is likely to be perceived as lacking gravitas. Here is one example. Suppose that the interviewer asks the following question: "Morale is low in the division you would be responsible for. What first step would you take to improve morale?" An answer reflecting gravitas might go something like this: "I would work carefully with human resources to identify the reasons the employees have low morale. I would interview a sampling of employees myself. HR would be asked to also conduct interviews and an attitude survey. After we had an analysis of the causes of low morale, we would work to resolve the problems that were feasible to fix right now." The following answer, however, reflects a lack of gravitas: "At the end of the day, morale boils down to every employee being on board with a great purpose. I would articulate the purpose of the company. I would even explain the purpose of our purpose. Morale would be high quite quickly."

*Gravitas Helps Attract Mentors and Mentees.* The vast majority of successful people have had one or more mentors during their careers. In the past, mentors were almost always higher-ranking people. Today, mentors can be peers and even lower-ranking individuals. A lower-ranking organization member, for example, can educate you on how other parts of the organization work—something you may need to know to advance. Being mentored by a young person, usually for the purpose of learning a new technology, is referred to as *reverse mentoring.*

Many companies assign mentors to company newcomers, but still a person might want to supplement company-assigned mentoring with a mentor found on his or her own. It is particularly helpful to find a mentor with the skills and characteristics you would like to develop. For example, if you want to develop charisma, attempt to find a charismatic mentor. Sometimes you can develop a mentor from contacts made on social media.

Whether a person attracts a mentor from in-person physical contacts or online, projecting gravitas is a major factor in attracting the mentor you want. The reason is that desirable mentors are in demand, yet they have limited time for mentoring. It might be true that part of a leader's role is to mentor, but mentoring must be squeezed into a busy schedule. Coworkers and reverse mentors also have full work schedules, and mentoring is unlikely to be part of their job description. Potential mentors are therefore selective in whom they choose to mentor. Mentees, or protégés, are often chosen based on gravitas-related factors such as:

- the person's perceived advancement potential
- whether the potential mentee can offer something of value in return, such as industry knowledge
- whether or not the person looks to be a "winner"
- the extent to which the person appears serious about his or her career
- the level of commitment the person appears to have to the organization

If part of being a leader, or a corporate professional, is being a mentor, it helps to attract quality mentees. The question the leader or professional might ask is "Why would a high-quality person want me as a mentor?" The answer is that displaying gravitas helps make you an attractive potential mentor. Among the criteria a desirable potential mentee might have in wanting to be mentored by a specific individual are:

- how much influence the person has in the organization
- the depth of knowledge the person has in his or her field
- the seriousness the person might have about the mentorship role
- how committed this person might be to helping the mentee in his/her career

In sum, being perceived as a person with gravitas is an asset for attracting mentors or mentees. Even if people are not aware of the term *gravitas*, they are aware of its attributes.

*Gravitas Helps Lead People Through a Crisis.* Crisis leadership is so important that it has become the subject of hundreds of books, articles, and Internet posts. Among the potential crises facing organizations are drastic revenue decline; pending bankruptcy; homicide in the workplace; scandalous or criminal behavior by executives; natural disasters, such as hurricanes, floods, and earthquakes, and epidemics; terrorist attacks and violent protests; and a cruise ship being shipwrecked. Even a less dramatic event, such as a spike in interest rates, can create a crisis for a home builder. Here we focus on several approaches to crisis leadership that require the leader to have gravitas.

Displaying optimism is helpful during a crisis. Pessimists abound in every crisis, so an optimistic leader can help group members overcome the bad times. A helpful starting point is to model an optimistic attitude by such means as celebrating when a team hits a milestone like winning back a major customer. Building relationships, a key gravitas quality, is particularly important during a crisis.

A leader who displays sadness and compassion helps group members work through a crisis. An organizational crisis is a sad event, making it imperative that leaders deal with their emotions as well as those of the group. Leaders should be able to express sadness about the crisis, such as expressing sadness that a former employee has injured several current employees. Compassion is also important because it shows that the leader cares about the plight of employees caught up in the negative consequences of the crisis.

Effective leaders exhibit gravitas by staying calm and performing steadily under heavy workloads and uncertain conditions. Remaining steady under crisis conditions contributes to effectiveness because it helps team members cope with the situation. When the leader remains calm, group members are reassured that things will work out. Stability also helps the leader appear cool and professional under pressure—a key gravitas component.

The ultimate gravitas-related approach to helping an organization or organizational unit through a crisis is transformational leadership (making big, positive changes). Leadership coach Gordon Tredgold writes that when leaders face a volatile, uncertain, complex, and ambiguous environment, the transformational leadership style is best.[20] The transformational leader can often lead that organization out of its misery. Transformational leadership is likely to benefit the troubled organization both in dealing with the immediate crisis and performing better in the long run. Another way a transformational leader helps a company or work unit cope with a crisis is to establish a climate of trust long before a crisis strikes.[21] If workers and other stakeholders trust the leader, they will take more seriously the leaders' directives during a crisis.

*Gravitas Prompts Workplace Associates to Quote You.* A personally gratifying positive consequence of having gravitas is that you are likely to be quoted more than others in the organization. Holding a high-level position also facilitates being quoted frequently, but the combination of a high-status position and gravitas has a more powerful effect. Quotes in organizations are frequently based on comments made during in-person meetings, video conferences, or social media posts. Yet one-on-one statements made during conversations or through emails and text messages might be a source of quotes. Here are a few examples of how high-gravitas people might be quoted:

- "I heard Tanya [the chief marketing officer] say that half of our product line well be obsolete in four years, so we better do some heavy product brainstorming soon."
- "Jared in HR told me that if we don't start hiring more refugees soon the EEOC [Equal Employment Opportunity Commission] will be on our back. He could be right."
- "Conrad, one of our facilities engineers, said that the office tower we are in is sinking one-eighth of an inch each year. He's a sharp engineer, so maybe we should find a new building or work from home."

*Gravitas Helps Build an Enterprise from Scratch.* Launching almost any kind of successful business requires multiple skills. Among them are in-depth knowledge of your product or service, imagination, perseverance, and often the ability to convince investors that you should be taken seriously. Being taken seriously also helps develop the network of influential people who might become early customers. A robust example of a person who helped build an enterprise from scratch is Brian Chesky. Along with Nathan Blecharczyk and Joe Gebbia, he founded the peer-to-peer and home rental company Airbnb in 2008. A former body builder, Chesky attended the Rhode Island School of Design. After graduation he worked as an industrial designer in Los Angeles before Airbnb achieved success as an enterprise.

Chesky has embedded his creative talents in Airbnb's culture, product, and community. The design-driven approach has fostered a system of trust that enables strangers to live together and developed a business model that facilitates connections and belongings. (That's not to say that Airbnb is devoid of problems such as renters wrecking people's homes and Airbnb rentals sometimes being used for illicit purposes.) Here is a sampling of Chesky's gravitas-style thinking that might also be referred to as strategic in nature.

- In 2023, Chesky thought it was time to reboot his entire business back to its roots. Airbnb emphasized renting single rooms as opposed to whole houses or apartments. The company began as a way to stay in another person's house. "When we came up with the idea," Chesky recalled, "people thought the idea was crazy. They said, 'Strangers will never stay with other strangers.'" But the idea worked well.
- Chesky said that a lot of founders, especially those who have a largely successful app, get a little bored with their core business. Airbnb started focusing on a lot of new offerings. Over the years, Chesky felt like the company needed to get back to its roots, back to the original ethos of sharing. Affordability is a key factor.
- Chesky observed that, as a company succeeds, a founder may come to have less in common with customers. Airbnb doesn't cater just to 41-year-old tech founders, after all, so Chesky has to remember who he was when he started the company: a 26-year-old with limited money.
- According to Chesky, a challenge Airbnb faces is that it has only so many marketing dollars. Is it best to spend them to build demand or supply? The best answer, in Chesky's view, is to try to create one marketing message that speaks to both audiences. The idea is to promote rooms to stay in but at the same time

prompt people to consider spare rooms in their own homes as potential moneymakers.

- In 2022, the company initiated a policy that stated Airbnb employees could live and work anywhere. Yet Chesky thinks the future of work is not remote per se, but flexible. He wants to combine the best of Zoom with the best of working in physical proximity. The company does not want to recreate the world of Wall-E where everybody is staring at screens the entire day, and no one has any interaction in the physical world.[22]

## *The Potential Downside of Gravitas*

As with almost all human attributes, it is best to have an optimum level of gravitas. An analogy can be drawn to the personality trait of conscientiousness. We choose conscientiousness as an analogy because it is but one component of gravitas. It is well known and well documented that conscientiousness relates positively to job performance. Workers who score low on this trait are often poor performers, are neglectful about their responsibilities, and might be frequently late and absent. Workers with a high standing on conscientiousness take their responsibilities seriously and diligently pursue work goals. Yet there is a downside to being super-conscientious in the workplace. Super-conscientious workers follow rules and processes so carefully that they are sometimes reticent to inject a little creativity into accomplishing their work.

Having too much gravitas also has a potential downside. The leader who is overly infused with gravitas might project so much weight, seriousness, and authority that others perceive him or her to be unapproachable and distant. Equally bad, the leader with excessive gravitas might be perceived as boring. As reported by an executive coaching firm, signs of being stuck in the gravitas trap include the following:

- being perceived as unapproachable
- having a tendency to ignore negative feedback because of high self-confidence
- relying on a small range of facial expressions
- believing that the high stakes responsibilities of his or her office do not allow for spontaneity or risk-taking[23]

We emphasize that the above downsides would most likely surface only in those leaders and professionals who are smug and low on self-awareness. Few people have to worry about having excessive gravitas.

---

# Guidelines for Action

1. Being taken seriously merits serious attention. Unless you are taken seriously you may not be chosen for a leadership position. Once in a leadership position, you need to be taken seriously to influence others.

2. Gravitas warrants your attention because it is part of what garners leaders attention, respect, and choice opportunities.

3. Carefully examining a variety of definitions of gravitas as it applies to the workplace will help clarify what being taken seriously means in practice.

4. Gravitas is not fake seriousness to enhance your image or distancing yourself from others by acting superior to them. Nor does it mean putting up a front that masks your true personality.

5. If you develop gravitas as a leader and have other talents, you will be able to receive better performance evaluations, advance further in your career, and hold on to key positions.

6. If you develop gravitas, you will be able to connect with others on a more personal level based on behaviors such as actively listening to people even when they have an opinion contradictory to yours.

7. If you have gravitas, work associates are much less likely to ignore you.

8. If you have gravitas, work associates will often ask your opinion on important job-related issues.

9. Having gravitas is a major consideration in being evaluated positively for a major leadership role during a job interview.

10. Projecting gravitas is a major factor in attracting the mentor you want, as well as in attracting quality mentees.

11. Should you be leading a group through a crisis, gravitas will help you display optimism, sadness, and compassion; stay calm; and perform steadily.

12. A personally positive consequence of having gravitas is that you are likely to be quoted by other organizational members.

13. Gravitas can contribute to your ability to start an enterprise from scratch by helping you develop the social network you need and be taken seriously by potential investors.

14. As with almost all human attributes, it is best to develop an optimum level of gravitas, to avoid being perceived as unapproachable and distant.

**2**

# Components of Gravitas
# Relating to the Self

The journey toward understanding gravitas in depth is to examine its components or elements. Because gravitas is a comprehensive concept, it has many components. In this chapter we concentrate on those components of gravitas that primarily focus on individual attributes such as values and big-picture thinking. In the following chapter we emphasize attributes that focus more on interpersonal relationships. The categories, however, blur, such as emotional intelligence being an individual attribute that involves interpersonal relationships.

## Displaying Gravitas Through Your Work

Gravitas goes beyond such factors as speaking well, dressing well, and making interesting comments. Gravitas can also be expressed through one's work. Leaders and professionals with gravitas are typically passionate about their work. Before delving into several ways in which gravitas can be displayed through work, take the accompanying self-quiz about work attitudes. It will help you think through some of the thought patterns involved in whether work is a force for gravitas in your life.

---

### The Work Attitude Quiz

**Directions:** Indicate how well you agree with the following statements by circling the appropriate response: strongly disagree (**SD**), disagree (**D**), neutral (**N**), agree (**A**), or strongly agree (**SA**).

## Gravitas for Leadership

| Statement about work | SD | D | N | A | SA |
|---|---|---|---|---|---|
| 1. My work is a direct expression of me. | 1 | 2 | 3 | 4 | 5 |
| 2. Sometimes I'm oblivious to the rest of the world when I am working. | 1 | 2 | 3 | 4 | 5 |
| 3. At times I am so absorbed in my work that I forget to stop for food or drink breaks. | 1 | 2 | 3 | 4 | 5 |
| 4. I often get drowsy at work. | 5 | 4 | 3 | 2 | 1 |
| 5. The best part of my work is the fact that I get paid. | 5 | 4 | 3 | 2 | 1 |
| 6. My work is a source of major excitement in my life. | 1 | 2 | 3 | 4 | 5 |
| 7. My workspace is a mess. | 5 | 4 | 3 | 2 | 1 |
| 8. During the day I waste a lot of time accessing websites not directly related to my work. | 5 | 4 | 3 | 2 | 1 |
| 9. My projects and assignments are almost always finished on time. | 1 | 2 | 3 | 4 | 5 |
| 10. My work is a great source of fun for me. | 1 | 2 | 3 | 4 | 5 |
| 11. At times in my life when I have been lonely, my work has been a source of solace to me. | 1 | 2 | 3 | 4 | 5 |
| 12. Coworkers and managers marvel at my productivity. | 1 | 2 | 3 | 4 | 5 |
| 13. I don't recall a boss of mine complimenting me on my dedication to work. | 5 | 4 | 3 | 2 | 1 |
| 14. Watching my favorite shows (including news and sports) on TV or by streaming is more exciting to me than my work. | 5 | 4 | 3 | 2 | 1 |
| 15. At the start of most workdays, I tingle with excitement. | 1 | 2 | 3 | 4 | 5 |

**Scoring and Interpretation:** Add the numbers you have circled, then look at the interpretation for the range into which you fall.

| | |
|---|---|
| **60–75** | You are so passionate about your work that it probably adds to your gravitas. |
| **46–59** | There are times when your work attitudes and approach to work contribute to others perceiving you as having gravitas, but the tendency is not pronounced. |
| **15–45** | The way in which you perform your work, and your attitudes toward your work, probably detract from the serious image you want to project. A role in which you could become more passionate about your work might enhance your gravitas. |

## 2. Components of Gravitas Relating to the Self

*Strive for Peak Performance.* At their best, people with gravitas experience *peak performance,* or total absorption in what they are doing at the time. This type of total absorption is frequently referred to as *mindfulness.* Total absorption helps you perform at close to your capacity. The total absorption and passion for the task project gravitas. The attributes of peak performers point toward how this total absorption or *flow experience* can be attained.[1]

1. *A sense of mission.* Peak performers almost always have a sense of mission. They strive for a broader purpose and motivate others with their mission, which contributes directly to their gravitas. The mission might touch thousands of people, such as the mission to build and distribute safe gas stoves. Or the mission might be more limited in scope, such as sheltering people without housing in one neighborhood.

2. *Concern about results and processes.* Peak performers want to achieve outstanding results, so they set high goals consistent with their mission. Yet they also care about how they achieve these results. The peak performer cares about the minute details involved in a project.

3. *Mental and physical calmness.* A remarkable attribute of peak performers is their mental and physical calmness as they proceed with their work. While focusing on the task they love, they are at ease. The ease and calmness of peak performers adds to their gravitas. It is impressive to observe somebody producing outstanding results so calmly.

4. *Great powers of concentration.* Mental and physical calmness enable the peak performer to concentrate hard enough to attain high performance. An ability to concentrate intently contributes mightily to gravitas because others will be impressed by your focus.

5. *Sensory acuity.* Being mentally and physically calm also assists the peak performer in sensing and responding to relevant cues in the environment. Although the peak performer experiences total concentration, he or she will still respond to important signals. For example, the peak performing industrial sales representative will detect a prospect's facial expression indicating it is not quite the right time to say, "I have the contract ready for your e-signature." Instead, he or she might say, "I think we should talk about any other concerns you may have about committing your company."

6. *A results orientation.* To achieve peak performance, a person must produce meaningful results. As obvious as this statement may

seem, think about the people you know who work hard but produce very little. In the workplace, these people conduct a lot of meetings, produce exquisite computer graphics, and talk impressively, yet useful output can rarely be found.

7. *An ability to correct course.* Peak performers can detect when they are off course. The peak performer senses when he or she has strayed from the best path toward goal attainment and then redirects activity. The ability to process feedback from the environment is an important part of knowing when you are off course. Suppose that middle-manager Natalie wants to lighten up her seriousness by telling jokes around the office. She tries a series of jokes and receives very few laughs or smiles. Natalie then shifts to making humorous comments rather than telling jokes and receives more favorable reactions from office mates.

8. *A penchant for self-management.* Peak performers practice self-management in the form of achieving results without constant prodding by a supervisor. Achieving difficult goals reinforces the belief that they can attain even more difficult goals whether set by themselves or their managers.

9. *Reinvention of the self.* A core value of the corporate athlete is continual renewal and continual self-reinvention. (Being a "corporate athlete" enhances your gravitas.) Self-renewal refers to the conscious, ongoing efforts to rejuvenate and regenerate oneself. In practice, self-renewal might refer to quickly adapting to a new role, such as logistics specialist taking on a human resources management assignment.

*Be a Fixit Person.* Being a troubleshooter or a leader who can turn around a troubled situation adds immensely to a person's gravitas. At a high organization level, the fixit person is considered a transformational leader. An example of a business leader with exceptional fixit and transformational abilities is Mark Thompson, who was named chairman and CEO of CNN in September 2023. CNN, a once dominant network, had drifted away from objective news reporting and shifted to strongly liberal commentary. CNN fell far behind both Fox News and MSNBC in viewership.

Before joining CNN, Thompson received considerable credit for transforming the *New York Times* into a digital newsroom, as the print edition was losing many subscribers. The digital overhaul included the addition of podcasting, the acquisition of a shopping recommendations website, and the addition of new digital subscriptions such as NYT Cooking. Thompson had also fixed major problems at the British Broadcasting Company (BBC). At BBC, Thompson pioneered on-demand viewing, launching iPlayer long before Netflix popularized streaming.

When Thompson joined CNN, David Zaslav, the CEO of the company that owns CNN, made a comment that illustrates the fixit capability and gravitas of Thompson: "Mark is a true innovator who has transformed for the digital age two of the world's most respected news organizations." In 2023, restoring CNN to its past glory was considered a Herculean task, but those who know him agreed that if anyone is capable of the task, Thompson can.[2] Yet, by 2025, the restoration still had a long way to go.

*Display High-Level Skills and Abilities.* A foundational component of gravitas is a person's skills and abilities, as implied in the mention of Mark Thompson. At the beginning of a person's career the foundation of being perceived as a person of substance is to display competence in your field. You might refer to this knowledge as functional, discipline related, or technical. The word *technical* today connotes information or communication technology, but all fields have technical details. Technical knowledge usually must be combined with interpersonal skills to advance into a leadership role. Yet without performing well in a person's own discipline, he or she will not be taken seriously enough to be considered for a leadership role.

Displaying high-level skills and abilities gives a person authority that is based on how that person brings experience, knowledge, and qualifications to the work task at hand.[3] An extreme example is that during a major forest fire, people with authority in fighting fires are called in from around the world. Authority is a key component of gravitas.

## Self-Confidence and Decisiveness

Another foundational component of gravitas is to project the image that you believe in yourself and that you can accomplish almost all tasks within your field of competence. We mention *within your field of competence* because a person with sensible self-confidence recognizes that his or her skill set has limits. A self-confident finance executive, for example, would be hesitant to suggest a new method of routing the company truck fleet to save on energy costs.

A leader who is self-confident—self-assured without being bombastic or overbearing—instills self-confidence in team members. A self-confident team leader of a group facing a seemingly impossible deadline might tell the group, "We are understaffed and overworked, but I know we can get this project done on time. I've been through tough demands like this before. If we work like a true team, we can pull it off."

Decisiveness stems from self-confidence and is a key component of gravitas. The leader or professional with self-confidence can say something to the effect, "If we take the following action, we will get the results we want." Visualize Nikki, a human resources recruiter with a high level of self-confidence. She tells the chief human resources director, "If we recruit IT talent in four-year colleges and career schools in obscure locations, I am certain we will find the talent we need. Good talent is not confined to students who attend schools with a reputation for academics or sports. Our selection procedures will uncover undiscovered talent."

Gravitas researcher Sylvia Ann Hewlett notes that self-confidence includes grace under fire and is a major component of gravitas. During a high-pressure or crisis situation, the person who possesses grace under fire will take appropriate action. The person will not worry about possible personal shortcomings that could make resolving the problem difficult. Grace under fire also includes being able to absorb disappointing news without throwing a temper tantrum. So doing projects strengths to work associates.

Hewlett emphasizes that another major component of gravitas is *speaking truth to power*, which can be framed as a manifestation of self-confidence.[4] Speaking truth to power is an affirmation of courage because the person tells someone in power the truth rather than what he or she might want to hear. Sharing your convictions regardless of whether they might conflict with those of a superior is another face of speaking truth to power.

Evan, a customer care manager, observes that the revamped company shopping website that his boss championed results in considerable user confusion. With self-confidence, Evan explains to his boss, "I understand that the new website was supposed to be more useful for our customers and result in more sales. But the truth is that it is too confusing. Our agents spend far too much time in phone conversations with customers trying to navigate our website."

Another facet of self-confidence that contributes to gravitas is courage. Courage comes from the heart, as suggested by the French word for heart, *coeur.* Leaders must face up to responsibility and be willing to put their reputations on the line. It takes the courage of a leader to suggest a new undertaking, because if the undertaking fails, the leader is often seen as having failed. For example, a handful of business leaders have had the courage to emphasize hiring formerly incarcerated people to work as entry-level employees. The "second chance" hiring has been generally successful, but when one formerly incarcerated person fails as an employee, the leader takes the blame.

Sara Nelson, the president of the Association of Flight Attendants, is a leader with self-confidence and courage who has gained the respect of both workers and the corporate leaders she challenges. The TravelPulse website describes Nelson as one of the most powerful union leaders in the aviation industry. In 2022, she was reelected as the international president of the Association of Flight Attendants-CWA, AFL-CIO. Nelson worked for 25 years as a flight attendant and has served as the AFA international president since June 2014. Nelson has been an outspoken advocate for flight attendants, especially when conditions on airplanes often became unruly and even violent starting with the pandemic.

Nelson was seen as instrumental in helping end the 35-day government shutdown in 2019. Her approach reflected bravado and gravitas, but if carried out would have done massive damage to the United States economy, workers included. Nelson's suggestion was a general strike, referring to work stoppages across key sectors of the economy. Her words were, "End this shutdown with a general strike."

*InStyle* magazine once placed Nelson on their "Top 50 Badass Women" list. Nelson led the AFA to some of the most consequential legislative wins in the union's history. An especially notable win was obtaining COVID relief that totaled $54 billion in payroll support to keep aviation workers receiving paychecks, healthcare, and other benefits for 16 months.

Nelson is passionate about AFA's mission to achieve fair compensation, job security, and improved quality of life for flight attendants. She also believes in the importance of a safe, healthy, and secure aircraft cabin for passengers and crew alike.

At Yale Law School, Nelson once gave a lecture titled "Women and Unions: Solidarity Is a Force Stronger than Gravity" (an interesting link to gravitas!). A key point of the lecture was that the AFA's approach to tackling union objectives is to define the problem, state demands, and add urgency. Nelson said that this formula helped keep knives off airplanes, starting in 2013. She also mentioned the FAA's strike tactic

CHAOS, or "create havoc around our system," referring to the practice of unannounced, intermittent strikes, as permitted in labor laws.[5]

## Emotional Intelligence

Emotional intelligence deals in general with managing your emotions effectively, as well as those of work associates. As with gravitas, emotional intelligence is a broad attribute that encompasses several other attributes.[6] Here we mention several aspects of emotional intelligence that contribute the most to gravitas. Emotional intelligence frequently enters into interaction with people but is still a personal attribute.

*Self-Awareness.* Having high self-awareness enables people to know their strengths and limitations and have high self-esteem. High self-esteem, in turn, contributes to gravitas. Self-awareness helps people accurately measure their own moods, and they intuitively understand how their moods affect others. A leader with good self-awareness would recognize such factors as whether he or she was liked or was exerting the right amount of pressure on group members. As a result, the leader would be taken more seriously.

*Self-Management.* This aspect of behavior is the ability to control one's emotions and act with honesty and integrity in a consistent and adaptable manner. The right degree of self-management helps prevent a person from throwing temper tantrums when activities do not go as planned. Throwing temper tantrums quickly reduces a leader or professional's gravitas.

*Social Awareness.* This attribute includes having empathy for others and organizational problems and is considered an essential component of gravitas. Empathy has surged in importance as a key leadership quality. Socially aware leaders go beyond sensing the emotions of others by showing they care and receive respect in return.

*Relationship Management.* This attribute includes the interpersonal skills of being able to communicate clearly and convincingly, disarm conflicts, and build strong bonds. A leader with good relationship skills would not burn bridges and would continue to enlarge his or her personal network to win support when needed, thereby displaying considerable gravitas.

## Defined Set of Values

A value refers to the importance a person attaches to something. Values are also tied into the enduring belief that one's mode of conduct is better than another mode of conduct. Suppose a business leader believes that imitating already successful products is better than spending large amounts of money on research and development. That leader will think that business leaders who invest large sums in research and development are frivolous with money.

Group members are likely to take a leader more seriously when that person has a transparent set of values, meaning that other people can observe those values in action. Suppose that CEO Claudia believes strongly that taxpayers should be able to retain a large amount of their earnings. Simultaneously, she believes the federal and local governments should only tax enough of their money to pay for essential services. To demonstrate her values in action, Claudia would therefore not look for government subsidies for her company.

Claudia's actions demonstrate the integrity aspect of values. According to ethics researcher Thomas E. Becker, integrity goes beyond honesty and conscientiousness. *Integrity* refers to loyalty to rational principles and practicing what one preaches regardless of emotional or social pressures.[7] For example, a leader with integrity would believe that employees should be treated fairly, and the pressure to cut costs would not prompt the leader to renege on paying for fertility treatments for employees. As another example, a leader who preaches cultural diversity would assemble a diverse team.

An executive who leads by values will fortify his or her gravitas. Leading by values means that the leader influences people by demonstrating values that guide the behaviors of others. One opinion is that the ideal values for a leader to pursue would be mutual respect, trust, honesty, fairness, kindness, and doing good.[8] These "ideal values" reflect the values of the person who says they are ideal. Another leader might think the most appropriate value in business and politics is to "do whatever you have to do" to win.

Values are also important in the workplace because they are tied in closely with goals. Our values create within us a desire to behave consistently with them. If an executive values honesty, the executive will establish a goal of presenting only true facts to work associates. Goals are also linked to gravitas because a person who consistently attains useful goals adds to his or her gravitas. Imagine that plant manager Nick establishes the goal of increasing plant productivity by one percent a quarter for the next four quarters. After one year, plant productivity has increased by four percent. Nick will be perceived as a heavyweight by top-level management and his plant management team.

A useful approach to understanding your own values is to clarify them, meaning that you rank various values in terms of their importance to you. After you have identified several values that you consider to be highly important, they might serve as guides to behavior including goal setting and interactions with work associates. If you behave consistently in the pursuit of these values, you will strengthen your gravitas. The accompanying exercise presents an opportunity to clarify your values mostly related to the workplace.

---

# Value Clarification Exercise

Clarifying your values can be uplifting and at the same time help you make decisions based on these values. Rank from 1 to 15 the importance of the following workplace-related values to you as a person. The most important value on the list receives a rank of 1, the least important a rank of 15. Use the space next to "Other value" if the list has omitted an important workplace-related value of yours.

- _____ Being kind to coworkers
- _____ Being admired by coworkers
- _____ Achieving outstanding job performance
- _____ Working for a high-prestige organization
- _____ Operating my own business
- _____ Earning a high income
- _____ Being regarded as having strong leadership ability
- _____ Treating all workers fairly
- _____ Being a knowledgeable, informed person
- _____ Being regarded as a person of high potential
- _____ Being considered as the "Most Valuable Player" on my team
- _____ Being perceived as a highly ethical person
- _____ Helping other people develop and grow
- _____ Being a positive role model for others
- _____ Other value

*Do you find any surprises in these rankings?*

## Positive Reputation

Another noteworthy component of gravitas related to the self is a positive reputation. A reputation is based on a multitude of factors, including accomplishments, problem-solving ability, ethical behavior, fair treatment of others, and strong interpersonal skills. Physician Carmen W. Landrau writes that a positive reputation means that your character and actions are respected and perceived as worthy. People regard you as a true leader, and you are held in high regard.[9]

Ajay Banga, the World Bank president and former CEO of Mastercard, represents a high-level example of a person whose reputation has contributed to his gravitas. After Mastercard, Banga was the vice chairman of the private equity firm General Atlantic. Banga's reputation has been built on kindness to employees, technological acumen, and strategic thinking. During his more than a decade as CEO of Mastercard, shareholders received a total return of close to 1,600 percent, nearly five times the return attained by the S&P 500 index fund. Profits climbed 18.7 percent annually. Mastercard became the 21st most valuable company in the world, up from 256th when Banga was appointed CEO.

Banga explained that he is a traditional believer in capitalism, because the system has lifted so many people out of poverty. He thinks, however, that the system must be repositioned as stakeholder capitalism, or simply capitalism with guardrails. The first guardrail is to take care of employees, such as some kind of stock incentive award. A stock plan aligns two stakeholders, employees and investors. A key value of Banga is that profits are needed to help people. He says, "You've got to do well and do good at the same time. It's not either/or."

Banga has built part of his reputation on his strong conviction about human decency. He says that you need your decency quotient when you come to work every day. "You have to care about the people who work with you, for you, above you, and around you."

On his first day on the job at the World Bank in June 2023, Banga displayed gravitas by asking all employees to work toward his vision "to create a world free from poverty in a livable planet." Banga also interjected his business acumen by noting that the bank had to become more efficient by reducing the approval time for projects that could take up to three years.

During his job interview with the World Bank executive board, Banga demonstrated the type of big-picture thinking that has contributed to his reputation. He estimated that annual investments of trillions of dollars were needed to stop the forces of climate change and fragility, while building up human capital and combatting inequality in health, education, and income. The first month on the job, Banga engaged in another reputation-building activity. He conducted a listening tour of World Bank employees to help understand the complexity of his new role.

A small part of Banga's reputation was based on his enthusiasm. Shortly after joining MasterCard (the previous styling of the company name) in 2009, he developed the reputation of being the company's cheerleader. Banga attempted to shake up the company's low-key culture with hugs and fist bumps in the hallway.[10]

## Grit

Another component of gravitas is a person's ability to keep plugging away at reaching a long-term, worthwhile goal, often referred to as *grit*. As defined by Angela L. Duckworth and her colleagues, who have researched this human quality, grit is perseverance and passion for long-term goals.[11] Other people are likely to take you seriously when you have the fortitude to work diligently toward worthwhile purposes.

The person with grit often wins out over even the more talented person because grit gives you the stamina for the long haul. As is frequently observed by industrial sales managers, the sales representatives who earn the most commissions are not necessarily those with the best persuasive skills or personal appearance. Instead, the winningest reps are those who have decent natural sales skills and who keep plugging along with logical proposals for the long haul. Indeed, the person with grit pursues external goals, but at the same time, he or she enjoys the excitement and inner satisfaction derived from working toward the goal.

The idea that grit is necessary for high achievement evolved during interviews conducted by Duckworth and her colleagues with professionals in a variety of fields, including investment banking, painting, journalism, college teaching and research, medicine, and law. When asked which personal attribute distinguishes star performers in their field, the professionals pointed to grit or a close synonym as frequently as they mentioned natural talent. Many of the interviewees were highly impressed by the achievements of colleagues who did not seem particularly gifted at first but whose sustained commitment to attaining their goals was intense and exceptional. Even more penetrating was the observation that many of the more gifted colleagues did not reach the top of their field.

## Big-Picture Thinking

A major contributor to being perceived as having gravitas is a person's ability to see the big picture or think strategically. The ability of Ajay Banga to see the big picture was mentioned above. The term *big-picture thinking* has several closely related definitions and meanings. A good starting point is to recognize that a big-picture thinker is conceptual thinker—he or she has an overall or global perspective on a situation. The little-picture retail executive thinks, "If we can close two more stores in the Chicago area, we can save $5 million per year in annual operating costs." The big-picture executive says, "True, we can save $5 million in operating costs per year, yet there is a cost. Each store that stays open functions like a permanent advertisement. It reinforces in the consumer's mind that our chain exists, and that we are conveniently located."

The big picture has also been defined as the main or important part of something. A person is said to be a big-picture thinker when he or she can understand a situation or concept as a whole rather than getting bogged down in specific details. Similarly, the big-picture thinker gets the gist of something without getting caught in the details. A couple might be contemplating the purchase of a 300-year-old armoire at an antique store. The detail-oriented husband says, "Forget this ragged old armoire. I see three scratches and one chip." The big-picture-thinking wife says, "This is a magnificent piece of furniture that will blend in perfectly with our other antiques. A few small imperfections do not detract from its beauty and value."

Big-picture thinking can also be described as the way a person perceives problems, opportunities, and situations. A big-picture thinker will often generate many alternative solutions to problems. He or she is likely to be an idea-generator who thinks of huge changes, large projects, and opportunities to start a new business. Big-picture thinking often leads to creativity and innovation.[12] The effective big-picture thinker might rely on others to execute his or her big ideas but does not totally neglect the details, such as an automotive executive making design suggestions about a new model.

An analogy can be drawn between big-picture thinking and the direction of a play. A blogger wrote that if she were the director of a play, she would not be able to see the whole representation or gestalt of a scene if she were on stage directing mixed in with the characters. "Seated off stage in the audience or even in the balcony, I can see the bigger picture of how the actors engage with each other, the lighting, the set design, and the sound quality. I can see things I wouldn't be able to if I didn't set myself apart to view the big picture."[13]

To pursue a big picture of this lofty nature, a person does not have to occupy a position of power or earn a high income. For example, a kindergarten teacher might have what she perceives to be one of the most important purposes in her life. She might explain, "One of my responsibilities is to get five-year-old children on the path to becoming good readers. Without my help these children could never escape poverty or live a comfortable life." Parents and school administrators are likely to perceive this teacher as having gravitas.

*Big-Picture Thinking as Strategic Thinking.* The term *strategy* has several different meanings, with the popular one referring to a person's technique or approach for getting something accomplished. For example, a person might say, "My strategy for keeping ants out of my kitchen is to sweep the floor twice a day to get rid of crumbs, and spray ant-killer poison on the floor." *Strategy* in reference to business and related activities also has several meanings. As used here, strategy refers to an integrated overall concept of how the organization will attain its objectives. Strategy is therefore a master plan for getting big things done. An example of a business strategy is "sticking to core competency." The organization focuses its effort on what it does best to become world-class. A sterling example is the watch company Citizen; it manufactures and sells only watches and has been in business since 1931.

An amusing, but telling, illustration of how big-picture thinking is tied in with strategic thinking is the story behind the Aflac duck. Daniel P. Amos, now the chairman of Aflac (originally, American Family Life Assurance Company) writes that the origins of the ubiquitous duck trace back to the year 2000. At the time, American Family Life Assurance Company was suffering from low name recognition. A radical name change would have required obtaining new insurance licenses in every state, so the company decided on Aflac. The creative group at a New York advertising agency came up with the idea for the Aflac duck because they had difficulty remembering the company name. One day an advertising copywriter asked, "What is the name of the account we're pitching?" A colleague replied, "It's Aflac, Aflac, Aflac." Someone said he sounded like a duck, and the idea for the advertising campaign was born.

The Aflac duck scored well in tryouts by the advertising agency, and the light went on for Amos. He sensed that this duck could somehow help Aflac attain its strategic goals of becoming a leading insurance company. When Amos mentioned the Aflac duck to other executives, all he received was a silent stare. Amos then decided to tell colleagues only that he had decided on a new advertising campaign that attained amazing numbers in preliminary testing.

Visualizing the potential of the duck-themed advertising campaign, Amos decided to run the commercial for two weeks and carefully monitor the results. The first Aflac duck ad was launched on New Year's Day, 2000, on CNN, and ran four times per hour. Again, seeing the big picture, Amos sensed that businesspeople would be watching CNN regularly to see if Y2K was really going to wreak havoc on computer systems. Overwhelming success was attained immediately. On the first day of the telecast, the company had more visits to its website than in the entire year before. Within weeks, Aflac was getting requests for a stuffed animal version of the duck. A subcontractor was hired to manufacture the ducks, and all the proceeds were donated to the Aflac Cancer and Blood Disorders Center in Atlanta.

The Aflac duck was also a sensation when displayed at an event at Disney Studios (even though Donald Duck is king at Disney). Amos knew he'd found a winner, but the big question remained of whether the Aflac duck would help the company attain its business goals. The answer was affirmative, with first-year sales in the United States up by 29 percent. In three years sales had increased 100 percent. Today the name recognition of Aflac is higher than 90 percent.

Aflac was then brought to the Japanese market in 2009 when the company's Japanese marketing team introduced a new version of the duck for a new insurance product. The duck was a blend of the North American duck and the traditional Asian good luck white cat, Maneki-neko. The commercial focused on the cat duck was an enormous success in terms of rated popularity, and increased Aflac revenues by 44 percent over a seven-year period. More than one-half of the company's revenues stem from Japan.

The Aflac duck story is certainly impressive, but for the present purpose, the big-picture thinking of Daniel P. Amos must be scrutinized. Before moving forward with the campaign, Amos reasoned: "Having gotten my college degrees in risk management, I was committed to making the decision the way I'd been taught: Don't risk a lot for a little; don't risk more than you can afford to lose; and consider the odds." The plan was to invest $1 million in the initial campaign, an affordable sum for the company. Amos also felt that the odds were reasonable of getting a good return on the money invested. The big picture was moving Aflac forward on a grand scale, and the little picture was squandering $1 million and some executive time.[14]

The business concept of strategy also has considerable relevance to the individual. The majority of successful people did not attain their goals through simply working hard or being lucky. Instead, they had an overall plan for success including establishing career goals, obtaining the right formal education, continuous learning, and building a network of valuable contacts. Many of these people got the big picture early in life, such as studying a second language seriously in high school to fit better in the new global economy.

An individual within a firm who is not part of top-level management can also profit from thinking strategically and looking at the big picture. Leanne Hoagland-Smith observes that the highest-performing sales professionals schedule time to plan, strategize, and think. They think of the long term, such as "Am I getting the most out of my territory?" They also ponder whether they are investing their time in the areas that produce the greatest return. Successful sales representatives look at each sales opportunity strategically, starting with their goal in mind. They develop tactics to get them to the end goal as quickly and effectively as possible. Should surprises happen, rather than reacting impulsively, they pause to understand, and adjust their strategies as needed.

Top sales professionals understand the value of planning: planning a sales call, planning to make a deal, planning how to maximize growth in their territory, and planning how to most effectively spend their time. Strategic thinking is the way top sales professionals approach every aspect of their jobs. Understanding the big picture is what separates the high-level sales professionals from their counterparts who chase transactions.[15] The strategic thinking of these sales professionals adds to their gravitas.

*Asking Big-Picture Questions as Part of Strategic Thinking.* The big-picture thinker who contributes to business strategy not only has some grand ideas of his or her own but also asks questions that enhance the big-picture thinking of others. If you have formal authority, such as being a high-level manager, others are more likely to answer your questions. Yet asking such questions of coworkers, and even your boss, will also enhance your skills and reputation as a strategic thinker. Here are a few provocative big-picture questions:[16]

- Why is your idea important?
- What will be the impact of your project on the rest of the organization?
- If your project is not approved, how will this hurt the organization?
- Who cares about your proposal? Who will be affected both directly and indirectly?

After these big-picture questions are answered, the effective strategic thinker responds to the answers in a thoughtful way. For example, "I agree that outsourcing our manufacturing of American flags to Mexico would save us considerable money in labor costs, but let's also talk about the potential negative publicity for our company."

The accompanying self-quiz provides you an opportunity to reflect on your present tendencies toward big-picture thinking.

## My Tendencies Toward Big-Picture Thinking

Indicate your strength of agreement with each of the following statements: strongly disagree (SD), disagree (D), neutral (N), agree (A), strongly agree (SA).

| Statement About Big-Picture Thinking | SD | D | N | A | SA |
|---|---|---|---|---|---|
| 1. I get upset if my checkbook does not balance even to the dollar. | 5 | 4 | 3 | 2 | 1 |
| 2. I often think about the meaning and implication of news stories. | 1 | 2 | 3 | 4 | 5 |
| 3. A top-level manager is usually better off finding ways to cut costs than thinking about the future of the business. | 5 | 4 | 3 | 2 | 1 |
| 4. I like(d) to argue with an instructor about what the correct answer to a multiple-choice question should be. | 5 | 4 | 3 | 2 | 1 |
| 5. So long as a company provides good customer service with its present product line, its future is very secure. | 5 | 4 | 3 | 2 | 1 |
| 6. I prefer acquiring knowledge and skills that can help me with my job during the next month rather than those that might help me in the future. | 5 | 4 | 3 | 2 | 1 |

## Gravitas for Leadership

| Statement About Big-Picture Thinking | SD | D | N | A | SA |
|---|---|---|---|---|---|
| 7. It makes me laugh when a CEO says a big part of his or her job is creating visions. | 5 | 4 | 3 | 2 | 1 |
| 8. I have already created a vision for my life. | 1 | 2 | 3 | 4 | 5 |
| 9. I am a "big-picture" thinker. | 1 | 2 | 3 | 4 | 5 |
| 10. If people take care of today's problems, they do not have to worry about the future. | 5 | 4 | 3 | 2 | 1 |
| 11. World events have very little impact on my life. | 5 | 4 | 3 | 2 | 1 |
| 12. An organization cannot become great without an exciting vision. | 1 | 2 | 3 | 4 | 5 |

**Scoring and Interpretation:** Find your total score by summing the point values for each question.

| 52–60 | You are probably already a big-picture thinker, which should help you in your career and will probably add to your gravitas. |
|---|---|
| 30–51 | You probably have a neutral, detached attitude toward thinking big. |
| 12–29 | Your thinking probably emphasizes the here and now and the short term. People in this category usually do not focus on the implications of their work and might not be perceived as having gravitas. |

---

# Guidelines for Action

1. Having passion for your work is a strong building block for developing gravitas because it helps you be taken seriously.

2. Total absorption in your work helps you attain peak performance, which is a component of gravitas.

3. If you can attain mental and physical calmness it will assist you in attaining peak performance.

4. If you want to attain peak performance, it is necessary to produce results that are helpful to the organization. Although this may appear to be an obvious statement, many people still think that activity is as important as results.

5. Being a troubleshooter and/or a leader who can turn around a troubled situation will add immensely to your gravitas.

6. Another foundational component of gravitas is to project the image that you believe in yourself and that you can accomplish all tasks within your field of competence—thereby displaying self-confidence.

7.  Being able to remain calm and rational under pressure is an aspect of self-confidence that contributes to gravitas.

8.  Self-management helps you control your emotions, thereby minimizing temper tantrums that could detract from your gravitas.

9.  If you are in a leadership role, group members will probably take you more seriously if they can observe your values in action. For example, if you profess to value merit, you make choice assignments based on merit, not political factors.

10.  A comprehensive way of projecting gravitas is to develop a positive reputation. A positive reputation means that your character and actions are respected and perceived as worthy. Reputation development is a career-long pursuit.

11.  Grit will enhance your gravitas, and the word refers to the ability and desire to keep plugging away at reaching a long-term, worthwhile goal.

12.  A major contributor to you being perceived as having gravitas is your ability to see the big picture or think strategically.

13.  One way to be a big-picture thinker who contributes to strategy is to ask provocative questions, such as, "Why is your idea important?"

# 3

# Interpersonal Components
# of Gravitas

Gravitas is measured and recognized by its impact on other people. It therefore follows logically that many components of gravitas are linked to interpersonal relationships. Keep in mind, however, that personal attributes associated with gravitas fuel the impact on interpersonal relationships. For example, if you have a strongly developed trait of conscientiousness, you will follow through on the commitments you made to work associates. Having a reputation for following through on your commitments will, in turn, enhance your gravitas. In this chapter we focus on the interpersonal or external components of gravitas.

## Positive Interactions with Work Associates

Engaging in positive interactions with work associates is a broad subject that essentially encompasses the study of human relations. In recognition of this reality, here we focus on several aspects of positive workplace interactions characteristic of high-gravitas people.

*Have High Self-Esteem and Be at the Center of a Communication Network.* A starting point in having positive interactions with work associates is to have the right personality structure and to be at the center of a communications network. Brent A. Scott, a professor of management at Michigan State University, and Timothy A. Judge, an eminent professor of industrial-organizational psychology at Ohio State University, conducted two studies to investigate what made workers popular, or generally accepted by their peers.

The study with the most informative results involved 139 healthcare employees from 22 groups of a large hospital, with most of the work being conducted in teams. Popularity was measured in terms of how well the employee was liked by coworkers on a 1-to-5 scale. Self-esteem was measured by significant others of the study participants completing a core self-evaluation quiz about the participant. Work communication central-ity was measured by asking each coworker to "check the names of people with whom you communicate as part of the job during a typical workweek."

The results showed that having a high core self-evaluation (a mea-sure that includes self-esteem) and being at the center of communi-cations were related to popularity. The more popular employees also received more citizenship behavior from coworkers and fewer inci-dences of counterproductive, or disruptive, behavior—both of which reflect better coworker relationships.[1] Being popular adds to having gravitas and therefore being taken seriously.

*Develop Allies Through Being Civil.* Incivility detracts from gravi-tas. Leaders who are courteous, kind, cooperative, and cheerful develop allies and friends in the workplace. Practicing basic good manners, such as being pleasant and friendly, is also part of being civil. Being civil helps make you stand out, because many people believe that crude, rude, and obnoxious behavior has become both the norm and a national prob-lem. Leaders and professionals typically have high standing on civility, but there are exceptions. Uncivil behaviors characteristically involve rudeness and discourteousness. A study of three midwestern business organizations across different industries found that 86 percent of the employees surveyed said they had experienced some form of incivility within the last year.[2] Examples of incivility include the following:

- A salesperson makes sarcastic comments about another employee in front of a customer.
- A coworker initiates smartphone calls while listening to a presentation at a meeting.
- A supervisor continues responding to email messages while a group member is talking to him in person.
- A leader gives a dirty look to another leader during a meeting.
- A person whistles or sings constantly in the office (an intensely annoying behavior for many people).

Closely related to being civil is maintaining a positive outlook. Everyone knows that leaders gain more support by being optimistic and positive than by being pessimistic and negative. Nevertheless, many leaders ignore this simple strategy for getting along well with others. Group members are more likely to solicit the leader's opinion or offer to help when the leader is perceived as a cheerful person.

*Make Other People Feel Important.* A fundamental principle of fos-tering good relationships with subordinates and colleagues is to make them feel important. Making others feel important is honest because everybody in an organization has a contribution to make, including the CEO, payroll coordinator, and parking lot attendant. The link between making other people feel important and gravitas is that that when you make another person feel important, the person is likely to think you have good judgment. One approach to making a subordinate feel important would be to bring a notable accomplishment of his or hers to the attention of the group. The accompanying self-assessment quiz gives you an opportunity to think through your tendencies to make others feel important.

## How Important Do I Make People Feel?

Indicate on a scale of 1 to 5 how frequently you act (or would act if the situation presented itself) in the ways indicated: very infrequently (**VI**), infrequently (**I**), sometimes (**S**), frequently (**F**), very frequently (**VF**). Circle the number in the column that best fits your answer

| Statement about Importance or Unimportance | VI | I | S | F | VF |
|---|---|---|---|---|---|
| **1.** I do my best to correctly pronounce a team member's name. | 1 | 2 | 3 | 4 | 5 |
| **2.** I avoid letting other people's egos get too big. | 5 | 4 | 3 | 2 | 1 |
| **3.** I brag to others about the accomplishments of my group members. | 1 | 2 | 3 | 4 | 5 |
| **4.** I recognize the birthdays of friends in a tangible way. | 1 | 2 | 3 | 4 | 5 |
| **5.** It makes me anxious to listen to others brag about their accomplishments. | 5 | 4 | 3 | 2 | 1 |
| **6.** After hearing that a group member has done something outstanding, I shake his or her hand or give the person a fist bump. | 1 | 2 | 3 | 4 | 5 |
| **7.** If a group member or coworker recently received a degree or certificate, I would offer my congratulations. | 1 | 2 | 3 | 4 | 5 |
| **8.** If a group member or colleague finished second in a contest, I would inquire why he or she did not finish first. | 5 | 4 | 3 | 2 | 1 |
| **9.** If a group member showed me how to do something, I would compliment that person's skill. | 1 | 2 | 3 | 4 | 5 |
| **10.** When a group member or coworker starts bragging about a family member's accomplishments, I do not respond. | 5 | 4 | 3 | 2 | 1 |

**Total Score** _____

### 3. Interpersonal Components of Gravitas

**Scoring and Interpretation:**

Total the numbers corresponding to your answers.

| | |
|---|---|
| **40–50** | Suggests that you typically make people feel important. |
| **16–39** | Suggests that you have a moderate tendency toward making others feel important. |
| **10–15** | Suggests that you need to develop skill in making others feel important. |

*Minimize Complaints.* Being open and honest in expressing your feelings and opinions is part of having positive interactions with work associates. Nevertheless, this type of behavior, when carried to excess, could earn you a reputation as a whiner. Few higher-level managers or colleagues want to have a leader around who constantly complains about working conditions, coworkers, working hours, pay, and so forth. Furthermore, excessive complaining detracts from a person's gravitas.

Another important reason a boss usually dislikes having a direct report who complains too much is that listening to these complaints takes up considerable time. Most managers spend a disproportionate amount of time listening to the problems of a small number of ineffective or complaining employees.

To make valid complaints to the next-level manager, complain only when justified. And when you complain, back it up with a recommended solution. Anyone can take potshots at something. The valuable leader is the person who supports these complaints with a constructive action plan. An example follows of a complaint, supported by action plans for its remedy.

> When a potential customer wants a discount of more than 3 percent, we must receive authorization from you. The problem is that you may be out of contact with us temporarily, even by phone. The 3 percent rule was probably established before there were so many overseas suppliers. If authorization were required only for discounts of 5 percent or more, our team could close more sales quickly.

One possibility for minimizing the need for complaints is to attempt to look at decisions from the point of view of higher management. The company might decide to prohibit workers from using text messaging for personal reasons during working hours. Instead of a team leader complaining that the prohibition on text messages creates problems or is unjust, the team leader might attempt to understand why company management thinks instant messages lower productivity.

*Give Appropriate Compliments.* An effective way of developing good relationships with work associates is to compliment something with which they closely identify, such as their children, spouses, hobbies, or pets. Compliments are also effective because they are a form of flattery. Giving sensible compliments adds to a person's gravitas because the compliment giver will often be perceived as a person of substance.

Another way of complimenting people is through recognition. The suggestions made earlier about making people feel important are ways of recognizing people and therefore are compliments. Investing a small amount of time in recognizing work associates can pay large dividends in terms of cultivating an ally. Recognition and compliments are more likely to create a favorable relationship when they are appropriate. *Appropriate* in this context means that the compliment fits the accomplishment. Praise that is too lavish may be interpreted as belittling and patronizing. Let's look at the difference between an appropriate and an exaggerated compliment over the same issue.

An executive secretary gets a printer operating that was temporarily not printing documents. ***Appropriate compliment:*** "Nice job, Suzanne. Fixing the printer took considerable skill. We can now resume making hard copies of documents when the occasion arises." ***Exaggerated compliment:*** "Suzanne, I'm overwhelmed. You're a world-class printer specialist. Are there no limits to your talents?" Observe that the appropriate compliment is thoughtful and is proportionate to what Suzanne accomplished. The exaggerated compliment is probably wasted because it is way out of proportion to the magnitude of the accomplishment.

An important factor in making effective use of compliments is not to use them in a manipulative way to attain personal gain. An example would be to compliment a colleague and then follow up the compliment with a request to hire your nephew into your department for a summer job.

## Gaining the Respect of Others

Gaining the respect of others is a major component of gravitas, because people who are taken seriously are usually respected unless they engage in immoral and/or criminal behavior.

Respect and gravitas run in two directions. If other people have high respect for a person, it facilitates the person having gravitas. Yet the opposite is also true: a person who has gravitas tends to be respected. A good starting point in understanding how respect contributes to gravitas is to dig into a sampling of the many meanings of *respect*. A general guideline is that respect as defined in the *American Heritage Dictionary* is "to feel or show deferential regard for; esteem."

An analysis of academic studies conducted over a 70-year period arrived at various definitions and meanings of respect as it applies to leadership.[3] We focus here on a sampling of these definitions and meanings that have the most relevance for understanding how respect is a component of gravitas for leaders and professionals.

1. Respect is showing care and concern for followers as individuals.

2. Respectful leaders possess a high degree of respect for others and treat individuals with respect simply because they are people.

3. Respect stems from actions that show the leader cares about group members, such as expressing congratulations to individual group members for their achievements.

4. Respect is the degree to which a leader shows concern and respect for subordinates, looks out for their welfare, and expresses appreciation and support.

5. Respect is a judgment of worthiness based upon some perceived quality of another person.

6. Group members respect the leader when they sense that they are all valued in the organization.

7. Respect is the quality of how people are treated.

8. Respectful behavior is the result of believing another person has value.

A type of respect that has a weak relationship to gravitas relates mostly to the position a person holds. Certain individuals based solely on the position they hold in organizations or society appear to receive respect. This type of respect is based on station or position and not necessarily on the accomplishments, virtues, or values of the person so positioned.

Based on the various meanings of respect, a brief explanation of respectful leadership that can be put into practice is as follows: Respectful leadership is an appreciative attitude toward group members. As a result of this attitude the leader pays attention to subordinates. In response the group members feel that they are important, of equal worth, and treated respectfully.[4] As the leader shows respect for group members, he or she is more respected and therefore more likely to be perceived as having gravitas. Leaders also gain respect by displaying effective leadership in hundreds of different ways. Here we focus on a sampling of the most potent ways for a leader to gain respect.[5]

*Establish a Climate of Respect.* To establish a climate of respect the leader should lead by example in such ways as carefully processing suggestions from group members and showing the same amount of friendliness and kindness to group members at every job level. A less direct way of establishing a climate of respect is to set high standards for the group and support group members in their quest to meet the high standards. Workers who attain the high standards should be recognized by both formal rewards and words of appreciation.

*Earn Respect by Giving Respect.* As just implied, a key way for the leader to earn respect is by showing respect for others. Respect is reciprocal: when you respect others, they respect you. Small actions are frequently the path to success. Among these actions are conducting performance appraisals when due; showing up for meetings on time; paying full attention to the other person during one-on-one meetings; and not laughing at the mistakes of team members.

*Be Dependable.* Dependability contributes to being perceived as having gravitas and is also an effective way of gaining respect. Suppose that department head Haley says that she will carefully review department member Aaron's request for hybrid work within one week. When Haley gets back to Aaron in seven days with her answer, she will earn Aaron's respect—especially if the answer is affirmative. Dependability on the part of the leader also garners trust, which also leads to respect.

*Lead by Example.* A foundational approach for the leader to gain respect is to lead by example or be a positive role model. As is well known, "walking the talk" is a synonym for leading by example. The leader carries out actions that he or she recommends or requires for the group. For example, if the division president demands that workers at all levels be frugal in spending company money, the president should stay at modestly priced hotels or motels and rent non-luxury vehicles during business trips.

Another meaning of leading by example is for the leader to work 60 or more hours per week and expect subordinates to do the same. During a crisis, some employees will find the long hours acceptable. Yet most employees will not respect a leader who has such little respect for their work and family life balance.

*Give Criticism or Negative Feedback in a Respectful Way.* A component of effective leadership is to candidly discuss poor performance or behavior with direct reports. Delivering this negative feedback without belittling the recipient helps gain respect for the leader. Imagine data scientist Rajah has prepared several reports for CEO Edwin that the latter does not understand. Edwin is discouraged because Rajah is earning a giant salary.

A disrespectful way for Edwin to deliver the criticism to Rajah would be to say, "We are paying you far too much for you to give me reports so complicated and confusing that they are useless. I thought that an applied data scientist had common sense." A respectful way for Edwin to give Rajah negative feedback would be to say, "Your last few reports might show brilliance on your part, Rajah. But I need you to present your reports such that I as a non–data scientist can interpret them in a meaningful way. Let me give you a few examples of aspects of your reports that I cannot understand."

*Take Ownership of Mistakes and Failures.* Leaders who take risks have a high probability of making some mistakes and experiencing some failures. Accepting responsibility or "owning" these mistakes and failure generates considerable respect. A CEO of a tech company might say, "We bought this software startup for $15 million. Their main product, an AI-generated dating website, is a complete farce. It would be unethical to try to sell the startup, so we are absorbing the loss. My bad, and I apologize."

Owning lesser mistakes than a failed acquisition provides more opportunities for gaining respect because lesser mistakes are more frequent. Cora, the head of human resources, convinces the CEO that a Take Your Pet to Work Day would be a useful morale booster for the company. One day each month workers would be eligible to take their dog or cat to the office. After three months of implementation, the new initiative resulted in loads of complaints from workers who did not participate. Among the complaints were too much noise in the office, people distracted from work while tending to their pets, dog droppings in the workplace, and two workers being bitten by dogs on the premises.

Cora gained the respect of most employees and the CEO by distributing a company-wide email admitting her mistake. Cora explained that the company still loved pets and pet owners, but that the office proved not to be a suitable environment for pets. The company was, however, exploring the possibility of offering pet insurance as an employee benefit.

*Coach and Mentor Others.* A major responsibility of leaders not tied directly to earning a profit or serving the public is coaching and mentoring subordinates. Given that coaching and mentoring appeal to the need of people to grow and develop, the leader who is an effective coach and mentor gains considerable respect. A leader with an already heavy work schedule, such as a C-suite executive, will gain considerable respect for taking time from his or her heavy schedule to coach and mentor.

*Listen.* Once again listening is woven into gravitas. Listening to employee input about what should be done to resolve problems is especially important. The reasoning is straightforward. Workers respect a boss who respects their opinion. Another way in which listening triggers respect is when the leader listens to a group member's input about what went wrong when a problem develops. The opposite approach is telling the group member how the problem should be fixed or blaming the person. Here is an example of how a leader listening to the cause of a problem helps the leader earn respect.

Wealth manager Gordon loses a major account that the bank has been managing for a decade. Stacy, the team leader of the wealth manager group, thinks she knows why Gordon lost the account: His client saw below-average returns for three consecutive months because Gordon has a bias against international stocks. Before jumping in with her analysis of what went wrong, Stacy asks Gordon's opinion about how the bank lost this valuable account. Gordon then explains that the client has a nephew who recently became a certified financial planner and works for a small wealth management firm. The client wanted to make her nephew happy, so she had the account transferred to his firm. Gordon elevates his respect for Stacy because she listened to his explanation rather than casting blame—and did not suggest that he be fired.

A strong example of a business leader who gains respect from company insiders and outsiders alike is Karen S. Lynch, the former president and CEO of CVS Health. She was ranked number 1 on *Fortune*'s Most Powerful Women list, among many other power rankings by the media including *Forbes* and *Bloomberg*. Lynch was selected for the 2023 *TIME* annual list of the 100 most influential people in the world. She was the top executive of the highest-ranking Fortune 500 company ever led by a woman. CVS Health generates over $200 billion annually, with profits of about $8 billion. The company has more than 300,000 employees and upward of 40,000 physicians, pharmacists, and nurses on staff.

Lynch took over as CEO in the middle of the COVID-19 pandemic. She remarked that throughout her entire career she had been faced with many kinds of challenges and changes and big strategic issues. As a result, Lynch believed that she was up to the task of leading the company through the pandemic. During and after the pandemic, Lynch saw the opportunity to expand the impact of CVS Health on the community. The company offered an alternative site of care, either in its retail locations, or in the home via the internet. Under the guidance of Lynch and her executive team, CVS Health has entered the primary care space in the form of Minute Clinics. The company's primary health-care initiative received a boost during the pandemic. Millions of people who visited their local CVS for tests and vaccinations saw for the first time that they could also get a cholesterol screening or complete physical exam inside the same store. (The Minute Clinics proved not to be as successful as planned, and the number of locations was reduced.)

Lynch has been said to know her way around a microphone and a camera, with a willingness to address the public. She readily expresses her opinions and views, with confidence that those opinions are backed by knowledge, which has added to her respect. Lynch says she likes to create change and execute on that change. Yet she notes that an effective leader is willing to listen to the ideas of other people before charging down the path of change, a strategy that enhances the respect she receives.

Prior to CVS, Lynch was president of Aetna (later merged with CVS). While at Aetna, Lynch said there were many ways the company measured its impact on the people it served. Aetna employees start by asking themselves, "Are we improving access, affordability, and quality in the health-care system?" "Are we helping people achieve more healthy days?" Aetna also measured its impact by understanding the engagement level of its employees. Lynch said that engaged employees interact with the company's members in a unique and caring way and that that type of personal connection with members is critical in the new consumer marketplace. Her commitment to employee engagement was another way in which Lynch received the respect of employees.[6]

## Projecting Power

A leader or professional who projects power, or appears to be powerful, has one more factor in his or her favor to be perceived as having gravitas. Two robust categories for projecting power are knowledge and personality. Power can also be projected through nonverbal communication. The more of these approaches to project power the leader or professional uses, the more likely the person will gain gravitas through the projection of power.

*Expert Power.* A highly effective way to project power is through one's specialized knowledge, skills, or abilities. For expertise to be an effective source of power, group members must respect that expertise. Exercising expert power is the logical starting point for building one's power base. Powerful people in business, government, and education almost invariably launched their careers by developing expertise in a specialty of value to their employers. When work associates recognize your expertise, you automatically project power.

Here are two high-profile examples of business executives who project power through their expertise: Mary Barra, the CEO of General Motors (GM), began her career right out of college, as an electrical engineer at GM. Michael Dell began Dell Computers (now Dell Technologies) by selling computers as a college student. His expert knowledge of how to sell computers directly to customers highlighted his credibility. Barra and Dell possess gravitas in multiple ways, but their projection of expert power is a major contributor.

*Desirable Traits and Characteristics.* Another way of projecting power stems from one's desirable traits and characteristics. This type of power is based on the desire of others to be led by or to identify with an inspiring person. Making a positive impression through speech and appearance is therefore a source of power. Warmth and charm contribute to leadership effectiveness, partially because these attributes project power.

Personal power can sometimes be diminished by frequent use of the expression "I'm sorry." It might be acceptable to say "I'm sorry" for major offenses, but too frequent use of the phrase makes a person appear weak and therefore detracts from gravitas. Jeffrey Pfeffer, a professor of organizational behavior at the Stanford Graduate School of Management and Business says, "Don't give away your power."[7]

*Projecting Power through Nonverbal Communication.* A variety of nonverbal signals, including body language, help project a power image. These approaches are best considered to supplement the deeper strategies of having expert power along with desirable traits and characteristics. Almost anybody with good acting skills could learn to use nonverbal signals of power even if the person had no real power to project. Following is a list of power signals that would be the most effective if combined with expert power and desirable traits and characteristics.[8]

### 3. Interpersonal Components of Gravitas

1.  Use expansive posture by keeping your limbs away from your body. People posed in expansive postures, such as with the arms about six inches from the body, tend to feel more powerful. Expansive posture is part of taking up space, which also projects power.

2.  Make occasional eye contact while talking but be willing to look away when others do.

3.  Point toward people occasionally in a firm, positive way without making the gesture so strong that you appear to be accusatory.

4.  Keep the head straight up, by minimizing head tilts. Keeping the head in a neutral position tends to connote power.

5.  Smile occasionally but avoid excessive smiling. The obvious reason is that a person with gravitas is taken seriously, and excessive smiling detracts from an image of seriousness. Excessive smiling while talking about a serious subject such as layoffs or a labor strike detracts strongly from projecting a power image.

6.  Nod occasionally to help project a power image. Frequent nodding might connote deference. As with other nonverbal forms of communication, there are cultural differences in the interpretation of nodding. For example, Chinese and Japanese people in power positions tend to nod more frequently than their American and Canadian counterparts.

7.  Use firm but not punitive handshakes and fist bumps. In the post-pandemic era handshakes in the workplace came back in style, even though many people still prefer fist bumps. To project power, use the *professional shake* as follows: Square off your body to the other person, facing him or her fully. Make palm-to-palm contact and ensure that the web of your hand (the skin between your thumb and first finger) touches the other person's web.

8.  Use the *authoritative arc* when making an important point. The rising and lowering of the voice is considered nonverbal communication because it refers to how something is said rather than what is said. If your voice rises at the end of sentences, listeners may think that you are asking for approval. To project a power image, use the authoritative arc, meaning that your voice begins on one note, rises in pitch through the sentence, and drops back down at the end. Recording yourself on a video is a helpful way to practice the authoritative arc.

We emphasize again that the most robust way of projecting power is to combine expert power and desirable traits and characteristics with a type of nonverbal communication. The three-way combination is likely to enhance your gravitas.

## Engaging Communication Skills

Probably almost every reader of this book has studied many times how to improve spoken and written communication skills. Here we highlight a few aspects of communication skills that facilitate demonstrating that you are a person with gravitas.

*Vocal Attractiveness.* A group of researchers devised a complicated study to examine whether vocal attractiveness is positively related to perceptions of leadership effectiveness. One study involved a vocal analysis of U.S. presidents and Canadian prime ministers who left office by 2005. A second study involved 255 subjects distributed into 85 teams in a laboratory setting. Vocal attractiveness was defined as a voice that reveals confidence and lacks tension. Perceived leadership effectiveness is related to gravitas, because a leader whose is perceived to be effective will usually be taken seriously. The authors concluded that there is compelling evidence that vocal attractiveness contributes heavily to perceptions of leadership effectiveness.[9]

*Clear Speaking.* Speech coach Laura Mathis reminds us that to demonstrate gravitas, it is essential to speak clearly. Mumbling or combining words too quickly can send a message that what you are saying lacks importance. You might have insightful ideas that would impress people, but the impact is lost if listeners cannot hear and understand what you are saying. Recording your own voice while talking to work associates will provide feedback that could indicate if you need to speak more clearly.[10]

*Deep Listening.* Engaging in deep or active listening is a bedrock communication skill for the person with gravitas. Deep listening takes place when we listen to understand the other person, to understand not just the content but also the motivation and purpose of what the person is saying. Suppose that plant manager Derek is making the rounds at his plant to get a personal feel for employee morale and potential problems. He drops by the final assembly department headed by the supervisor, Coleen. When asked by Derek how things are going, Coleen replies, "Not bad, but the work ethic of some new entry-level workers is a challenge."

Instead of just shrugging off the comment, Derek reflects, "Does Coleen think the new generation of workers are lazy? Does she think that our HR department is letting her down with the quality of job candidates?" Instead of just assuming what Coleen means by her statement, Derek digs further and says: "Coleen, your opinion is important. You are supervising our frontline workers. In what way is the work ethic of our new hires a challenge for you?" Coleen now feels free to discuss her concerns about the work ethic of the recent group of new hires. She feels that her opinion is respected and thus has more respect for Derek.

*Anecdotes to Communicate Meaning.* Anecdotes are a powerful part of a leader's kit of persuasive tactics and bolster the leader's gravitas. Although storytelling is an ancient art, it is more in vogue than ever as a method for leaders to influence and inspire others. The title of the marketing manager at the software giant SAP is "Chief Storyteller Executive Advisory and Architecture." A carefully chosen anecdote is also useful in persuading group members about the importance of organizational values. So long as the anecdote is not repeated too frequently, it can communicate an important message.

Zippo is a consumer products company that has hundreds of anecdotes to share about how those sturdy steel cigarette lighters saved somebody's life by deflecting a bullet. It seems that the stories originated in World War II but have continued into more recent times, such as how a Zippo in the pocket of a police officer prevented a criminal's bullet from killing him. Zippo leaders can inspire workers with such heroic tales starring the Zippo lighter. In recent years, Zippo has shifted into many products not related to smoking, but the anecdotes are still inspiring for the nonsmoker.

*Data to Back Up Conclusions.* Backing up your conclusions with data is a persuasive communication technique that links directly to being taken seriously. You will be more persuasive if you support your spoken and written presentations with solid data, adding to your credibility and weight. One approach to obtaining data is to collect them yourself—for example, by conducting an online survey of your customers or group members. Published sources also provide convincing data for arguments. Supporting data for hundreds of arguments can be found on appropriate websites, in the business pages of newspapers, and in business magazines and newspapers. *The Statistical Abstract of the United States*, published annually, is an inexpensive yet trusted reference for thousands of arguments.

Relying too much on research has a potential disadvantage,

however. Being too dependent on data could suggest that you have little faith in your own intuition. For example, you might convey an impression of weakness if, when asked your opinion, you respond, "I can't answer until I collect some data." Leaders are generally decisive. An important issue, then, is for the leader to find the right balance between relying on data and using intuition alone when communicating an important point.

*Business Jargon in Appropriate Doses.* Business and government executives and professionals make frequent use of jargon. Workplace jargon is a natural part of almost any organization. (Only athletic coaches exceed businesspeople in the heavy use of jargon and clichés.) Often the jargon is used automatically without deliberate thought, and at other times jargon words and phrases are chosen to help establish rapport with the receiver. An appropriate amount of jargon therefore helps the leader or professional to be a person of substance. A vastly overused phrase these days is "at the end of the day," with "scale" fighting for second place. "The end of the day" has come to replace "in the final analysis," "space" has replaced industry sector, and "buckets" replace "categories." Many businesspeople say "at the end of the day" twice in the same few sentences.

Six major executives and management professors were asked which buzzwords they would ban from conversation in the boardroom, office, and beyond: The six disliked buzzwords, or jargon words, were "push the envelope," "de-layering" (in place of "downsizing"), "dynamic resilience," "out-of-the-box thinking," "passionate," and "viral."[11]

Sprinkling business talk with jargon does indeed help establish rapport and adds to a person's popularity. But too much jargon makes a person seem stereotyped in thinking and perhaps even unwilling to express an original thought—and therefore lacking power and credibility.

*Minimal Language Errors, Junk Words, and Vocalized Pauses.* Using colorful, powerful words enhances the perception that you are self-confident and have leadership qualities. It is also important to minimize the use of words and phrases that dilute the impact of your speech, such as "like," "you know," "you know what I mean," "he goes" (to mean "he says"), and "uh." Such junk words and vocalized pauses convey the impression of low self-confidence, especially in a professional setting, and detract from a sharp communication image. As a result, the person's gravitas diminishes.

An effective way to decrease the use of these extraneous words is to video-record your side of a phone conversation and then play it back. Many people are not aware that they use extraneous words until they hear recordings of their speech.

An effective leader should be sure always to write and speak with grammatical precision to give the impression of being articulate and well informed, thereby enhancing his or her leadership stature. Here are two examples of common language errors: "Just between you and I" is wrong; "just between you and me" is correct. "Him and I" or "her and I" are incorrect phrases despite how frequently they creep into social and business language. "He and I" and "she and I" are correct when used as the subjects of a sentence. "Him and me" or "Her and me" are correct when used as the objects of a sentence. For example, "She and I greeted the client" and "The client greeted her and me" are both correct.

Perhaps the most common language error business leaders make is to convert hundreds of nouns into verbs. Many nouns do become legitimate verbs, such as using the noun *phone* for a verb, such as "I will phone you later." The leader has to set a limit, and perhaps not use such verb-to-noun conversions such as, "Facebook me tonight," "Focus-group this problem," and "Zoom me a message." Yet, the cool leader will correctly use nouns that have been converted into dual use as a verb and noun, such as "google some potential customers for this product." Judgment is called for with respect to which nouns should be used as verbs to avoid sounding silly, and therefore weak.

When in doubt about a potential language error, consult a respected dictionary or guide to business communications. With printed information, you at least know that the suggestions have usually been edited by a knowledgeable person.

---

## Guidelines for Action

1. If you are popular with work associates it will contribute to your gravitas.

2. A fundamental principle of fostering good relationships with subordinates and colleagues is to make them feel important. Making others feel importance can contribute to your gravitas.

3. Excessive complaining on your part could detract from your gravitas.

4. Investing a small amount of time in recognizing work associates can pay large dividends in terms of cultivating allies.

5. A key approach to being perceived as having gravitas is to be respected by others in the workplace.

6. As a leader, if you pay respect to group members, you will be more respected, and therefore more likely to be perceived as having gravitas.

7. A recommended way to establish a climate of respect is to lead by example in such ways as processing suggestions from group members and showing the same amount of friendliness and kindness to group members at every job level.

8. Dependability contributes to being perceived as having gravitas and is also an effective way of gaining respect.

9. A foundational approach for the leader to gain respect is to lead by example or be a positive role model.

10. Delivering negative feedback to an employee without belittling the recipient helps gain respect for the leader.

11. Accepting responsibility or "owning" mistakes and failures generates considerable respect.

12. The leader who is an effective coach and mentor gains considerable respect.

13. A leader or professional who projects power, or appears to be powerful, has one more factor in his or her favor to be perceived as having gravitas.

14. A highly effective way to project power is through your specialized knowledge, skills, and abilities.

15. Your personal power might diminish a little with too frequent use of the words "I'm sorry."

16. Excessive smiling can detract from your gravitas because you might be taken less seriously.

17. Engaging in deep or active listening is a bedrock skill for the person with gravitas.

18. Anecdotes are a powerful part of a leader's kit of persuasive tactics and bolster the leader's gravitas.

19. Backing up your conclusions with data is a persuasive communication technique that links directly to being taken seriously.

20. Extensive use of junk words and vocalized pauses convey the impression of low self-confidence, especially in a professional setting, and detract from a sharp communication image.

21. An effective leader should write and speak with grammatical precision to give the impression of being articulate and well-informed, thereby enhancing his or her leadership stature.

# 4

# Key Leadership Gravitas
# Actions and Behaviors

To acquire an in-depth understanding of gravitas as practiced by leaders and professionals, it is helpful to look at what they actually do. What people actually do refers to their actions and behaviors. Suppose vice president of finance Carmen puts extra effort into seeing what he can do as a leader to help his staff members be more productive and happier. Carmen's activities and behaviors in serving his staff are well received, and as a result he is taken quite seriously. In this chapter we describe an assortment of actions and behaviors that contribute to leadership and professional gravitas.

## Language and Thinking Patterns for Gravitas

In Chapter 3, it was mentioned that certain aspects of communication skills are components of gravitas, including clear communication and projecting powerful body language. Being perceived as having gravitas goes beyond these aspects of communication. The perception extends to the type of language the leader uses as well as distinctive thinking patterns. Here we describe three language and thinking patterns characteristic of high-gravitas leaders and professionals.

*Constructive Insights.* A distinguishing intellectual strength of people with gravitas is that they can size up people and situations and arrive at in-depth understandings that others might miss. Constructive insights lead to being taken seriously because they offer people assistance with spotting trends and interpreting events they might not have seen for themselves. A major advantage of an insight is that it helps another person understand a situation more clearly, including the illogic in his or her own thinking.

A leader with the insights that contribute to gravitas tends to interpret feedback deeply. Whereas others might accept feedback

55

superficially, the person with intellectual gravitas is likely to wring much more meaning out of it. Consider Luna, who has lost three key group members over a six-month time span. A superficial mental approach would be for Luna to dismiss the problem by saying, "I guess we just don't pay enough to keep good people." Feedback is involved because the people quitting are a message back to her from the environment. Instead of making a superficial analysis, Luna uses her well-disciplined self-awareness orientation and digs deeper for the reasons behind the turnover.

Luna asks herself, "Is there something in my leadership approach that creates turnover problems?" Luna decides to dig even further into the turnover problem. She requests the results of her staff's exit interviews because these sometimes provide valuable information about the reasons for turnover. Workers leaving the company are more likely to be more candid about their work experience than those who are still employed.

*Becoming Better at Achieving Insights.* Even if you are convinced by now that making insightful interpretations of events will contribute to your gravitas, there is plenty of hard work ahead. Enhancing your insights is a form of mental discipline that requires concentrated listening and frequent practice. The opposite of insightfulness is letting messages from others go right over your head. The following suggestions will help you sharpen your insights:

1. When you receive feedback, ask yourself, "Does this have implications for my usual modus operandi?"
2. When observing general news events or those related to business, ask yourself, "What is the implication of this information for my role?"
3. When you receive an ambiguous message from someone in the organization, or a customer or client, ask yourself, "What is this person really telling me?" Maybe ask for clarification.
4. When anything goes wrong at work or home, ask yourself, "Is this a random event, or is it a wake-up call?" If you lose your keys, ponder whether this is something that will never happen again or whether it means that you need a fixed place to park your keys.
5. When engaged in a business activity or pastime, ask yourself, "What are the key factors that make for success in this activity?" For example, an indoor athletic club needs to attract people who can attend during the day such as full-time homemakers, retirees, and perhaps a few remote workers on a break.

6.  After experiencing a stunning insight, share it with others as a vehicle for enhancing your gravitas.

*Expressing Innovative Thoughts.* The same kind of mental toughness that enables people with gravitas to arrive at insights contributes to innovativeness. The term *innovative* in this context refers to close-to-original, imaginative, or non-stereotypical ideas that can be put into practice or monetized. Creativity generally refers to any imaginative idea, whereas innovation refers to commercializing the idea. For example, it would be considered creative to think of a video hookup that would record dreams from the brain while the person sleeps. It would be innovative to develop a "dream machine" that could be manufactured and sold. Before reading further, take the accompanying self-quiz to think through your current level of innovative thinking.

## The Imagination Checklist

Indicate whether you tend to agree or disagree with each of the following statements.

| Statement About Imagination or Creativity | Mostly Agree | Mostly Disagree |
|---|---|---|
| Note 1: A novel suggestion of mine has been accepted by my manager or my employer at least once in my career. | | |
| Note 2: If going on a vacation, it is best to visit only well-known tourist destinations. | | |
| Note 3: I have entered at least one contest that required the contestants to name a product, name a mascot, or develop a slogan. | | |
| Note 4: I am seriously involved in a hobby such as photography, art, woodworking, or making pottery. | | |
| Note 5: Virtually all the photographs I take are of family members and friends. | | |
| Note 6: I almost never make up my own invitations or greeting cards but rely on those available online or printed. | | |
| Note 7: Several times in my life, work associates or friends have referred to me as creative. | | |
| Note 8: When involved in a group effort, I usually go along with the thinking of the team. | | |

| Statement About Imagination or Creativity | Mostly Agree | Mostly Disagree |
|---|---|---|
| Note 9: I have published something in my life even it was only a letter to the editor, a blog, or an online comment in response to an article. | | |
| Note 10: When faced with a problem, I typically accept the first solution that comes to mind. | | |
| Note 11: I make frequent us of everyday expressions such as "You can choose your friends, but you can't choose your family," and "You don't have to be a rocket scientist to...." | | |
| Note 12: Each year I take the same kind of vacation. | | |
| Note 13: There are only about four different foods I order when dining out or ordering in from a restaurant. | | |
| Note 14: At least one manager or supervisor of mine has said that I am creative. | | |
| Note 15: I frequently make comments on the job or in my personal life that make people laugh. | | |

**Scoring and Interpretation:** Give yourself a 1 for *mostly agreeing* with questions 1, 3, 4, 7, 9, 12, and 15. Give yourself a 1 for *mostly disagreeing* with questions 2, 5, 6, 8, 10, 11, 12, and 13. A score of 12 or higher indicates that you probably have good imagination and it enhances your gravitas. A score of 11 or lower suggests that you need to think more imaginatively to enhance your gravitas.

*Emphasizing Positive Thoughts.* A winning thought pattern of people with high gravitas is their propensity to express positive thoughts when appropriate. Being grumpy limits a person's influential appeal. Changing a tendency toward being negative requires considerable discipline. The reason is that people appear to have a genetically based predisposition to seeing either the positive or negative content in their lives. People are therefore apt to generally look at situations positively or negatively.

Even if you are a natural pessimist, you can learn to express optimism in the presence of others whom you want to influence positively and therefore project gravitas. A few suggestions for the aspiring positive thinker are as follows:

1. *Frame negative messages in positive terms.* Imagine you are a retail executive and you discover that your annual turnover rate is 60 percent. Your analysis is that such high turnover is too costly and

creates customer service problems. You tell your store managers, "If we can reduce our turnover rate by just 10 percent we will beat the industry average, reduce costs, and improve customer service."

2. *Frame scenarios in terms of what can be done or what will be done.* Like the suggestion just made, tell people how conditions can or will be improved. An inspiring, high-gravitas leader would make a pronouncement such as, "If we can develop one new successful product this year, we can avoid a downsizing."

3. *Provide a clear-cut course of action.* In the example just provided, explain the action plan for developing a new product.

4. *Substitute positive terms for negative ones when feasible.* Examples include *challenge* for *problem, major investment* instead of *major cost*, and *developmental opportunity* for *personal weakness.* Pushing this technique one step further, how about *best suited for yesterday's challenges* for *obsolete*?

The most dynamic person must at times point out the negatives in a situation to avoid not being taken seriously. Yet even during the worst adversity the high-gravitas person will deliver a positive message about working out of the adverse situation. A firm that provides coin-counting machines for supermarkets and transit companies had filed for bankruptcy. Surrounding its bankruptcy was a question of approximately $250,000 that appeared not to have been deposited in the customer's bank accounts.

The CEO told the workers, "We have hit rock bottom, and I'm sure the social media accounts of what happened will be very negative. Please do not despair. All the missing funds can be accounted for. We are going to stay in business, and we do not intend to lay off anyone. I am as upset as anyone in this room. Let's stick together and gain our good reputation back."

## Eagerness to Serve Others

An eagerness to serve others will often enhance a leader's gravitas because such willingness increases the leader's respect and seriousness of purpose. A true servant leader is one who serves constituents by working on their behalf to help them achieve their goals, not the leader's own goals. A servant leader is self-sacrificing and humble. A servant leader, for example, might take over the responsibilities of a team member so that person can take care of an ailing family member. A high-gravitas leader is usually not a total servant leader because he or she tends more to stand out from the crowd. Yet certain aspects of servant leadership are part of having gravitas. The aspects of servant leadership likely to be incorporated into the repertoire of a leader with gravitas are described next.[1]

1. *Place service before self-interest.* A servant leader is more concerned with helping others than with acquiring power, prestige, financial reward, or status. The servant leader seeks to do what is morally right, even if it is not financially rewarding. Such a leader is conscious of the needs of others and is driven by a desire to satisfy them. By placing service before self-interest, servant leaders might also be characterized as givers rather than takers. Givers are people who frequently give their time, effort, and resources to help others without expecting a return. Takers do the opposite, taking other people's time, effort, and resources with no intention of reciprocity. This aspect of servant leadership adds to the seriousness of purpose of the leader.

2. *Listen first to express confidence in others.* The servant leader makes a deep commitment to listening to get to know the concerns, requirements, and problems of group members. Instead of attempting to impose the leader's will on others, the servant leader listens carefully to understand what course of action will help others accomplish their goals. After understanding others, the best course of action can be chosen. Through listening, for example, a servant leader might learn that the group is more concerned about team spirit and harmony than striving for companywide recognition. The leader would then concentrate more on building teamwork than searching for ways to increase the visibility of the team. Listening, as has been mentioned before in previous chapters, is a key component of gravitas.

3. *Recognize personal limitations.* Servant leaders acknowledge their limitations and therefore actively seek the contributions of others to compensate for these limitations. Servant leader and marketing manager Lance might say to marketing assistant Brooklyn, "I'm not good at using Big Data to make a sales forecast for the next fiscal year. How about you taking over the task?" Recognizing personal limitations is part of self-awareness and therefore contributes to gravitas. Yet too strong a focus on these limitations will detract from the leader being perceived as a formidable individual.

4. *Show boldness with respect to values, morality, and doing the right thing.* Servant leaders can be very bold with respect to their sense of values, morality, and doing what is right. These behaviors are part of the strong ethical code of most servant leaders. For example, a servant leader might insist that two people who are equally qualified for a position, have comparable experience and skills, and perform comparably be paid equally. Acting boldly is an important behavior of the leader or professional who is perceived as having gravitas.

5. *Inspire trust by being trustworthy.* Being trustworthy is a foundational behavior of the servant leader. The leader is scrupulously honest with others, gives up control, and focuses on the well-being of others. Such leaders usually do not have to work hard at being trustworthy because they are already moral. Being trustworthy helps a person be perceived as a person of substance.

6. *Focus on the development of people.* Servant leaders focus on the development of people, such as giving them opportunities to acquire new skills and become leaders. The developmental focus requires humility in contrast to the politically motivated leader who prefers to avoid developing a person who might replace him or her. If someone helps you develop, you tend to perceive him or her as having gravitas.

7. *Lend a hand.* A servant leader looks for opportunities to play the Good Samaritan. A supermarket manager might help store associates by bagging groceries during a busy period. Or a servant leader might help clean out mud in the company lobby after a hurricane. Lending a hand might give a leader a few modest gravitas credits but does not project a power image.

8. *Acquire power to serve others.* The motivation to acquire power is strong for leaders, particularly for those who aspire to an executive position. Servant leaders also like power but not for the purpose of self-aggrandizement. Instead, servant leaders seek power so the power can be used to serve the needs of constituents. For example, a servant leader might want to acquire resources (a form of power) to create a pleasant and safe physical working environment for the workforce. Using resources in this manner helps the leader be perceived as a caring power user.

## Empathy, Compassion, and Gravitas

Empathy has become a buzzword in organizations with several different meanings. The original meaning of *empathy* is to understand another person's point of view, and this definition remains useful in understanding leadership behavior. Microsoft executive CEO Satya Nadella has touted empathy for many years, as will be illustrated in the story a little later in this chapter. He once said, "There is no way we are going to succeed if we don't have a strong sense of empathy." Brian Chesky, the CEO of Airbnb, was noted for the empathic way he communicated staff layoffs during COVID-19. He wrote in an internal company memo, "I have a deep feeling of love for all of you."[2] The leader who expresses empathy is perceived as a person of substance.

Compassion goes one step beyond empathy because it involves understanding the problem a person is experiencing and wanting to help with its resolution. Compassionate behavior on the part of a leader with gravitas is strongly needed during an organizational crisis, such as a hurricane or massive explosion. A leader who displays compassion during the crisis is likely to be perceived as strong and effective.

Displaying compassion with the concerns, anxieties, and frustrations of group members is also a key interpersonal skill for crisis leadership. The type of compassionate leadership that brings about organizational healing involves taking some form of public action that eases pain and inspires others to act as well. Compassionate leadership encompasses two related sets of actions. The first is to create an environment in which affected workers can freely discuss how they feel, such as a group meeting to talk about the crisis or disaster. The second is to create an environment in which the workers who experience or witness pain can find a method to alleviate their own suffering and that of others. The leader might establish a special fund to help the families of workers who were victims of the disaster or give workers the opportunity to receive grief counseling.[3]

Compassionate leadership also involves taking some form of public action, even if the action is modest, that is intended to relieve the pain of constituents.[4] A noteworthy example of a leader being compassionate and taking public action at the same time took place after massive flooding in Louisiana in 2016. Paul Kusserow, the chief executive of Amedisys Inc., based in Baton Rouge, showed active concern for the company employees and clients. (Amedisys provides home health and hospice care.) Among the 13 people who died in the flooding was company founder Bill Borne.

The disaster left about 100 of the company's 400 employees with flooded homes, and the firm's local hospice patients were at risk. Limited supplies of gasoline were available in the community. Kusserow arranged for fuel trucks to be brought in and dispensed fuel to caregivers so they could visit their patients. Employees with substantial property damage were wired $2,500 into their bank accounts. Kusserow went to a Lowe's store in the middle of the night with the company general counsel. He said, "We bought mops, buckets, fans, bleach, and anti-mold spray, anything that was on the shelf." Kusserow's decisive and compassionate actions helped the company, its employees, and patients get through the disaster.[5] As a result of these actions and behaviors, Kusserow can be viewed as a high-gravitas leader.

As mentioned above, Satya Nadella is known for his empathy.He is regarded as an unconventional CEO because empathy and compassion are the core of his business strategies. After 22 years of holding a variety of leadership positions at Microsoft Corp., Nadella was appointed CEO. He began his new position by establishing a new mission and vision for Microsoft. Nadella's primary focus was to make the company more innovative as the company was losing some of its dominance in software for business and personal use. He said that information technology only respects innovation, not tradition. A new mission and vision for the company was needed also because, throughout the industry, software as a product was gradually being replaced by software as a service. Many companies now run their IT infrastructure off cloud-based servers.

As articulated by Nadella, the mission of Microsoft is "to empower every person and every organization on the planet to achieve more." Nadella admits that the mission is ambitious but says that the company has the unique capability to harmonize the needs of both individuals and organizations because this capability is in Microsoft's DNA.

Nadella believes that it is incumbent upon him to teach, listen, and absorb new ideas rather than thinking he has all the answers. As with other effective leaders and managers, Nadella uses listening combined with empathy to build relationships with people. He says, "As a leader, I'm interested in fighting the new battles. You need new concepts with new innovation, and you have to have new capability and culture to go after those new concepts."

Nadella's empathy and compassion have been noted as a major contributor to the resurgence of Microsoft. He traces part of his empathy to having raised a child with cerebral palsy whose vision, hearing, and communication abilities were severely impaired. When Nadella began as the Microsoft CEO, he took a series of initiatives to ensure that empathy and compassion were integrated into Microsoft's mission and vision. One example is that he encouraged the teams to engage with customers and create products that met their needs, rather than innovating without customer input. The Xbox Adaptive Controller was developed based on an idea from a Microsoft employee with a disability who found it difficult to use traditional game controllers. The employee was given the resources to develop the new product, and the Xbox Adaptive Controller met with widespread acclaim. (The subtle point here is that the employee with a disability was also a customer.)

Another example of Nadella implementing empathy and compassion was the launch of the One Microsoft strategy. Teams were encouraged to break down silos and collaborate to create products and services that customers loved. Nadella's initiative was based on his vision of a united Microsoft serving customer interests, versus self-interest. The collaboration led to the development of new products and services including Microsoft Teams, and the Surface line of products.[6]

## *Expression of Gratitude*

The basic human principle of giving recognition by thanking people for a job well done and expressing gratitude has received considerable attention from leadership writers. The technical meaning of gratitude is a feeling of appreciation in response to an experience provided by another person that benefits you.[7] Gratitude specialist Adrian Gostick puts it this way: "It's vital to pay people appropriately, but there is only so much money to go around. That makes gratitude all the more meaningful and useful as a leadership tool." Showing gratitude is sometimes difficult because it makes managers as uncomfortable to praise employees as to criticize them.[8] Yet when a leader or manager expresses gratitude convincingly, it will add to his or her gravitas.

An easy approach to giving thanks and expressing gratitude is to compliment a group member. A field research project revealed that people underestimated how good their compliment would make the recipient feel and how much it would contribute to the recipient's sense of well-being. Compliment givers tend to believe that the compliment recipients will not enjoy the interaction as much as they do. A frequent thought is that giving a compliment will make the recipient uncomfortable. The same research project also found that people underestimate how much recipients appreciate gratitude. The implication of this study for leaders is not to underestimate the positive impact of compliments and grattitude.[9]

Another way to show appreciation and gratitude for motivational purposes is to begin team meetings with shout-outs for accomplishments of team members.[10] The team members receiving these accolades are likely to take the team leader quite seriously.

Research has uncovered an unusual twist about people receiving gratitude for their good deeds. A person is more likely to receive gratitude when the person helps another person in response to the latter's request for help.[11] In contrast, when a person takes the initiative to help another without being asked, the helper is less likely to receive gratitude. An extrapolation of this research is that a leader is more likely to receive gratitude when the team member asked for his or her help. In other words, to get another deposit in your gravitas account by expressing gratitude, wait until a team member asks you for help.

## Humility as Part of Gravitas

Leader humility is a positive force because it frequently improves subordinates' performance, job satisfaction, and creativity. A technical definition of humility helps explain why these positive outcomes are forthcoming. *Humility* is (a) self-awareness, (b) appreciating the strengths and contributions of others, and (c) openness to ideas and feedback regarding one's performance.[12] Leaders and professionals who act with a moderate degree of humility toward group members and clients will therefore often be perceived as having gravitas. Humility may be a personality trait, but being humble during interactions with others is a behavior. Here we describe a variety of leader actions and behaviors that demonstrate humility to subordinates.

*Placing Others in the Spotlight.* Pointing to the success of others is a robust way to be perceived as a person of substance. A key reason that leaders with humility place others in the spotlight is that they find joy in the success of others, similar to parents who find joy in the success of their children. Humble leaders also believe that the success of group members is not a threat to their own identity as a leader. A positive consequence is that the leader is willing to promote others and to celebrate the achievements of team members.[13]

Susan Brust is the senior vice president and director of new product development for Nordic Ware. She is recognized as having an advanced ability to allow others to shine as leaders themselves. Her humble leadership approach has several key elements. First, she gives all staff members and opportunity to lead. Brust leads by surrounding herself with good people and then finding ways to let them be visible. She says that rather than leading by "pulling people along," she leads by "pushing people ahead." When a variety of people are given the responsibility to step up, action happens.

Second, Brust acknowledges what the whole person brings to the workplace. In addition to acknowledging good work performance, she makes a point to acknowledge Nordic Ware employees for who they are as people. Sometimes this means that Brust must overcome her introverted tendencies and engage in everyday workplace small talk that can reveal a lot about the non-work side of people. Brust does this because it helps her build deeper connections, particularly with employees who are not her direct reports.

Third, she accepts acknowledgment and credit from others. Shrugging off a compliment—such as by saying "No big deal"—downplays the relevance and judgment of the compliment giver. Fourth, Brust does not assume that people know they are performing at a high level. Receiving recognition from the leader gives group members the reassurance that their contribution is recognized. Fifth, Brust recognizes that when they do well, you do well. She understands that when subordinates perform well, the leader has contributed to their success.[14] The humble leader does not see success as a zero-sum gain.

The most direct way for a leader to place others in the spotlight is to brag about their accomplishments to people outside and inside the group. Yet bragging too strongly to insiders about the accomplishments of one team member has the potential to create feelings of rivalry.

A prototypical example of bragging about a team member would be when a team leader says to his manager, "We never would have had this breakthrough without the creative thinking of Bree."

*Being a Team Player.* A basic approach for a leader to demonstrate humility is to work alongside team members. An example of showing humility by being a team player took place during the pandemic. Hint Water founder and CEO Kara Goldin stocked shelves with the company's product alongside her employees. Goldin illustrates that an empathetic leader knows when the team member needs help and works directly with them to get the work completed.[15]

*Helping Others Grow.* As Bradley P. Owens and David R. Hekman concluded in their pioneering study of humility and leadership, humble leadership can lead to employees who constantly keep growing and improving. Although the 55 leaders interviewed were from totally different organizations, they all agreed that the essence of leader humility involves being a model for subordinates of how to grow. The humble leaders in the study were described as "models of learning."[16] Being a model of learning contributes to a leader's gravitas because he or she will be admired by many group members.

Leaders with humility displayed openness to new ideas and information, listened before speaking, and were highly receptive to feedback. Humble leaders would also be models of personal growth and learning by initiating role reversals with group members. This meant the leaders would assume the group member role and place the group member in the leader/trainer role.

Rather than only telling subordinates how to do things, humble leaders were described as showing group members how to perform a task and then seeking feedback from the learners. For example, a leader might say, "Hey, let's learn this together. Let's make some sales calls together. Maybe you can see me making a call and can give me some pointers in what I do right and what I do wrong. Then you can try it."

It seemed that no group member task was too menial for leaders with humility. They would serve as a model of a wide variety of follower tasks from sales calls to custodial work to basic labor. In one extreme example, a high-ranking military leader broke his leg helping lift a large generator off a truck with his soldiers. The officer's only lament was that he would not be able to run with his soldiers in the immediate future.

By being a model of eagerness to learn, the humble leaders appeared to be intent on fostering a positive, proactive attitude about acquiring new knowledge. At the same time, the same leaders gained a deeper understanding about how to best help group members overcome challenges. Humble leaders not only talked about the importance of continual learning or supporting training programs for learning and development. They also provided an example of how to develop by being honest about areas for improvement including acknowledging mistakes and limitations.

An attitude of humble leaders that catalyzed an interest in growth was to tell group members that it is okay to be a "work in progress" here. The leaders emphasized that mistakes in acquiring new skills are almost inevitable and are therefore tolerated. Subordinates were influenced to believe that apprehension was natural and acceptable when acquiring new knowledge. A leader might say, "I can see what a whale of a challenge it is to learn how to incorporate artificial intelligence into your analysis. Take the time you need to learn how to apply AI to our problems."

*Macro-Managing Subordinates.* Leaders with humility take naturally to avoiding micromanagement because they usually assume that the person performing a task has more job-relevant knowledge than they do. As noted by management consultant Jeff Kirschner, the ability to step away from micromanagement and trust the team is a good demonstration of humility. When a CEO demonstrates humility, he or she builds trust and fosters followership for executives. They are provided with the bandwidth to carry out their roles with more freedom.[17]

Leaders who are deficient in humility tend to be micromanagers. They are so focused on ensuring everything is done their way that they lose sight of the group goal. Humble leaders are aware that micromanagement can backfire, so they work hard to promote group member autonomy. Humble leaders are comfortable in backing off and practicing *macro-management* because they accept the reality that they are not always the person with the best answer to an individual or group problem. Equally important, humble leaders are confident in their employees' skills and knowledge and are open to new ideas.[18]

As a macro-manager, the humble leader takes a hands-off approach to leading employees and allows group members to perform their tasks without much supervision. A potential pitfall of macro-management is that many employees want and need close supervision and feedback, particularly when they are acquiring new skills. Take the example of a woman who has a key position as a wedding planner for a company that specializes in organizing weddings. She might want to be supervised closely as she plans her first few events. An effective humble leader knows when the time is right to back off from micromanagement and shift to macro-management.

*Reverse Mentoring and Humility.* Another effective way a humble leader can build effective relationships within the group is through *reverse mentoring*, that is, being taught something specific by a younger group member. The typical scenario is for the younger group member to coach the leader about computer technology. Yet younger people have valuable skills and knowledge in many areas in addition to computer technology. Among the dozens of possibilities would be knowledge about a second language, the cultural values of a particular group, packaging design, fashion design, and mathematics.

Humble leaders take naturally to building relationships through reverse mentoring because one of their fundamental beliefs is that they do not have all the knowledge to perform their work in an outstanding manner. Stanley McChrystal, a retired four-star general, was a strong believer in practicing reverse mentoring. The Army's tactics and equipment changed dramatically between the time McChrystal joined the Army and his promotion to four-star general. During his later years in command, McChrystal recognized that his decades of experience were not directly relevant to the younger soldiers. With humility, he wondered if he should still be in charge.

McChrystal recognized that he had to be honest with himself and his troops. He admitted he had some knowledge gaps and asked his direct reports to teach him. In return, McChrystal promised to provide them with wisdom based on his lengthy experience. Rather than questioning his capability and legitimacy as a leader, the troops gave McChrystal credit for admitting where he needed fresh knowledge. The entire battalion benefited from the exchange of knowledge.[19]

A caution about humility and its impact on gravitas is that if group members think that the leader is using impression management to act humble, humility can backfire. A set of studies conducted with both working adults and college students suggested that leaders who were perceived to be humble just to create a positive impression were perceived as hypocritical.[20] A closely related finding is that when group members perceive the leader to be using humility in a self-serving way, they might engage in negative behavior such as lowering productivity.[21] The pretend humble leader therefor does not gain in gravitas.

## Appropriate Expression of Anger

A leader who expresses a reasonable degree of anger but is not outright hostile and aggressive will often be perceived as a person to be taken seriously. Part of the reason is that anger in the workplace can be a powerful force in motivating workers to achieve. Evidence from several fields suggests that anger may fuel the ambitions and creativity of some workers. Surprisingly, anger can help people calm down and get ready to address a problem. Anger appears to stimulate the frontal cortex, the part of the brain associated with pushing us to pursue desired goals in a logical, systematic manner.[22]

A scholarly review of research and opinion about workplace anger revealed several ways in which expressing this emotion can be beneficial. Appropriate expression of anger can therefore enhance the leader's stature. The more formal power a leader possesses, the more anger is accepted and tolerated by subordinates. Several of these potentially valuable outputs from anger follow.[23]

- Anger can serve a valuable function by alerting employees to violations of rules and norms including injustice and inappropriate behavior on the job. For example, the head of the department of neurosurgery might say in an angry tone to a surgical resident, "You are absolutely forbidden to ask a teenage patient to become one of your Facebook friends."
- Anger can get a group member energized toward goal accomplishment in a hurry. A CEO might say with an enraged look on her face to the head of cybersecurity, "Get this ransomware problem fixed by midnight, or we will lose one-third of our customers."
- Anger is often an effective negotiating tactic because negotiation counterparts take the negotiator seriously who expresses anger in a reasonable fashion.
- Anger can be a useful form of feedback because the subordinates often think they would not be recipients of anger if they were performing better. As a result of the anger, the subordinate may work toward improved performance.

To reinforce a key point, a reasonable display of anger makes the leader appear formidable. And being formidable adds to gravitas.

---

# Guidelines for Action

1. A distinguishing intellectual strength of people with gravitas is that they can size up people and situations and arrive at in-depth understandings that others might miss.

2. Whereas others might accept feedback superficially, the person with intellectual gravitas is likely to wring much more meaning out if it.

3. After experiencing a stunning insight, sharing it with others is a vehicle for enhancing your gravitas.

4. A winning thought pattern of high-gravitas people is their propensity to express positive thoughts when appropriate.

5. Even during the worst adversity, the high-gravitas person will deliver a positive message about digging out of the adverse situation.

6. An eagerness to serve others will often enhance a leader's gravitas because such willingness increases the leader's respect and seriousness of purpose.

7. As with all humble leaders, servant leaders acknowledge their limitations and therefore actively seek the contributions of others to compensate for these limitations.

8. The leader who expresses empathy is perceived as a person of substance.

9. Compassionate behavior on the part of the leader with gravitas is strongly needed during an organizational crisis, such as a hurricane or massive explosion.

10. When a leader or manager expresses gratitude convincingly, it will add to his or her gravitas.

11. Pointing to the success of others is a robust way to be perceived as a person of substance.

12. A basic approach for a leader to demonstrate humility is to work alongside team members.

13. Leaders with humility take naturally to avoiding micromanagement because they usually assume that the person performing the task has more job-relevant knowledge than they do.

14. A caution about humility and its impact on gravitas is that if group members think that the leader is using impression management to act humble, humility can backfire. The leader might be perceived as hypocritical.

15. A leader who expresses a reasonable degree of anger but is not outrightly hostile and aggressive will often be taken seriously.

5

# Key Leadership Skills
# for Gravitas

Having almost any valuable leadership skill might add to a leader's gravitas. For example, a team leader with expertise in conducting performance appraisals might be taken more seriously than a leader who botched performance appraisals. In this chapter, however, we focus on five leadership skills that make a major contribution to the leader's gravitas. We begin with the heavyweight skill of strategic thinking. Thinking strategically is so important for gravitas that it was described as a component of gravitas in Chapter 2. Here we frame strategic thinking as also a skill that contributes to gravitas.

## *Strategic Thinking*

One of the central challenges of modern organizations is for leaders at all levels in the organization to think strategically, including seeing the overall picture as they go about their work. Strategic thinking heavily emphasizes long-term thinking. A business leader might want to make major capital expenditures that will have a payoff in the long run but reduce short-term earnings. Effective strategic thinkers are likely to be perceived as having gravitas because they point the organization or organizational unit in a successful direction.

Professional service firm leader Julie Sweet represents a strong example of a strategic and big-picture thinker. In 2023, *Fortune* magazine ranked Sweet, the chair and CEO and of the professional services giant Accenture, as the most powerful woman in business. Accenture has over $62 billion in annual revenues and more than 720,000 employees worldwide. For many years, the company has focused on cloud, digital, and security businesses. Prior to becoming CEO in September 2019, Sweet served as the chief executive officer of the company's North American business. Sweet was previously the company's general counsel, secretary, and general compliance officer for five years. Sweet's in-depth professional expertise was used extensively in all these roles.

An example of Sweet's strategic thinking is her explanation of how macroeconomic trends impact Accenture clients. She noted that macro trends in 2022 were making it clearer that clients need to change more rather than less. She noted that the need for total enterprise reinvention, enabled by tech, data, and AI, and the ability to access, create, and unlock the potential of talent are critical for success now and in the future.

During Accenture's presentation to financial analysts for the first quarter of fiscal year 2023, Sweet made the following big-picture analysis: Customers' requirements for growth, cost optimization, and resilience suggest a very positive sign for the company. Sweet added that Accenture has unique strengths that customers need to navigate today and succeed tomorrow. "We are able to do so because of our deep strategy and consulting expertise across industries, allowing us to be a trusted advisor during different economic cycles because we bring the expertise coupled with the real-life practical experience we need."

Among her accomplishments, Sweet led the company through the COVID-19 pandemic, while simultaneously redefining Accenture's growth model, strategy, purpose, and brand. All these accomplishments took place during her first year as CEO. A new dimension *Fortune* used in ranking the most influential woman was, "Is the leader using their influence to shape the company and the wider world for the better?" Sweet has been using her role as CEO to place additional emphasis on important issues such as environmental sustainability and racial equality.

During an interview Sweet said, "Our new purpose is to deliver on the promise of technology and human ingenuity. And our new brand campaign is, 'Let there be Change,' because we have only one choice, and that is to embrace change and make it for the benefit of all." Accenture helps clients reimagine everything about their business, and rebuilding industries and economies for the benefit of all. Sweet believes technology today is our lifeline.

At Accenture, Sweet has made promoting women a priority, establishing aggressive targets for gender parity, and working hard to move more women into the executive ranks. Accenture aims to have 50/50 gender parity across the organization and for the managing director role to attain 25 percent women.

When hiring new people into Accenture, Sweet emphasizes two

attributes. The first is curiosity, because the new normal is continuous learning. The second attribute is leadership in the sense of having the courage to deliver tough messages to clients. Accenture clients are constantly saying, "The most important thing that you do is tell me what I need to hear, not what I want to hear." Sweet believes that the CEO of today must articulate moral purpose and compass to their stakeholders. They need a message that inspires purpose in people.

During the pandemic, many CEOs told Sweet they thought they needed to get rid of all their real estate. She told them not to move too fast. Even though there are many ways to work remotely and collaboratively, the human connection is still important. In-person collaboration is still critical.[1]

## Creative and Innovative Thinking

A major contributor to a leader's gravitas is the complex skill of creative and innovative thinking. By thinking creatively, a person can form a new enterprise or enlarge an existing one that can keep many people engaged in productive activity. However, the creative idea must be executed properly for innovation to take place. Although the terms *creativity* and *innovation* are often used interchangeably, *innovation* refers to the creation of new ideas and their implementation or commercialization. True innovation involves breakthrough development and is regarded by some management thinkers as the only sustainable source of competitive advantage.[2] The type of creativity under focus here is business creativity rather than scientific or technical, such as developing a chip to implant in the brain of people with quadriplegia to improve their ability to communicate and move physically.

The role of a creative leader is to bring into existence ideas and things that did not exist previously or that existed in a different form. Leaders are not bound by current solutions to problems. Instead, they create images of other possibilities. Leaders often move a firm into an additional business or start a new department that offers another service. A synthesis of 185 studies indicates that the leaders' efforts in facilitating creativity and innovation are worthwhile. The analysis found clear theoretical and empirical evidence demonstrating that leadership is a key variable that can enhance workplace creativity and innovation.[3]

*Cognitive Skills.* Creative individuals have been studied from many different perspectives. Yet examining the cognitive abilities of leaders is highly relevant in understanding how creativity and innovation enhance the gravitas of leaders. Cognitive abilities comprise such abilities as general intelligence and abstract reasoning. Creative problem solvers characteristically have well above-average cognitive intelligence, and being bright is yet another contributor to listening to what a person has to say.

Creative people are facile at generating creative solutions to problems in a short period of time. Creative people also maintain a youthful curiosity throughout their lives, and the curiosity is not centered just on their own field of expertise. Instead, their range of interests encompasses many areas of knowledge, and they are enthusiastic about puzzling problems. These mental workouts help sharpen a person's intelligence.

Creative people show an identifiable intellectual style: being able to think divergently. They can expand the number of alternatives to a problem, thus moving away from a single solution. (The essence of creativity is to identify multiple alternatives to a problem, including the familiar "thinking outside the box.") Yet, the creative thinker also knows when it is time to narrow the number of useful solutions. For example, the divergent thinker might think of 27 ways to reduce costs, but, at some point, the person will have to move toward choosing the best of several cost-cutting approaches.

A hallmark of a creative businessperson's intellect is to spot opportunities that others might overlook. A case in point is Hamdi Ulukaya, a Turkish immigrant who launched Chobani brand yogurt in 2007. At the time, the Greek market share of yogurt in the United States was less than 1 percent. Today the share is over 60 percent. Ulukaya says that the growth of his enterprise began when he spotted an abandoned and dilapidated yogurt plant Kraft Foods was looking to sell. With only $3,000 left in his pocket, Ulukaya needed an opportunity to make a living.[4]

A natural way for creative and innovative thinking by a leader to manifest itself is to choose a profitable direction for the company. Laura Alber is the CEO of home furnishing retailer Williams-Sonoma. An example of Alber's imaginative (as well as strategic) thinking took place during a time of high interest rates and inflation that threatened sales volume. "You can't wait for a macro trend to improve your business," she said. "You have to make it happen and look for other opportunities to grow." In recent years the Williams-Sonoma focus on high-earning consumers, luxury products, and multichannel selling has helped the company prosper. Several other home-improvement retailers have not performed as well.[5]

*Intuition.* A major cognitive contributor to creative thinking is *intuition.* The term refers to an experienced-based way of knowing or reasoning in which weighing and balancing evidence are done unconsciously and automatically. The *aha!* experience is an example of intuition. The yogurt entrepreneur mentioned above showed strong intuition when he saw the possibilities in an abandoned and dilapidated yogurt plant. The rise of data analytics has prompted many executives and management writers to think that intuition has become less important in making creative decisions. Brad Fisher, the U.S. leader of data and analytics at the consulting firm KPMG, said that companies beefing up their analytics must also find ways to sharpen executives' instincts (intuition). Fisher says, "You should collect as many data points as you can, but don't throw out your intuition."[6]

Take the accompanying self-quiz to think through your own intuition tendencies.

---

## The Intuitive Problem-Solving Style Quiz

Indicate your strength of agreement with each of the following statements: strongly disagree (**SD**), disagree (**D**), neutral (**N**), agree (**A**), strongly agree (**SA**).

| | | *SD* | *D* | *N* | *A* | *SA* |
|---|---|---|---|---|---|---|
| 1. | Most of my hunches prove to be correct. | 1 | 2 | 3 | 4 | 5 |
| 2. | Details tend to take care of themselves providing you are on the right track with your plans. | 1 | 2 | 3 | 4 | 5 |
| 3. | Before attempting to solve a problem, I gather many relevant facts. | 5 | 4 | 3 | 2 | 1 |
| 4. | Relying on gut feel is a terrible way for a business executive to make a decision. | 5 | 4 | 3 | 2 | 1 |
| 5. | When I meet a person for the first time, I take my time in deciding whether that person and I will get along. | 5 | 4 | 3 | 2 | 1 |
| 6. | It takes me about 10 seconds to know if I am physically attracted to another person. (Skip this question if you are in a committed relationship.) ☺ | 1 | 2 | 3 | 4 | 5 |
| 7. | It takes me a long time to decide whether I like the color on a vehicle I am thinking about purchasing. | 5 | 4 | 3 | 2 | 1 |

| | | SD | D | N | A | SA |
|---|---|---|---|---|---|---|
| 8. | I need, or would need, to gather a lot of facts before I would purchase stock in a specific company. | 5 | 4 | 3 | 2 | 1 |
| 9. | When making an important decision, it is much better to gather new facts rather than rely on experience. | 5 | 4 | 3 | 2 | 1 |
| 10. | When making an important decision, it is much better to gather new facts than to rely on experience. | 5 | 4 | 3 | 2 | 1 |
| 11. | Common sense is an effective source of information for making decisions. | 1 | 2 | 3 | 4 | 5 |
| 12. | I usually "jump to a conclusion" when making a decision. | 1 | 2 | 3 | 4 | 5 |
| 13. | My best ideas have come from flashes of insight. | 1 | 2 | 3 | 4 | 5 |
| 14. | Unless a person is rational and systematic, that person is unlikely to make effective decisions. | 5 | 4 | 3 | 2 | 1 |
| 15. | I am more impulsive than reflective. | 1 | 2 | 3 | 4 | 5 |
| 16. | When the "light bulb goes on," I know that I have a useful idea. | 1 | 2 | 3 | 4 | 5 |

*Scoring and Interpretation:* Find your total score by summing the point values for each question.

**65–80** You probably have a strong intuitive decision-making style that facilitates being a creative thinker.

**36–64** You probably have a balanced approach between an intuitive decision-making style and one that relies more on facts and research.

**15–35** Your decision-making style probably emphasizes basing your decisions on facts and careful observation rather than on intuition, which could be a deterrent to your creativity.

---

## Sensemaking of Ambiguous Events

Group members often look to the leader to help make sense of, or explain, what is happening during an ambiguous event. A leader engages in sensemaking by explaining the nature of what is happening, or literally making sense of events.[7] Sensemaking also refers to helping stakeholders understand the implications of what is happening. The leader who succeeds in making sense of what is happening will gain in stature and be taken seriously. Imagine that a company is going through bankruptcy. The CEO could make sense of the situation by explaining that the bank will continue to operate, employees will be paid, and there will be only a 6 percent reduction in force.

Sensemaking also applies to helping customers unravel ambiguity. The research firm Gartner surveyed 1,100 B2B (business-to-business) customers about the problem of being blitzed with enormous amounts of product information. Nearly 90 percent of the respondents agreed that the information they encountered as part of making a purchase is generally of high quality. The information is believable, relevant, and conveyed in an interesting manner. Nevertheless, the respondents struggle to make sense of all the information.

Fifty-five percent of the respondents found the information to be trustworthy but unclear as to which information is the most relevant. B2B buyers felt strained to identify useful criteria to make trade-offs among suppliers. Forty-four percent of the buyers found the information to be trustworthy but contradictory. Although the various pieces are relevant and believable, they suggest opposing directions.

Sales professionals who use sensemaking methods capitalize on the problems caused by the information blitz by aiding, organizing, and simplifying buyers' product research. What follows are several of these sensemaking methods that help clarify ambiguity for customers and potential customers.

- Emphasize simplicity over comprehensiveness.
- Instead of telling customers what to think, help them create a framework within which they can make their own decisions.
- Connect customers with relevant resources. Provide customers with only information that will help them advance with increasing confidence toward the path to making a major purchase.
- Clarify information. Help customers feel they have asked the right questions, examined competing perspectives, and accounted for problems that might arise.
- Collaborate on customer learning. Buyers should be guided on a learning journey, not told what to do. Customers should be encouraged to independently verify information provided by the seller. Provide guidance on verification resources.

Expecting sales professionals to engage in sensemaking with customers may seem to be an unrealistically high expectation, yet here is one small component of the sensemaking process. Expedient is a cloud-based disaster recovery software company that wanted to simplify the complexities of purchasing their software. Expedient created a seller training and certification program for all frontline reps and managers. Sales representatives were asked to identify the sources of information most frequently used by customers. Market research facilitated Expedient identifying priority questions customers were likely to ask. Expedient then developed an assessment tool that gave buyers a realistic means of answering these questions on their own. The framework enables customers to quickly organize, analyze, and prioritize information used to purchase the software in question.

A key result of sales professionals using the sensemaking approach is that approximately 80 percent of customers interacting with sensemaking reps completed high-quality, low-regret purchases. Two-thirds of buyers said they believed the claims of sales representatives who engaged in sensemaking. In contrast, when customers are struggling with an overload of high-quality information and looking to move forward, being presented with even more information can backfire. Placing even more information on the table, with limited guidance on how it fits or why it matters, results in more confusion for the buyer. Pushing even more information on the buyer feels pushy and self-serving and decreases customers' confidence that they can take decisive action.[8] The sales representatives who helped customers make sense of the mass of information were taken seriously.

## Effective Coaching

A robust way to gain stature with direct reports is to coach them in a way that helps them develop professionally. As with every contributor to gravitas, coaching is a broad subject of study itself. Our focus here is on several aspects of coaching that both help the person being coached and contribute to the perception that the leader or manager in the coaching role has a serious purpose.

*Apply the GROW Model of Coaching.* An effective way of projecting gravitas is to use a systematic framework for coaching. The GROW model devised in the 1980s is a plausible approach because it is field-tested. "GROW" is an acronym for the action steps of goal, reality, option, and will. Applying the model well requires mental discipline and practice.[9]

- **Goal.** At the start of coaching someone about an issue or topic, establish a goal of what he or she hopes to accomplish from this exchange. You might ask the person being coached, "When our coaching session is completed, what do you want to be the takeaway?"
- **Reality.** The second action step of the GROW model is to focus on specific facts. Two effective reality-focused questions to ask are "What are the most important things we need to know?" and "What is the real problem that you are facing in completing the project on time?" The reality action step is critical because it lessens the probability that the person being coached with overlook pertinent variables and jump to an unwarranted conclusion.
- **Options.** People who come to their manager for coaching often feel stuck in the sense of seeing no options or useful alternatives to the problem they are facing. In the coaching role, you want the other person to engage in creative thinking in the sense of generating more alternative solutions. As the options surface, the advantages and disadvantages of each one might be explored. Several options in relation to getting a project completed on time are (a) temporarily borrowing a few workers from another department, (b) hiring a couple of gig workers for the project, (c) asking team members to work longer hours until the project is completed, and (d) suggesting that all team members use better time-management skills.
- **Will.** The first part of this action step is to ask, "What will you do?" In responding to this question, the person must define how he or she will approach the problem. The second part of this action step focuses on the motivation to implement the action step. As a coach you might ask, "How likely is it that you are going to ask team members to work longer hours so the project will be completed on time?"

*Build Relationships.* Effective coaches build relationships with team members and work to improve their interpersonal skills, thereby facilitating being taken seriously. Having established rapport with team members facilitates entering a coaching relationship with them. Carefully listening to group members and providing emotional support are part of relationship building.

*Give Feedback on Areas That Require Specific Improvement.* To coach a group member toward higher levels of performance, the leader pinpoints what specific behaviors, attitudes, or skills require improvement. A coach with gravitas might say, "I read the product-expansion proposal you submitted. It's OK, but it falls short of your usual level of creativity. Our competitors are already carrying each product you mentioned. Have you thought about...?"

Another important factor in giving specific feedback is to avoid generalities and exaggerations such as, "You never come up with a good product idea" or "You are the most unimaginative product development specialist I have ever known." To give good feedback, the leader or manager must observe performance and behavior directly and frequently, such as watching a supervisor deal with a safety problem.

A major challenge in giving feedback is that many people find negative feedback to be uncomfortable. It is therefore helpful to get the person's buy-in—or at least willingness to receive feedback. For example, if coaching on the fly, the leader might ask, "Tyrie, I'd like to offer some quick feedback because I want to help you. Is this a good time?"[10]

It also helps to be quite specific about the negative feedback. Begin the conversation by noting where and when the behavior you want to discuss occurred.[11] For example, you might say, "During our product launch meeting last week you joked about the physical appearance of one of our support staff who fortunately was not in the room. Joking about another worker's appearance does not fit our culture." If the recipient of the negative feedback believes it to be warranted, the feedback giver will be taken more seriously.

Feedback is also likely to be less intimidating when the coach explains which behavior should decrease and which should increase. This approach is a variation of combining compliments with criticism to avoid insulting the person being coached. You might say, "Mia, I need you to place more emphasis on quality and less on speed."

Feedback can also be made less intimidating when the coach begins with a question such as "How do you think you are doing?" The question gives the person being coached joint ownership of the problem and helps him or her feel included rather than excluded.[12] The question also helps feedback become a conversation rather than the coach focusing on telling the group member what performance or behavior requires change.

Should the coach be dealing with a person who is highly sensitive to criticism, it can be helpful to convert the criticism into a positive suggestion to avoid intimidating the person being coached. For example, replace "A few of your facts were way off in your last report" with "You could improve your accuracy by double-checking your facts."

*Provide Regular On-the-Spot Feedback on What Is Going Well.* A modern twist on using feedback in coaching is to reinforce the desired performance or behavior when it is observed in the day-by-day work environment.[13] Text messaging is an effective medium for on-the-spot positive feedback. A facilities manager might say to a mechanic, "I saw what you did today. The air conditioning was down in the east-wing office. You dropped everything to rush in and fix the problem before half the staff fainted from the heat. To me that is superior performance. Keep it up." The facilities manager in this scenario had the coaching objective of getting the mechanic to respond more quickly to problems so he reinforced the speedy response.

We have devoted a lot of space to giving feedback because it lies at the heart of coaching and affects the coach's gravitas. Constructive feedback facilitates the coach being taken seriously.

*Help Remove Obstacles.* An act indicative of gravitas is making life easier for the person coached. To perform anywhere near capacity, individuals may need help in removing obstacles such as a maze of rules and regulations and rigid budgeting. An important role for the leader of an organizational unit is therefore to be a barrier buster. A leader or manager is often in a better position than a group member to gain approval from a higher-level manager, find money from another budget line, expedite a purchase order, or authorize hiring a temporary worker to assist. Yet if the coach is too quick to remove the obstacles, the group member may not develop enough self-reliance.

*Give Emotional Support and Empathy.* Being helpful and constructive, the leader provides much-needed emotional support to the group member who is not performing at his or her best. A coaching session should not be an interrogation. An effective way of giving emotional support is to use positive rather than negative motivators. The leader might say, "I liked some things you did yesterday, and I have a few suggestions that might bring you closer to your best performance."

Displaying empathy is an effective way to give emotional support. Indicate with words that you understand the challenge your direct report faces with a statement such as, "I understand that working with a reduced staff has placed you under heavy time pressures."

*Work on a Solution Together.* Particularly when an employee is struggling to overcome a problem, it is best to work with that person to find a solution together. Giving the subordinate a chance to take ownership of the difficult situation is empowering and often provides extra initiative for improvement.[14] A logistics specialist might say to the manager, "I am trying hard to keep up with my work, but I get so many digital messages every hour, it throws me off track." The leader as coach might reply, "What steps could you take to block out time for these messages, and still get your core work done?"

*Give Some Gentle Advice and Guidance.* Too much advice-giving interferes with two-way communication, yet some advice can elevate performance. Furthermore, workers being coached usually expect to receive some advice. The leader should assist the group member in asking the question, "What can I do about this problem?" Advice in the form of a question or suppositional statement is often effective. One example is, "Could the root of your problem be insufficient planning?" A direct statement such as, "The root of your problem is probably insufficient planning" often makes people resentful and defensive. By responding to a question, the person being coached is likely to feel more involved in making improvements.

Part of giving gentle guidance for improvement is to use the word *could* instead of *should*. To say "You should do this" implies that the person is currently doing something wrong, which can trigger defensiveness. Saying "You could do this," leaves the person with a choice: accept or reject your input and weigh the consequences.[15] (You *could* accept this advice to become a better coach!)

A key point about advice and guidance for our purposes is the advice that works enhances the perception that the advice giver has gravitas. The fact that the advice works is more important than how adroitly the advice was administered.

*Cheer Progress.* Corporate executive coach John Baldoni explains that cheering the progress of the person being coached contributes substantially to effective coaching. Cheering on people being coached affirms their progress and helps them gain more self-confidence to continue along the path to improvement. Visualize middle-manager Amanda coaching logistics specialist Matt to rely more on data when choosing a new supplier. During their second coaching session Matt says, "I did a thorough Internet search on Bandwidth Electronics before I offered them a contract. I looked at customer reviews and a Bloomberg report on their financial status." Amanda cheers Matt by saying, "You have built skills in precisely the area we pinpointed for improvement. I applaud your progress."[16]

## *Resolving Conflict Between Two Team Members*

A high-level leadership and managerial skill is to help two or more team members resolve conflict between or among them. Much of the time a manager or leader invests in conflict resolution is geared toward assisting others to resolve their conflict. Often, the conflict is between the heads of two different departments or divisions. A team leader will sometimes be placed in the position of having to resolve conflict between or among team members. Considering that resolving conflict successfully is an admired skill, the manager who can carry it out projects gravitas.

One analysis suggests that destructive conflict stems from perceived incompatibility in the way the team members operate. Among the contributing factors are differences in personality, industry background, gender, and age.[17] An incompatibility problem that surfaces frequently is that a couple of team members might be big-picture thinkers, while a few others focus carefully on details. Big-picture-thinking Arriana might say, "I see our team having a major impact on the total organization," Detail-thinking Tim might say angrily, "Arriana, will you please tells us exactly what you have in mind? Be specific about what we could accomplish."

The most useful approach is to get the parties in conflict to engage in confrontation and problem-solving. (*Confrontation* refers to discussing the true problem, and *problem-solving* refers to finding a way to resolve the conflict.) The manager sits down with the two sides and encourages them to talk to each other about the problem (rather than to the manager). This approach is preferable to inviting each side to speak with the manager or leader alone, because then each side might attempt to convince the manager that their side is right.

During the confrontation and problem-solving session, the leader/manager is placed in a mediator role of being impartial and wanting both sides to come to an agreement. As shown in the illustration below, the heart of the approach is *storytelling* in which each employee tells how and why the conflict started and persists. Each side must allow the other side to talk, and the leader maintains impartiality.[18] An abbreviated example follows:

> *LEADER:* I've brought you two together to see if you can overcome the problems you have about sharing the workload during a period in which one of you is overloaded.
>
> *MARISSA:* I'm glad you did. Calvin never wants to help me, even when I'm drowning in customer requests.
>
> *CALVIN:* I would be glad to help Marissa if she ever agreed to help me. If

**84**

she has any downtime, she runs to the break room so she can chat on her phone.

MARISSA: Look who's talking. I have seen you napping in your SUV when you have a little downtime.

LEADER: I'm beginning to see what's going on here. Each of you is antagonistic toward the other, and you look for little faults to pick. With a little more respect on both sides, I think you would be more willing to help each other out.

CALVIN: Actually, Marissa is not too bad. And I know she can perform well when she wants to. Next time I see her needing help, I'll pitch in.

MARISSA: I know that Calvin likes to joke around, but he has a warm heart. I'm open to starting with a fresh slate. Maybe Calvin can ask me politely the next time he needs help.

An effective component to this type of conflict resolution is for the leader to ask each side to restate what the other person has said. In the scenario just presented, Calvin might say, "I heard Marissa say that I never want to help her." Marissa might say, "I heard Calvin say that I run to the break room to talk on my phone when I have a little downtime."

Conflict specialist Patrick S. Nugent believes that being able to intervene in the conflicts of group members is a management skill that grows in importance. Such competencies are useful in an emerging form of management based less on traditional hierarchy and more on developing self-managing subordinates and teams. When the conflict is between two different groups, such as marketing versus manufacturing, a major goal of conflict resolution is to get the two sides to see the company's big picture.[19] The leader who can get both sides to see the big picture will be taken quite seriously.

## Appropriate Use of Humor

An effective sense of humor is an important part of a leader's role. Humor adds to the approachability and people orientation of a leader. Done effectively, humor adds to the leader or professional's stature. Because humor helps the leader dissolve tension and defuse conflict, it helps the leader exert power over the group. Here we look at aspects of humor that have a reasonable chance of adding to the leader's gravitas.

*Self-Effacing Humor Is the Safest Bet.* Self-effacing humor is the choice of comedians and organizational leaders alike. By being self-effacing, the leader makes a point without insulting or slighting anybody. Charismatic leaders are masters at mild self-effacement. Ronald

Reagan in the later years of his presidency jokingly referred to a conversation he had with Thomas Jefferson during his (Reagan's) youth. Instead of criticizing a staff member for being too technical, the leader might say, "Wait, I need your help. Please explain how this new product works in terms that even I can understand."

Self-effacing humor should be light and indulged in infrequently to avoid detracting from the humorist's seriousness of purpose. Carried to an extreme, self-effacing humor is a form of negative self-talk that will sooner or later begin to pall.

*Spontaneous Witty Comments.* Making a witty or clever comment on the spur of the moment makes a vastly bigger contribution to gravitas than does telling rehearsed jokes. Telling jokes can help you develop a reputation for being funny and a good storyteller. Yet a joke teller is rarely considered witty. The witty comment that follows helped establish the reputation of a product manager at a major consumer-products company. The product manager was walking in downtown San Francisco with three work associates. San Francisco, like most major cities, has at least one person per block holding out a Styrofoam cup in the retail and entertainment district.

The product manager flipped a five-dollar bill into the cup of a beggar, a healthy-looking man in his mid-forties. One of her work associates asked why she would give money to a healthy-looking beggar. The product manager replied: "I empathize with the guy. If our latest product fails to get the market share we forecast, we'll all be joining him next month."

*Avoidance of Insulting the People Present Is Important.* Insulting any member of a group on hand is usually an ineffective form of humor. When insults are perceived as an attack, the insulter loses in psychological stature. Insulting people who are not present can sometimes be effective. Even when outside groups are attacked, the attack should have a soft, human touch. A member of a sales group used this variation of a joke that achieved cliché status a few decades ago. "How many marketing analysts does it take to change a light bulb?" Answer: "Three. Two to conduct a nationwide online survey of whether changing a light bulb leads to customer satisfaction, and one to make the actual change if needed."

*Humor That Delivers an Uplifting Comment About Others Is a Winning Tactic.* A deeply ingrained behavior pattern of high-gravitas people is to make others feel good through their humorous comments. If this is a skill that does not come naturally, it takes a long time to develop. The starting point is to raise your level of self-awareness of the importance of building the self-esteem of others.

Humorous comments that enhance the self-esteem of people who are present physically or online typically exaggerate their capabilities. The sales manager of a company that makes car interiors for automotive manufacturers was holding a meeting. The sales representatives receive a base salary along with commissions. During a discussion of the recent surge in sales as automotive manufacturers outsourced more components, the sales director said with a straight face: "Right now, team, we are facing an internal problem. Jason, our CEO, said that at our present rate of sales, two of you will soon be earning more than he does. And he doesn't like it. I told Jason that he could join our sales team if he could prove that he can do the job."

The sales manager's comment complimented the outstanding performance of two group members. In addition, he added to team pride by pointing out that the sales team is so elite that it was uncertain if the CEO had the right capabilities to join them.

*Effective Workplace Humor Should Support a Serious Purpose.* Humor and creativity consultant Lindsay Collier advises his clients to use humor that focuses on, and if possible, supports a serious purpose. By being connected with the task at hand, the humor will be perceived as especially clever, thus contributing to the gravitas of the person making the comment.[20]

A principal in an investment firm told the staff at an 8:30 a.m. meeting: "I wish I had good news to tell you. But the truth is that the economic reports to be released this week show that almost all economic indicators are up. Housing starts are way up, inventories have declined, vehicle sales are way up, and consumer confidence has jumped three percentage points. You probably read the positive report on the Internet. The consequences for our clients should be disastrous."

Perhaps you are wondering why the staff chuckled at the principal's announcement. The explanation is that during the time when the principal made the comment, good economic news often meant that the major stock market indices moved downward. Portfolio managers feared that interest rates would climb and that stocks would not have much of an edge over fixed-income securities. The comment about the good news bringing bad news for the clients helped prime the wealth managers to meet the challenges of the day. Many clients would be worried about their stock and stock mutual fund investments.

*Effective Workplace Humor Makes a Point.* Akin to humor supporting a serious purpose, workplace humor should ideally also make a point. The humorous comment should alert another person to the need for change, compliment the person, or help solve an organizational problem. A CEO asked an information technology manager how well her assignment of updating the accounts receivable system was proceeding. He replied, "Pretty well, I've already obtained my first four approvals." Ouch! Yet the humorous comment helped the CEO to recognize how badly the company needed to reengineer its process for making changes in an important system.

---

# Guidelines for Action

1. Almost any valuable skill might add to your gravitas as a leader.
2. Effective strategic thinkers are likely to be perceived as having gravitas because they point the organization or organizational unit in a successful direction.
3. You are likely to be perceived as a big-picture thinker if you can understand a situation or concept from an overall perspective rather than getting bogged down in small details.
4. A major contributor to your leadership gravitas is the complex skill of creative and innovative thinking.
5. The role of a creative leader is to bring into existence ideas and things that did not exist previously or that existed in a different form.
6. A key skill for developing our creativity is to think divergently or expand the number of alternatives to a problem.
7. Another essential part of creativity is knowing when it is time to narrow the number of useful solutions.
8. Having intuition that is usually correct enhances your gravitas.
9. Collect as many data points as feasible but do not neglect your intuition.
10. Group members often look to the leader to make sense of or explain what is happening during an ambiguous event. As a result, the leader who succeeds in making sense of what is happening will gain in stature and be taken seriously.
11. A robust way to gain stature with direct reports is to coach them in a way that helps them develop professionally.
12. To coach a group member towards higher levels of performance, pinpoint what specific behaviors, attitudes, or skills require improvement.
13. If you have to deliver negative feedback to a subordinate or coworker, be quite specific about what you perceive to be wrong.
14. Feedback is likely to be less intimidating when the coach explains which behavior should decrease and which should increase.

15.  A modern twist on using feedback in coaching is to reinforce the desired performance or behavior when it is observed in the daily work environment.

16.  An act indicative of gravitas is to make life easier for the person being coached, such as helping remove obstacles to good performance.

17.  An effective way of giving emotional support is to use positive rather than negative motivators.

18.  Too much advice-giving can interfere with two-way communication, yet workers being coached expect to receive some advice.

19.  Cheering the progress of the person being coached affirms their progress and imparts a seriousness of purpose to the coach.

20.  Considering that resolving conflict successfully is an admired skill, the manager who can carry it our projects gravitas.

21.  A recommended approach to resolving conflict between two people is for the manager to have both sides sit down and encourage them to talk to each other about the problem rather than to the manager.

22.  Done effectively, humor adds to the leader's or corporate professional's stature.

23.  Self-effacing humor is recommended because it makes a point without insulting or slighting anybody.

24.  Making a witty or clever comment on the spur of the moment makes a vastly bigger contribution to gravitas than does telling rehearsed jokes.

25.  By being connected with the tasks at hand, the humor will be perceived as especially clever, thus contributing to the gravitas of the person making the comment.

# 6

# Charisma and Gravitas

A leader with a high level of charisma will usually be perceived as having gravitas. Conversely, a leader with a high level of gravitas will usually be perceived as charismatic. The reason is that the accomplishment that accompanies gravitas adds to a person's charisma. A leader who attains outstanding results is often perceived as charismatic. Before delving into the effects of charisma and how it can be developed, it is worth exploring its meaning in depth.

## The Meaning of Charisma

Charisma has been defined in various ways, yet there is enough consistency among these definitions to make it a useful concept in practicing leadership and enhancing gravitas. *Charisma* is a Greek word meaning "divinely inspired gift." For our purposes, charisma is a special quality of leaders whose purposes, powers, and extraordinary determination differentiate them from others.[1] In general use, the term *charismatic* means to have a charming and colorful personality, such as shown by many celebrities in various fields.

The various definitions of charisma have a unifying theme. Charisma is a positive and compelling quality that makes many others want to be led by the person who has the quality. The phrase "many others" must be chosen carefully. Few leaders are perceived as charismatic by all constituents. A case in point is Bill Gates, the cofounder of Microsoft and, in recent years, a climate and health activist. His technical savvy and contagious enthusiasm contributed to his charisma during the early years of Microsoft. Yet many Microsoft employees did not perceive him to be charismatic based on what they thought was his arrogant, know-it-all attitude. The latter qualities became much more pronounced during Gate's post–Microsoft years.

# *The Effects of Charisma*

The study of charisma grows in importance when its effects are recognized, such as whether by being charismatic a leader can enhance productivity, lower accidents, and enhance job satisfaction. (All of these outcomes add to a person's gravitas.) Much of the impact of charisma is based on the positive emotions the charismatic leader triggers among group members. A current theoretical analysis concluded that charismatic leaders elicit strong emotions from followers that encourage devotion and action. In turn, these emotions influence the effects of charisma. For example, if a charismatic leader's personality and behavior triggered devotion, group members would work tirelessly to attain workgroup goals.[2]

A group of researchers conducted a study of firefighters and their leaders to explore how the emotional component of charisma affects the mood and happiness of subordinates. The study involved 216 firefighters and 48 officers. Happiness, including positive affect and negative affect (unhappiness), was measured through a questionnaire. Leader charisma was measured by a questionnaire. The results suggested that firefighters under the command of a charismatic officer were happier than those under the command of a non-charismatic officer. Charismatic leaders who expressed positive emotion and thoughts tended to have an even stronger impact on the positive emotional state of firefighters. The positive affect of the officers also tended to reduce negative affect among the firefighters.

A conclusion of the study going beyond firefighters is that one of the ways by which charismatic leaders emotionally touch subordinates is through enhancing their positive affect. Furthermore, happier leaders spread their positive mood to group members.[3]

Another major impact of a charismatic leader in a senior-level position is that the leader leaves a personal stamp on the organization. For example, Mark Zuckerberg, the CEO of Meta (Facebook included), has become one of the world's best-known business leaders. At the same time, he is "the face of Facebook," whether or not one approves of his behavior.

An example of a high-charismatic leader who attains outstanding results is Doug McMillon, the president and CEO of Walmart. At the same time, he is an exceptional example of a leader whose charisma is intertwined with his gravitas. McMillon's charisma helps him be taken very seriously, and his seriousness of purpose contributes to his charisma. McMillon began his Walmart career in 1984 as an hourly employee unloading trailers. While at the business school at the University of Tulsa, he entered the Walmart training program for *buyers*—managers who choose which merchandise their stores will stock. The buyers program is an entry point for grooming management candidates who are judged to have high potential for advanced responsibility.

McMillon has held numerous positions at Walmart on his path to the executive suite. He has worked as a buyer, store manager, and district manager, enabling him to acquire knowledge in merchandising, sourcing, and logistics. The accumulated knowledge gave McMillon a deep understanding of the retail industry. As his career advanced, McMillon has held senior leadership roles in all of Walmart's business segments. McMillon became president and CEO in 2014, and from 2009 to 2014 he was president and CEO of Walmart International. Previously, he was CEO of Sam's Club for four years.

McMillon's imaginative leadership has revitalized Walmart. When he became CEO in 2014, company sales had plateaued, and thousands of customers were shifting to Amazon. During the next 10 years McMillon played a major role in building an e-commerce powerhouse, and Walmart has a steady hold on the number one rank of the Fortune 500. At the same time, Walmart has become the world's largest brick-and-mortar retailer.

McMillon's leadership style combines several aspects of a charismatic leader—humility, vision, and a strong dedication to his employer's principles. He listens carefully to associates and encourages them to participate in decision-making. In the process, he has helped build an organizational culture of teamwork and inclusivity. People of color comprise 49 percent of the Walmart workforce; 37 percent of executives are women; and 37 percent of executives are minorities.

In his leadership role, McMillon acknowledges the talent and creativity of Walmart store associates and expresses admiration for their ingenuity and adaptability. McMillon emphasizes that the spectacular success of Walmart is due primarily to its employees who are comfortable taking risks and swiftly implementing new ideas.

Business writer Dan Craft says that McMillon's leadership approach has certain key elements. He has a forward-thinking mindset, a willingness to take calculated risks, and a commitment to the long-range success of the business. Furthermore, McMillon deeply appreciates the company's associates, and he focuses on building trust. (All these attributes contribute to charisma and gravitas.)

## 6. Charisma and Gravitas

A pointed approach to describing McMillon's charisma and gravitas is through his interactions with Walmart associates. The company holds a few gatherings per year at its Bentonville, Arkansas, campus to celebrate the long tenure of about 150 employees. At a recent gathering McMillon was the person being mobbed, not the employees being celebrated. Coworkers rushed up to him to get an autograph or snap a selfie with their photogenic CEO. Once on stage, McMillon invited a variety of store associates to share their stories about their decades of employment at the company. A business reporter from *Fortune* observes that McMillon is skilled at maintaining eye contact with his communication partner and making that person feel that his total attention is focused on him or her.[4]

## Characteristics of Charismatic Leaders

The outstanding characteristic of charismatic leaders is that they can attract, motivate, or lead others. They also have other distinguishing characteristics. As we look at the characteristics of charismatic leaders, you will note that many of these characteristics apply equally to leaders with gravitas. The reason is that charisma is a major component of gravitas.

First, charismatic leaders are *visionary* because they offer an exciting image of where the organization is headed and how to get there. Charismatic leaders also possess *masterful communication skills*. To inspire people, the charismatic leader uses colorful language and exciting metaphors and analogies. Another key characteristic is the *ability to inspire trust*. Constituents believe so strongly in the integrity of charismatic leaders that they will risk their careers to pursue the chief's vision. Charismatic leaders are also *able to make group members feel capable*. Sometimes they do this by enabling group members to achieve success on relatively easy projects. They then praise the group members and give them more demanding assignments.

Charismatic people are typically tactful in social situations based partly on their ability to read other people's emotions (part of emotional intelligence). Related to reading emotions is the ability to connect with people, as in the now overdone phrase, *"I feel your pain."* For example, during a severe business downturn, a company leader might say, *"I know a lot of you are worried about losing your jobs. Working with you as a team, we are fighting to avoid layoffs."*

In addition, charismatic leaders demonstrate an *energy and action orientation.* Like entrepreneurs, most charismatic leaders are energetic and serve as role models for getting things done on time. *Emotional expressiveness and warmth* are also notable. A key characteristic of charismatic leaders is the ability to express feelings openly. A bank vice president claims that much of the charisma people attribute to her can be explained very simply: *"I'm up front about expressing positive feelings. I praise people, I hug them, and I cheer if necessary. I also express my negative feelings, but to a lesser extent."* (Recall that cheering is a technique used by a coach with gravitas.) Nonverbal emotional expressiveness, such as warm gestures and frequent (nonsexual) touching of group members, is also characteristic of charismatic leaders.

Another trait of charismatic leaders is that they *romanticize risk.* They enjoy risk so much that they feel empty in its absence. Jim Barksdale, now a venture capitalist for online startup companies and former CEO of Netscape, says that the fear of failure is what increases your heart rate. As great opportunists, charismatic people yearn to accomplish activities others have never done before. Risk-taking adds to a person's charisma because others admire such courage. In addition to treasuring risk, charismatic leaders use *unconventional strategies* to achieve success. (Risk-taking will be mentioned again later in the chapter with respect to the development of charisma.)

Another characteristic observed in many charismatic leaders is that they *challenge, prod, and poke.* They test your courage and your self-confidence by asking questions like "Do your employees really need you?" Larry Ellison, the celebrity charismatic who is founder and CEO of Oracle Corporation, often asks workers to explain how their job contributes to the organization.

Research conducted by William von Hippel of the University of Queensland suggests that people who think fast tend to be perceived as charismatic. Participants in the study were given intelligence and personality tests, and then asked 30 common-knowledge questions, such as "How many continents are there?" Participants also rated their friends' charisma and social skills. Individuals who answered the questions more rapidly were perceived to be more charismatic regardless of their cognitive ability, personality, or knowledge.[5]

Another major characteristic of charismatic leaders is an amalgam of the ideas already introduced: Being *dramatic and unique* in significant, positive ways is a major contributor to charisma. This quality stems from a combination of factors, such as being energetic, engaging in self-promotion, romanticizing risk, and being emotionally expressive.

## 6. *Charisma and Gravitas*

The late leadership scholar Warren G. Bennis contends that great leaders, particularly those in public life, are great actors. The effective leader sells people on a vision to elevate their spirits.[6]

A characteristic of many charismatic leaders that can backfire is *hubris*, a tendency to hold an overly confident view of one's capabilities and to abuse power for one's own selfish goals.[7] During his first week in office, the CEO of an industrial company fired the entire sales staff in a display of hubris and drama. The subsequent transition to distributors and online selling was slow and awkward, and the company suffered financially.

To personalize charisma characteristics, go through the accompanying charisma checklist. If you can respond to the checklist with a reasonable degree of objectivity, the quiz should enhance your understanding of how you might or might not be perceived as charismatic (and most likely having gravitas) by many people at this stage of your career.

---

# A Checklist of Behaviors and Attitudes Reflecting Charisma

*Instructions:* Indicate whether each of the following statements applies to you now, or whether it does not apply now or probably never will.

| | | *Applies Now* | *Does Not Apply or Probably Never Will* |
|---|---|---|---|
| 1. | Many people have said that I am likeable and charming. | ☐ | ☐ |
| 2. | In groups I have been part of or led, I have offered a vision that others accepted. | ☐ | ☐ |
| 3. | I have more physical energy than most people, and the energy is apparent to other people. | ☐ | ☐ |
| 4. | I do a good job of telling true stories and anecdotes to others on the job. | ☐ | ☐ |
| 5. | My appearance in terms of dress and personal grooming is well above average. | ☐ | ☐ |
| 6. | I communicate a lot of passion about my own work or about the task of the group. | ☐ | ☐ |

|  | | Applies Now | Does Not Apply or Probably Never Will |
|---|---|---|---|
| 7. | I am successful at making other people feel important. | ☐ | ☐ |
| 8. | I am candid without being offensive. | ☐ | ☐ |
| 9. | I make frequent use of a strong handshake or fist bump when greeting people I know or making first-time introductions. | ☐ | ☐ |
| 10. | My posture is good, and I look people in the eye without being accused of staring at them. | ☐ | ☐ |
| 11. | I have taken sensible risks at least several times in my life. | ☐ | ☐ |
| 12. | I am comfortable in letting other people know of my accomplishments. | ☐ | ☐ |
| 13. | I have been told that I have a warm smile. | ☐ | ☐ |
| 14. | People listen to me when I talk at a meeting. | ☐ | ☐ |
| 16. | I have an exceptional number of social media friends and followers. | ☐ | ☐ |

**Scoring and Interpretation:** The more of these 15 statements that apply to you now, the greater the probability that you are perceived to be charismatic by many people. If 12 or more of the statements in the checklist apply to you now, you have above-average charismatic tendencies. Answering these statements is so subjective that it would be helpful for one or two people who know you well to also respond to the checklist in relation to you. You might then compare your responses to the responses of the other person or persons.

---

## Charismatic Qualities and Behaviors Capable of Being Developed

A person can increase charisma by developing some of the traits, characteristics, and behaviors of charismatic people. Several of the charismatic characteristics described earlier in the chapter can be developed. For example, most people can enhance their communication skills, become more emotionally expressive, take more risks, and become more self-promoting. In this section, we examine several behaviors of charismatic people that can be developed through practice and self-discipline.

*Create Visions for Others.* Being able to create visions for others will be a major factor in your being perceived as charismatic and as having gravitas. A vision uplifts and attracts others. The visionary person looks beyond the immediate future to create an image of what the organization, or unit within, can become. A vision is designed to close the discrepancy between current and ideal conditions. The vision thus sees beyond current realities.

Another characteristic of an effective vision formulated by the leader is that it connects with the goals and dreams of constituents.[8] For example, the leader of a group that is manufacturing batteries for electric cars might listen to team members talk about their desires to help reduce pollution in the atmosphere and then base the vision statement on a "desire to save the planet" or "reduce global warming."

*Be Enthusiastic, Optimistic, and Energetic.* A major behavior pattern of charismatic people is their combination of enthusiasm, optimism, and high energy. Without a great amount of all three characteristics, a person is unlikely to be perceived as charismatic by many people. A remarkable quality of charismatic people is that they maintain high enthusiasm, optimism, and energy throughout their entire workday and beyond. Elevating your energy level takes considerable work, but here are a few feasible suggestions:

1. Get ample rest at night, and sneak in a 15-minute power nap during the day when possible. If you have a dinner meeting where you want to be impressive, take a shower and nap before the meeting.

2. Exercise every day for at least 10 minutes, including walking. No excuses are allowed, such as being too busy or too tired or the weather being a handicap.

3. Switch to a healthy, energy-enhancing diet.

4. Keep chopping away at your to-do list, so you do not have unfinished tasks on your mind—they will drain your energy.

An action orientation helps you be enthusiastic, optimistic, and energetic. "Let's do it" is the battle cry of the charismatic person. An action orientation also means that the charismatic person prefers not to agonize over dozens of facts and nuances before making a decision.

*Be Sensibly Persistent.* Closely related to the high energy level of charismatics is their almost-never-accept-no attitude. I emphasize the word *almost* because outstanding leaders and individual contributors also know when to cut their losses. If an idea or a product will not work, the sensible charismatic absorbs the loss and moves in another, more profitable direction.

*Remember People's Names.* Charismatic leaders, as well as other successful people, can usually remember the names of people they have seen only a few times. (Sorry, no charisma credits for remembering the names of everyday work associates.) This ability is partly due to the strong personal interest charismatic leaders take in other people.

The surest way to remember names, therefore, is to really care about people. You can also use the many systems and gimmicks available for remembering names, such as associating a person's name with a visual image. For example, if you meet a woman named Betsy Applewhite, you can visualize her with a white apple (or a white tablet computer) on her head. The best system of name retention remains to listen carefully to the name, repeat it immediately, and study the person's face.

*Develop Synchrony with Others.* A subtle, yet defining, aspect of a truly charismatic person is one who connects well with others. Psychology professor Frank Bernieri studies physical signals that people send to each other and concludes that being in synch physically with other people is part of charisma. If someone is in synchrony with you, you tend to think they are charismatic.

A practical method of being in synch with another person is to adjust your posture to conform to their posture. The other person stands up straight, and so do you; when they slouch, you do also. Charismatic people make these postural adjustments almost subconsciously, or at least without giving the process much thought. Highly skilled charismatic people through the timing of their breaths, gestures, and cadence can entrap listeners into synchrony to the point that they "breathe and sway in tune with the speaker."[9]

*Develop a Personal Brand, Including Making an Impressive Appearance.* A popular career advancement technique is to build a personal brand that in turn adds to your charisma and gravitas. Understanding your basket of strengths forms the basis for developing your *personal brand.* Your identity as shown on the Internet, including social networking sites such as Facebook, is also part of your personal brand. Your personal brand makes you unique, thereby distinguishing you from the competition.[10] Perhaps your brand will not reach the recognition of Adidas or Rolex, but it will help develop your reputation. Your personal brand also helps you attract people to accept your leadership.

## 6. Charisma and Gravitas

Another component of your personal brand is your appearance. By creating a polished appearance, a person can make slight gains in projecting a charismatic image. In most cases, the effect of appearance depends on the context. If exquisite clothing and good looks alone made a person a charismatic leader, those impressive-looking store associates in upscale department stores and boutiques would all be charismatic leaders. Therefore, in attempting to enhance your charisma through appearance, it is necessary to analyze your work environment to assess what type of appearance is impressive. A highly polished appearance would create a negative image at most high technology firms.

*Be Candid.* Charismatic people, especially effective leaders, are remarkably candid with people. Although not insensitive, the charismatic person is typically explicit in giving their assessment of a situation, whether the assessment is positive or negative. Charismatic people speak directly rather than indirectly, so that people know where they stand. Instead of asking a worker, "Are you terribly busy this afternoon?" the charismatic leader will ask, "I need your help this afternoon. Are you available?"

*Make Adjustments to Project E-Charisma.* Projecting charisma during a videoconference requires some strategies beyond what suffices when physically present with others. The online environment eliminates such physical cues as the way the person stands or moves. Instead, what people are saying takes on more weight, and facial expressions also count heavily. Some of the collective wisdom for projecting e-charisma follows.

To attain stage presence, your face should take up at least one-third of the screen. Strong lighting helps make your image look brighter, but avoid too much light, which produces a washed-out appearance. Nonverbal energy can be projected by a reasonable dose of nodding and smiling. Slouching while listening should be avoided. Speaking loudly is important because of electronic distortions. Speaking slowly and articulating carefully is highly recommended. To make better eye contact look at the computer lens or the top third of the screen. One way to project charisma is to acknowledge what the previous speaker said, perhaps paraphrasing in a few words. Speaking in short bursts of time, then pausing, shows you are charismatic enough to care about other people.[11]

*Take Sensible Risks.* Charismatic people not only have an action orientation but are willing to take sensible risks. The term *sensible* refers to situations in which the risk-taker believes that he or she has enough skills to control the uncertainties in that situation. To reflect on your won propensity for taking risks, take the accompanying self-quiz.

---

# My Propensity for Risk-Taking

Answer true or false to the following questions to obtain an approximate idea of your tendency to take risks or your desire to do so:

| Statement About Risk-Taking | True | False |
|---|---|---|
| 1. I send and receive text messages while driving. | | |
| 2. I would be willing to join a startup in my field and receive one-half of my pay in salary and the rest in stock options. | | |
| 3. I dislike trying foods from other cultures. | | |
| 4. I would choose fixed-income investments rather than growth stocks for most of my investments. | | |
| 5. I am hesitant to challenge people who have authority over me. | | |
| 6. I will eat fruit from a store or street vendor without first washing it. | | |
| 7. I will sometimes talk on my phone while driving at highway speeds. | | |
| 8. I would be thrilled to be an entrepreneur (or am thrilled at being one). | | |
| 9. I would like to help in a crisis such as a product recall. | | |
| 10. I would like to go cave exploring (or already have done so). | | |
| 11. I would be willing to have at least one-third of my compensation based on a bonus for good performance. | | |
| 12. I would be willing to visit a maximum-security prison on a job assignment. | | |

**Key:** *1. T; 2. T; 3. F; 4. F; 5. F; 6. T; 7. T; 8. T; 9. T; 10. T; 11. T; 12. T.*

**Scoring and Interpretation:** Give yourself one point each time your answer agrees with the key.

| 10–12 | You are probably a high risk-taker. |
|---|---|
| 6–9 | You are probably a moderate risk-taker. |
| 3–5 | You tend to be a cautious risk-taker. |
| 0–2 | You are most likely a very low risk-taker. |

## 6. Charisma and Gravitas

The story is frequently heard of entrepreneurs who started businesses by borrowing money on their credit cards and from friends, and by taking out a second mortgage. Being convinced that sensible risk-taking is associated with charisma is not sufficient to make you more charismatic. Others must be aware of your risk-taking so that it has an impact on their perception of you. You would have to make your risk-taking visible to people you want to influence. Talk widely about the sensible risk you have taken and explain the results you achieved.

There is another way to benefit from the link between risk-taking and charisma. As you become more comfortable taking risks, you will develop a more adventuresome personality. Given that an adventuresome personality is part of charisma and gravitas, you will have developed in a positive direction.

*Engage in Storytelling.* A significant aspect of the communication style of charismatic leaders is that they make extensive use of memorable stories to get messages across. *Leadership by storytelling* is the technique of inspiring and instructing team members by telling fascinating stories related to the organization. Storytelling as a leadership tool has been elevated to such a level that some companies hire corporate storytelling consultants to help their executives develop the art. Telling true stories is regarded as a useful tool for getting people to embrace change, because a well-crafted story captures people's attention.

Executive coach Jeff Gothelf recommends a touch of humility to add to the effectiveness of a story. One of his clients was attempting to gain enthusiasm for an Objectives and Key Results program that was not meeting with much enthusiasm. Telling a humble story helped build support for the program. Part of the story used by the CEO to show a dose of humility was as follows:

> Many of you remember when we tried to upgrade our goal-setting system. At the time I was the chief operating officer, and I was a major driver for that change. The initiative failed badly, and it was my fault. I pushed the change too fast without understanding clearly how to support the organization while the goal-setting program was being implemented. I learned a lot from that experience. Now, I'm looking to all of you for valuable suggestions and support to help make the OKR a success.[12]

*Be Humanistic.* A comprehensive characteristic of many charismatic people is their humanism. *Humanistic* is a catchall term that refers to almost any positive appeal to the emotions and feelings of others. An especially important part of humanism is showing concern for both the work and personal lives of others. If you express an interest in the total individual and his or her multiple roles in life, you are being humanistic. The leader is well positioned to display humanism on the job.

The perception of you as being charismatic and having gravitas will increase when you are humanistic. Leaders with a high standing on charisma are often those with a reputation for the kindness and warmth they extend to their constituents. The late Sam Walton, a charismatic and legendary company founder, was frequently lauded for the kindness he displayed toward Wal-Mart (now Walmart) employees. Many Walmart associates looked upon "Mr. Sam" as a father figure who had their best interests in mind.

Here are a dozen humanistically oriented attitudes and actions you can take in relation to group members.

1. *If you are a manager, initiate an extreme dress-down day.* Such a day would encourage employees to dress in the type of clothing they ordinarily wear while running, doing household chores, washing the car, or performing yard work.

2. *Purchase a gift for a new parent's child.* Most new parents are thrilled to receive yet another gift for their newborn.

3. *Ask group members about their career and lifestyle aspirations.* Ask how well their roles fit into their career plans and what aspirations they have for future roles.

4. *Ask group members what you can do to make their jobs easier.* A humanistic and high-gravitas leader will often find ways to lighten the workload of subordinates and facilitate them working more productively.

5. *Conduct a group meeting to discuss existing and potential company programs that could possibly make life easier for employees, such as childcare and parental care assistance.* A discussion of this type might point to programs some employees did not know were in place, such as loans to deal with emergencies.

6. *Grant an employee a day or two to work from home, even if your company does not have a hybrid work program.* In this way an employee might be able to put in a full day's work yet still take care of a personal problem such as accompanying a child to a medical appointment.

7. *Conduct a luncheon discussion about the major sources of work stress and what can be done about them.* For example, too many late afternoon or early morning meetings might be stressful for young parents.

8. *Write personal messages periodically to high-contributing group members.* Express appreciation for their help in keeping the organization operating and mention how they make life easier for you.

9. *Give employees proper credit for any of their ideas that you use.* A major employee complaint is that managers use their ideas without giving them appropriate credit. Furthermore, a leader who is perceived as stealing employee ideas will not be taken seriously.

10. *Invest at least a couple of hours per month in listening to the personal problems and complaints of employees.* Let them give vent to their confusion and anger but avoid becoming their counselor. If an employee's problems appear to be overwhelming, suggest that he or she visit the company employee assistance program or other form of outside help.

11. *Ask in a friendly, nonjudgmental way about the physical health of group members.* Ask about what the person is doing for physical exercise.

12. *Ask about the health, happiness, and major activities of family members.* Again, the question should be asked in a friendly, nonjudgmental way, such as, "How is your daughter enjoying being a member of her high school wrestling team?"

*Stand Up Straight and Use Other Nonverbal Signals of Self-Confidence.* Practice good posture, minimize fidgeting, scratching, floor tapping, and speaking in a monotone. Walk at a rapid pace without appearing to be anxious. Dress fashionably without going to the extreme that people notice your clothes more than they notice you. A fist can project confidence, power, and certainty. Waving a hand, pointing, or rapping a table can help get attention focused on you.

*Give Sincere Compliments.* Most people thrive on flattery, particularly when it is plausible. Attempt to compliment only those behaviors, thoughts, and attitudes you genuinely believe merit praise. At times you may have to dig to find something praiseworthy, but it will be a good investment of your time.

*Be More Animated Than Others.* People who are perceived to be more charismatic are simply more animated. They smile more frequently, speak faster, articulate better, and move their heads and bodies more often.

*Inspire Trust and Confidence.* A robust way of projecting charisma and gravitas is to make your deeds consistent with your promises. Get people to believe in your competence by making your accomplishment known in a polite, tactful way. For example, a sales manager might comment to a manager from another department, "I was so pleased that our team pulled together to exceed our sales goals by 21 percent this most recent quarter."

---

# Guidelines for Action

1. If you have a high level of charisma, you will usually be perceived as having gravitas. Conversely, if you have a high level of gravitas, you will usually be perceived as charismatic.

2. If you are charismatic, it will enhance the happiness of your subordinates.

3. Thinking fast will help you be perceived as charismatic.

4. Many characteristics of a charismatic person can be developed, such as communication skills, emotional expressiveness, risk-taking, and self-promotion.

5. Being able to create visions for others will be a major factor in you being perceived as charismatic and as having gravitas.

6. A major behavior pattern of charismatic people is their combination of enthusiasm, optimism, and high energy. Elevating your energy is therefore important and can be accomplished through such means as getting ample rest at night and sneaking in a 15-minute power nap during the day when possible.

7. Charismatic leaders, as well as other successful people, can usually remember the names of people they have seen only a few times. The surest way to remember names is to really care about people.

8. A popular career advancement technique that facilitates being charismatic is to build your personal brand. Understanding your basket of strengths forms the basis for developing your personal brand.

9. By creating a polished appearance, you can make slight gains in projecting a charismatic image.

10. Being convinced that sensible risk-taking is associated with charisma is not sufficient to make you more charismatic. Other people must be aware of your risk-taking so that it has an impact on their perception of you.

11. A significant aspect of the communication style of charismatic leaders is that they make extensive use of memorable stories to get messages across. Adding a touch of humility adds to the effectiveness of your story.

12.  A characteristic of many charismatic people is their humanism. An especially important part of humanism is showing concern for both the work and personal lives of others. For example, ask group members about their career and lifestyle aspirations.

13.  A basic part of being charismatic is to stand up straight and use other nonverbal signals of self-confidence. It is therefore helpful to practice good posture, minimize fidgeting, scratching, floor tapping, and speaking in a monotone.

14.  Inspiring the trust and confidence of others places you on the path to being perceived as charismatic and possessing gravitas. The most effective approach is to make your deeds consistent with your promises.

# 7

# Executive Presence and Gravitas

A person who commands the attention of other people has executive presence, thereby contributing to the person's gravitas. Simultaneously, the person with gravitas has a strong executive presence. The unavoidable tautology is that you need executive presence to have gravitas, and you need gravitas to have executive presence. Executive presence is about a leader's ability to inspire confidence in three key stakeholders. Subordinates must be confident that you are the leader they want to follow. Peers must be confident that you are capable and reliable, and senior leaders must have confidence that you have the potential for substantial achievements.[1] Executive presence is therefore important for success in your present role, as well as for career advancement. The bigger the position the more likely that executive presence (or gravitas) is a major qualification.

## Exploring Further the Meaning of Executive Presence

Given that executive presence is multifaceted and of profound career importance, it is useful to explore several of its meanings and interpretations. Presented next are several of the most insightful definitions and meanings of executive presence.

- The moment a leader with executive presence walks into a room, the leader is noticed because he or she has the *wow factor*. The *wow factor*, or executive presence, is about the capacity to mobilize others in the direction of accomplishing something worthwhile. To be influential and attain complicated business initiatives, executive presence is an essential quality.[2] Executive presence has also been labeled the "X factor" and the "It factor." Both labels suggest that executive presence is an elusive, difficult-to-pin-down quality of importance.

- Executive presence is analogous to purchasing a house based on *curb appeal.* What constitutes executive presence is therefore highly subjective. A quick look at the house signals to you that the house interests you but exactly why is difficult to specify.[3] Like quality and pornography, executive presence is difficult to pin down but "you know it when you see it."
- Executive presence can be considered *grace under fire.* A person with executive presence does not lose his or her composure in a high-stakes meeting. An example would be a presentation to the top-management team to convince them that you are the right candidate for an open executive position. To obtain a high-level executive position, a person is expected not only to have the right skillset, but to act, speak, and look the part.[4]
- Executive presence is a complex set of characteristics that convey the message that a person controls a situation. The characteristics include the ability to present oneself in a manner that inspires trust, credibility, poise, and unflappability in challenging situations.[5]
- Executive presence is the ability to project confidence and authority in any situation based on how you carry yourself, communicate, and interact with others.[6]

## *The Components of Executive Presence*

The several definitions of executive presence suggest its components, such as having the self-confidence to take charge of a situation. Nevertheless, to learn more about executive presence, and to develop this elusive quality, it is worthwhile to explore in depth the components of executive presence.

*Self-Awareness.* A foundational component of executive presence is awareness of who you are, including your key strengths and weaknesses and the impact you make on others. Suppose that team leader Marvin wants to project executive presence as a way of being perceived as a strong and confident leader. Yet Marvin does not recognize that he frequently stands so close to work associates that he violates their personal space. As a result, Marvin is not perceived as having as strong an executive presence as he would like.

Self-awareness is considered a key competency within emotional intelligence. Having high self-awareness enables people to know their strengths and limitations and have high self-esteem. A leader with good self-awareness would recognize such factors as whether he or she was liked or was exerting the right amount of pressure on people.

Self-awareness depends on self-knowledge and therefore requires careful observation to obtain. Spontaneous comments by work associates are one source of valuable feedback. Imagine that Tammy is joining the group in a physical or Zoom meeting. She hears meeting member Darwin say, "Great that Tammy is here. As she always does, she'll keep us focused on the problem we are trying to solve."

Comments made about you in a performance appraisal can be a helpful source of feedback for learning about how you are perceived, particularly if more than one manager made the same comment. Sam might have received that same comment from two different managers that he has a deadpan expression. To develop his executive presence, Sam would then need to become more animated.

Another source of useful feedback for work purposes is standardized psychological assessments. Among the many factors measured related to executive presence are agreeableness, extraversion, conscientiousness, emotional stability, and intellectual curiosity. (These are classified as the Big Five personality factors.) Two positive examples: If others perceive you as conscientious, it enhances your image because you will be regarded as a dependable person. Being intellectually curious adds to executive presence because if you ask work associates questions in an interested, but nonthreatening way, you will often be perceived as a person of stature.

*Self-Confidence.* Executive presence is highly dependent on projecting self-confidence. A leader who is self-assured without being bombastic or overbearing makes a positive impression on subordinates. To demonstrate executive presence, the leader must, in addition to being self-confident, project that self-confidence to the group. He or she may do so by unequivocal wording, maintaining good posture, and making appropriate gestures such as pointing an index finger outward. Standing up straight helps a leader come across as commanding, whereas slouching and looking down at your feet has the opposite effect. Taking long strides and walking with the chest held high also projects self-confidence. Maintaining eye contact is yet another subtle contributor to executive presence.

Taking ownership of your ideas and decisions is another manifestation of self-confidence.[7] *Ownership* refers to admitting that you are responsible for an idea or decision, good or bad. Baxter, a chief human resource officer, initiated a program of hiring documented refugees as production technicians. The initiative was a big success because the result was hiring two dozen competent and reliable workers with below average voluntary turnover. Eighteen months into the program Baxter said to the executive team, "I am so happy that the refugee hiring program has helped our manufacturing group. I admit I crossed my fingers when I suggested the program, and I am happy it worked out well."

*Outstanding Communication Skills.* Surveys of executives conducted by economist Sylvia Ann Hewlett reinforce the importance of outstanding communication skills as a component of executive presence. Several aspects of communication skills were noted in the survey.[8] Superior speaking skills were at the top of the list. The well-known aspects of high-level speaking skills include varying the voice tone, clear articulation, a wide vocabulary, colorful expressions, and maintaining eye contact with the audience. In recent years, the communication skill aspects of executive presence include performing well during a videoconference such as Zoom. In-person communication skills must be transferred to the virtual meeting. The suggestions for displaying e-charisma presented in Chapter 6 apply here.

Listening to receive valuable input and learn is another contributor to outstanding communication skills. A listening orientation is essential for making sound decisions, and making high-quality decisions enhances executive presence. Listening also contributes to the ability to reach an audience. In this sense *listening* also means observing the body language of members of the audience. For example, if the leader observes several dumbfounded expressions, it is time to rephrase or explain in more detail what he or she is communicating.

Hewlett includes authenticity as a trait that contributes to outstanding communication skills. In this context, authenticity refers to revealing who you fundamentally are, rather than pretending to have an idealized different self. To illustrate, there is pronounced tendency for many politicians and CEOs to emphasize their working-class roots to project the image of a "person of the people." The same person sometimes has an MBA from a prestigious university and has accumulated an impressive net worth.

*Inclusivity.* A component of executive presence geared to the modern world is *inclusivity.* The leader who facilitates inclusion makes a deliberate effort to ensure that all team members, group members, or other employees feel included and welcome with the organization. An advanced form of inclusivity does not focus exclusively on demographic factors such as gender, race, age, and physical status. Instead, and inclusive leader also welcomes thought diversity, such as a high-tech firm welcoming conservative thought, or a gun manufacturer welcoming employees with a liberal ideology. Here are three illustrative activities of an inclusive leader:

- seeking to build a demographically and culturally diverse workforce
- taking a personal interest in each member of the group or team
- encouraging team or group members to take the initiative to ensure that all coworkers are made to feel like "one of the gang"

A sensible approach for attaining executive presence via inclusivity is for the leader to emphasize inclusive language. Leaders can help create a more culturally diverse and inclusive organizational culture by avoiding terms that might make anybody feel excluded. An example is that some people feel rejected when sexes or genders are divided into only two categories. Yet a leader can go beyond these subtle nuances of language. A strong leadership initiative for fostering a diverse, equitable, and inclusive culture is to emphasize phrases that specifically welcome every organizational member as well as other stakeholders. Most charismatic leaders find this to be a natural communication style.

Two corporate communication specialists, Noah Zandan and Lisa Shalett, have identified three ways inclusive leaders talk and send written messages. First, they use audience-centered language. To be audience-centered, the leader needs to understand the needs of the group members and personalize the language. For example, members of the HR department have heard frequently enough that they are a staff rather than a line function and might find the reference to be annoying. Use the second-person pronoun "you" frequently to take the focus off yourself and bring the audience into your message.

Second, demonstrate subject matter expertise, such as providing relevant data. At the same time show a willingness to process new data that will enhance your expertise and incorporate new perspectives. An automobile marketing manager might say, "My research shows that we are losing a little market share because our dashboards are too complicated to use for some customers. What insights have you gathered on this problem?"

Third, be authentic. If you gain the trust of group members, you will convey that you really care that they feel included.[9]

Another approach to emphasizing inclusive language is to introduce humble phrases into a conversation, which creates the space for others to contribute and therefore feel included. To include more diverse opinions, a leader might say, "Our team has worked hard at fine-tuning the company vision. But please tell me how we can make our vision even more attractive to more people."[10]

An effective way to make people from diverse organizational functions feel included rather than excluded is to minimize negative categorization of work roles. Examples of exclusionary terminology include a division president referring to "non-technical staffers," or "non-business types." Another exclusionary term as perceived by many people is "foreign workers." "Foreign" sometimes connotes different in a negative way, such as having a foreign element in a tube of medicine or in the ear canal. A preferred phrasing would be "workers from other countries." Mentioning the contribution of all team members is inclusive, in contrast to mentioning only the contribution of one or two.

The final suggestion is the easiest of all to execute. The inclusive leader says frequently, "Welcome everybody"—in speaking, writing, and sign language.

It would be difficult to find an organizational leader today who is opposed to inclusion. The story of Emmanuel Roman, CEO of bond giant and money manager PIMCO, provides one example of a high-level leader who adds to his executive presence by being systematically inclusive. In November 2016, Roman, an ex–Goldman Sachs banker, was appointed CEO of PIMCO. His two key early initiatives were to leverage new technologies and hire new talent. Under Roman's leadership, PIMCO's growth in total assets has been dramatic. The firm now manages $1.89 trillion in assets for institutions and individuals including $1.51 trillion in third-party client assets.

For many years, the fixed-income firm Pacific Investment Management Co. (PIMCO) was proud of its cutthroat reputation. Ambitious young finance specialists have been attracted to PIMCO's trading floor to work alongside some of the bond market's most skilled investors. They might have had to endure aggressive colleagues, rapidly changing management decisions, and long working hours, but the excitement and exceptionally high paychecks made it all worthwhile.

The hypercompetitive culture at PIMCO began to soften in 2014, after its legendary investor, Bill Gross, left the firm following a series of disagreements with his colleagues. Yet conflict and discord at PIMCO did not disappear when Gross departed. Many lawsuits six years later alleging gender discrimination and harassment placed the spotlight on a problem-laden culture at PIMCO.

## Gravitas for Leadership

Roman has emphasized that the PIMCO of today is much different from the PIMCO of 10 years ago. In recent years the firm has overhauled how employees are evaluated, promoted, and trained. Management consultant McKinsey & Company was hired to conduct regular staff workplace surveys, and an employee ombudsman was appointed. PIMCO leadership has also worked to narrow the wide gaps in pay between top executives and those on a rung or two below. One of the approaches to narrowing the pay gap is to grant stock options that vest over time.

In response to charges from seven former female employees about discrimination, harassment, and retaliation, PIMCO engaged a highly experienced third-party expert to conduct an independent review of the accusations. The investigation did not find evidence of discrimination, harassment, or retaliation, and concluded that the company handled the complaints appropriately. Yet the report recommended that top-level management clarify how it makes decisions on promotions. Under Roman's leadership, the company now makes its basis for promotions more transparent. Leadership skills, values, and a variety of management skills are now factored into these decisions, screened by a committee and checked for any potential biases. The report also mentioned that PIMCO is a type A environment with high work expectations and high reward. One conclusion was: "Many flourish in this environment, but it does not fit everyone."

A key part of the cultural shift at PIMCO is to bring in a younger and more diverse group of candidates. About one-third of the firm's senior U.S. staff self-identifies as an underrepresented minority, an increase of 11 percent from 15 years ago. A quarter of the U.S. officers self-identify as women, also an 11 percent increase. Roman strongly endorses workforce diversity at PIMCO. He plays a major role in the CEO Leadership Alliance of Orange County, which is committed to expanding an inclusive cohort of high-skilled workers for the future of Orange County.

Roman points out that the way people think about and solve problems is influenced by their past, making it important to have employees from different backgrounds and geographic locations. "I really believe that the argument for diversity is that it is a plus from a business standpoint," Roman said. "Listen. I'm a French guy, and they were willing to embrace someone who thought differently."[11]

*Respect for Others.* Respect is closely related to inclusion because including people indicates that you respect them. As Hewlett found in her surveys about executive presence, showing respect for others helps give a leader stature.[12] Showing respect for the individual means that you recognize that everybody has some inner worth and should be treated with courtesy and kindness. An office supervisor demonstrated respect in front of the department when he asked a custodian who entered the office, "What can we do in this department to make your job easier?"

Another way in which respect for others enhances executive presence is in overcoming cross-cultural communication barriers. A widely used comment that implies disrespect is to say to a person from a different culture, "You have a funny accent." Should you be transported to that person's culture, you too might have a "funny accent." The attitude of highest respect is to communicate your belief that although another person's culture is different from yours, it is not inferior to your culture.

*Appearance.* A superficial, yet vital, component of executive presence is a person's physical appearance, including demeanor and clothing. Your appearance is also part of your personal brand. By creating a polished appearance, a person can make slight gains in projecting executive presence. In most cases, appearance depends on the context. People pay more respect and grant more privileges to people they perceive as being well-dressed and physically attractive.

Appearance has a heavy impact on first impressions, and making a positive first impression is a component of executive presence. Looking successful contributes to a positive first impression. Your clothing and speech should project the image of a successful, but not necessarily flamboyant person. Appearing physically fit is also part of the success image.

In attempting to enhance your executive presence through appearance, it is necessary to analyze what type of presence is impressive. Highly polished formal attire is more impressive in an investment bank than in a high-technology startup.

An analysis of hundreds of research studies about the impact of clothing in the workplace provides a few clues about how appearance contributes to executive presence. Here are six of the most relevant conclusions drawn from this mega study:

- The level of formality of clothing influences how competent the person appears to be. (In many situations wearing highly formal clothing makes you appear competent.)
- Wearing formal clothing in the workplace tends to make you

appear warm. (Context again is important. Wearing a three-piece suit would make anyone look stiff and cold in an AI startup.)

- People who wear fashionable clothing tend to be perceived as warm. (Warmth is part of executive presence, which makes dressing fashionably useful.)
- Formal clothing has a bigger impact on women being perceived as competent than it does for men. (As a contributor to executive presence formal clothing carries more weight for women than it does for men.)
- Wearing fashionable clothing contributes more to being perceived as competent for women than for men. (Fashionable clothing has a bigger positive impact on executive presence for women than for men.)
- A person's body size influences the impact of fashionable clothing on the perception of warmth and competence. (Wearing fashionable clothing contributes more to executive presence for people with large body sizes and body mass index.)[13]

Whether or not you want to take these six findings seriously, they are based on scientific analysis. Recognize that most conclusions about executive presence are based more on observations and opinions than rigorous research.

## *The Development and Improvement of Executive Presence*

The development and improvement of executive presence follows logically from understanding its components. For example, if you agree that a polished appearance enhances executive presence you can work diligently at improving your appearance, perhaps with the advice and counsel of a fashionable person or a clothing consultant. The general point is that with practice and concentration, executive presence can be developed and improved much like communications skills, or even pickleball.

*Self-Discipline.* As with other types of personal development, developing and improving executive presence requires considerable self-discipline. In the present context, *self-discipline* is mobilizing one's effort and energy to stay focused on attaining an important goal. A key component of being a self-disciplined learner is to set goals for development such as, "I am going to maintain appropriate eye contact with others on the job."

Self-discipline is required for almost all forms of enhancing executive presence. Suppose that a leader is convinced that superior speaking skills are a key component of executive presence. The leader reads about superior speaking skills, watches YouTube videos about the subject, and attends a workshop on oral communication skills. After the reading, video watching and workshop are completed, the leader will need to concentrate diligently to remember to speak with polish and refinement. Self-discipline is particularly necessary because the pressures of everyday activities often divert a person's attention from personal development.

Self-discipline plays an important role in the continuous monitoring of one's behavior to ensure that needed self-development occurs. After one identifies a need for improvement, it is necessary to periodically review whether one is making the necessary adjustments. Suppose that a person recognizes the developmental need to become a more colorful communicator as a way of enhancing charisma (a strong contributor to executive presence). The person would need self-discipline to make the conscious effort to communicate more colorfully when placed in an appropriate situation.

The accompanying self-quiz gives you an opportunity to think about your self-discipline tendencies.

---

## My Self-Discipline Tendencies

Indicate the extent to which each of the following statements describes your behavior or attitude by circling one number. The numbers refer to strongly disagree (SD), disagree (D), neither agree nor disagree (N), agree (A), and strongly agree (SA). Consider enlisting someone who knows your behavior and attitudes well to help you respond accurately to the statements.

| *Statement Related to Self-Discipline* | *SD* | *D* | *N* | *A* | *SA* |
|---|---|---|---|---|---|
| 1. I usually stay focused on whatever goal I am pursuing. | 1 | 2 | 3 | 4 | 5 |
| 2. I have a mission or purpose in life. | 1 | 2 | 3 | 4 | 5 |
| 3. Saving or investing for the future makes little sense when you can have fun with the money in the present. | 5 | 4 | 3 | 2 | 1 |

| Statement Related to Self-Discipline | SD | D | N | A | SA |
|---|---|---|---|---|---|
| 4. A highly talented person does not have to invest much time in practicing the skill related to that talent. | 5 | 4 | 3 | 2 | 1 |
| 5. I can work on my job for an entire hour without checking to see if I have a phone, text, or email message. | 1 | 2 | 3 | 4 | 5 |
| 6. I have developed a new skill in the last 12 months without being forced to by my employer or an instructor. | 1 | 2 | 3 | 4 | 5 |
| 7. I almost never bother retaining facts any longer because I can find whatever facts I need on the Internet. | 5 | 4 | 3 | 2 | 1 |
| 8. My days rarely turn out the way I hope. | 5 | 4 | 3 | 2 | 1 |
| 9. Given a choice between receiving a gift of $2,000 today versus receiving a gift on $4,000 three months from today, I would wait for the $4,000. | 1 | 2 | 3 | 4 | 5 |
| 10. I would be willing to devote 15 minutes per day for two years to learn another language. | 1 | 2 | 3 | 4 | 5 |
| 11. Working 60 hours per week for even a short period of time is something that I would never do. | 5 | 4 | 3 | 2 | 1 |
| 12. I tend to daydream a lot even on the job or during quiet moments with family and friends. | 5 | 4 | 3 | 2 | 1 |
| 13. I usually read the owner's manual before I spend much time operating a new vehicle or complicated piece of electronic equipment. | 1 | 2 | 3 | 4 | 5 |
| 14. When I'm involved in an important work project, I can enjoy myself fully at a recreational event after hours. | 1 | 2 | 3 | 4 | 5 |
| 15. I feel that I'm moving forward a little bit every day toward achieving my goals. | 1 | 2 | 3 | 4 | 5 |
| 16. I accomplish very little unless I am closely supervised. | 5 | 4 | 3 | 2 | 1 |
| 17. Several people have described me as being conscientious. | 1 | 2 | 3 | 4 | 5 |
| 18. My work area is neat, clean, and well organized. | 1 | 2 | 3 | 4 | 5 |
| 19. I become bored easily. | 5 | 4 | 3 | 2 | 1 |
| 20. I am willing to work hard and long at a task even if the payoff is uncertain. | 1 | 2 | 3 | 4 | 5 |

## 7. Executive Presence and Gravitas

| Statement Related to Self-Discipline | SD | D | N | A | SA |
|---|---|---|---|---|---|
| 21. It makes sense for a marathon runner to keep going even when it appears that the runner has almost no chance of being among the top group of finishers. | 1 | 2 | 3 | 4 | 5 |
| 22. I frequently misplace or lose items such as my keys, wallet, smartphone, or glasses. | 5 | 4 | 3 | 2 | 1 |
| 23. Planning is difficult because life is so unpredictable. | 5 | 4 | 3 | 2 | 1 |
| 24. I can concentrate on an entire news story if the subject interests me. | 1 | 2 | 3 | 4 | 5 |
| 25. I'm terrible at remembering names of people I meet only once or twice. | 5 | 4 | 3 | 2 | 1 |

*Scoring and Interpretation:* Calculate your score by adding up the numbers circled.

| | |
|---|---|
| **110–125** | You are a highly self-disciplined person who should be able to capitalize on your skills and talents. |
| **61–109** | You have an average degree of self-discipline. |
| **25–60** | You appear to have a below-average degree of self-discipline that could be interfering with your accomplishing goals and achieving satisfaction. |

*Know What You Are Trying to Accomplish and Articulate It with Clarity.* Executive coach Gerry Valentine explains that one of the most important parts of inspiring confidence is to have a compelling vision. He defines a vision as a well-conceived notion of what you are working to accomplish. Inspiring confidence is relevant here because it is a component of executive presence. The vision should be appropriate in scale for your level of seniority. You should be able to communicate your vision clearly in a variety of situations, be it a three-minute elevator ride with an executive, an offsite with the team, or a dinner with stakeholders. A robust, clearly articulated vision makes you unique and is a powerful tool for inspiring confidence.[14]

What Valentine refers to as a vision is essentially a goal, not necessarily a statement of where the entire organization is pointed. Suppose that Kaitlin is the vice president of finance for a technology company. She articulates clearly what she wants to accomplish by frequently telling other company executives, "We need to get our revenue per employee up to $1.5 million to compete successfully with other companies in our field." Kaitlin's goal is clear, valid, and perhaps inspiring to the other executives.

*Capitalize on the Impact of Brevity.* C-suite executives are typically strapped for time, which makes brevity of thought highly important. During most high-level meetings, you have about five minutes to convince the other participants that your idea has merit. How rapidly you get people to comprehend the potential contribution of your idea is a powerful part of executive presence.[15] Kaitlin's statement about revenue per employee is a useful example of a brief but powerful message.

A problem with not being brief (or being long-winded) is that it can detract from executive presence by making you appear boring. The totality of a complex idea perhaps cannot be explained in five minutes, but the significance of the idea can be given in a brief, front-loaded message. Imagine that data scientist manager Tyrod has worked on a presentation about how AI is likely to impact the organization. His report is complicated and esoteric, yet Tyrod can enhance his executive presence with an opening statement such as, "The good news is that AI is going to make us a much more productive company. The bad news is that at least 2,000 positions will be eliminated."

*Prepare in Advance for Stressful Situations.* To be perceived as having a strong executive presence it is necessary to perform well in stressful situations such as dealing with an angry employee group or labor union or defending a wrong decision. The usual anti-stress bromides apply, such as learning to relax, participating in physical exercise, eating well, and sleeping well. A field-tested, specific approach for dealing with an upcoming stressful situation is *rehearsal.* The basic idea is that you think in advance of the challenges you will be facing and then visualize how you will respond. You practice what you have visualized, such as this scenario: Pablo, the vice president of operations, wants to start a program of hiring previously incarcerated people for production technician positions. He imagines in advance he will receive a couple of hostile responses to his recommendation, such as, "Have you lost your mind? We'll have thieves and criminals on the payroll." Pablo thinks, "If I do get such negativity, I will respond calmly with facts such as pointing out that previously incarcerated people have proven to be dependable, hard-working employees. I will also give facts about their low quit rate."

The general idea of rehearsal is to imagine yourself feeling calm and confident in a potentially stressful situation so you can be relaxed when facing the situation. Proceed as follows:

1.  Close your eyes and relax your muscles as best you can. Concentrate for one or two minutes on feeling relaxed.
2.  For another one or two minutes imagine yourself going through the scenario you are practicing for.
3.  Concentrate again on feeling calm.
4.  Visualize the upcoming scenario again and create as many details as possible. (For example, who else will be present, what will you be wearing, and what will you say?)
5.  Imagine yourself being calm and self-assured as the scenario unfolds.
6.  Imagine a positive outcome, such as your boss and other people welcoming your suggestion and encouraging you to implement your idea.[16]

A rule of thumb is that you may need to use the rehearsal technique a few times to prepare for your first potentially stressful event. As you become more skilled with the technique it is plausible that one or two rehearsals will be sufficient. As your skill in rehearsal increases, you might need to use only steps 5 and 6. High-stakes events, such as a job interview or giving or receiving a performance appraisal, usually require more rehearsal.

*Communicate Assertively and Directly.* An obvious contributor to developing and improving executive presence is to communicate more effectively, particularly when speaking. Communicating assertively and directly is a notable way of displaying executive presence. Many people lower their executive presence by expressing their ideas in a passive or indirect mode. If instead they explain their ideas explicitly and directly—and with feeling—the message is more likely to be received with impact. Being assertive also contributes to effective communication because assertiveness enhances persuasiveness.

Notice the difference between a passive (indirect) phrasing of a request versus an assertive (direct) approach:

## Passive

*TEAM MEMBER:* By any chance would there be some money left over in the budget? If there would happen to be, I would like to know.
*MANAGER:* I'll have to investigate. Try me again soon.

## Assertive

*TEAM MEMBER:* We have an urgent need for a high-speed color copier in our department. Running to the document center to use their copier is draining our productivity. I am therefore submitting a requisition for a high-speed color copier.

*MANAGER:* Your request makes sense. I'll see what's left in the budget right now.

Being assertive also includes being direct, rather than indirect and evasive, when delivering bad news. A manager might say, "Today is a good day for a change," when he has to deliver some bad news about demoting a few staff members or the loss of a major customer. Indirect communication of this type is often referred to as *spin*, which is intended to look at the bright side of a bad situation.

A caution is to understand that communicating directly does not mean being rude. (Rudeness detracts from executive presence.) One example is to convert a hard "no" into a soft "no." If the message sender is too blunt in response to a request, the sender can readily be perceived as a person who does not want to collaborate or accept suggestions.[17] Suppose a team member suggests that all customer complaints be answered with generative AI, and the manager thinks this is a bad idea. The manager might respond, "Maybe we can answer a few routine requests with AI, but most complaints deserve more than an automated reply."

*Display Passion for What You Are Proposing.* A deep-level way of developing and improving executive presence is to purposely be passionate about your work. When interacting with others, this display of passion will enhance your executive presence. The passion can be for work and to some extent for the people who help accomplish the work. Passion goes beyond enthusiasm and often expresses itself as an obsession with achieving company goals. Many executives begin their workday at 6:00 a.m. and return to their homes at 7:00 p.m. After dinner, they retreat to their offices at home to conduct business for about two more hours. Communication technology devices feed the passion for work, making it possible to be in touch with the office even during a round of golf or a family picnic. Extreme work hours may not be for everybody, but such a strong work ethic is often associated with executive presence.

Passion for their work is especially evident in entrepreneurial leaders, no matter what size or type of business. A given business, such as refurbishing engines, might appear mundane to outsiders. The leader of such a business, however, is willing to talk for hours about tearing down old engines and about the wonderful people who help do the job.

Passion often stems naturally from a deep interest in one's work, but it can also be cultivated by the person who wants to develop executive presence. The process would be to think carefully about what component of a role is the most exciting, such as building teamwork or launching a new product. When interacting with work associates, spend some time talking about those aspects of your role about which you are passionate.

*Establish High Performance Standards.* Effective leaders consistently hold group members to high standards of performance. The high standards, if not arbitrary and outlandish, enhance executive presence. High performance standards can also take the form of challenging the thinking of others. For example, a member of the top management team might say, "There is no way we can find a manufacturer to produce tablet computers for less than $100." The CEO might respond, "Why not? Has anybody tried it?"

The lesson for developing and improving executive presence is to purposely set high performance standards. For example, a sales manager for construction equipment setting a goal of improving revenue by 10 percent over the previous fiscal year would constitute high performance standards.

*Give Emotional Support and Encouragement to Work Associates.* Going out of your way to be kind to people will often enhance your executive presence. A supportive leader gives frequent encouragement and praise and displays caring and kindness even about non-work matters such as the health of a worker's ill family member. Keep in mind that encouragement means to fill with courage. One of the many work-related ways of encouraging people is to ask for their input about important decisions. Emotional support generally improves morale and sometimes improves productivity. In the long term, emotional support and encouragement may bolster a person's self-esteem. Being emotionally supportive comes naturally to the leader who is empathetic and warm.

An indirect, but effective, way of giving emotional support to group members is to make them happy by creating conditions that foster happiness. Psychology professor Sonja Lyubomirsky has found that employees are happier when they are helping others. Based on a study at Coca-Cola in Madrid, she found that acts of kindness make employees feel more connected to one another and their jobs. Furthermore, coworkers observed what was happening and were inspired to replicate kindness in such ways as complimenting one another and bringing coffee.[18] The leader's role here would be to encourage employees to be kind to one another. The encouragement of kindness would, in turn, enhance the leader's executive presence.

*Take Sensible Risks.* Taking sensible risks is a contributor to executive presence. To bring about constructive change, the leader must take risks and be willing to implement those risky decisions. If the risky decision proves to be correct, the leader's stature increases. The relevance of risk-taking to leadership effectiveness is emphasized by Sarah Mensah, the president of Jordan Brand North America. She believes that the ability to welcome and seek out risks is a valuable skill: "I've learned that if there is no risk, there will be no reward."[19]

*Inspire Others and Be Visible.* Taking steps to inspire others is an elegant way of enhancing your executive presence. Inspiring people usually involves appealing to their emotions and values, such as when the head of a snowmobile business unit encourages workers to believe that they are making winters more enjoyable for people who live in regions that accumulate snow as well as facilitating rescue missions.

Because human contact and connections reinforce inspiration, another part of being inspirational is being visible and available. The act of being visible and available is easier to accomplish than changing your attitude or personality. One factor contributing to the popularity of Apple Inc. CEO Tim Cook is that he communicates freely with his executive team and many other workers. A market researcher said, "Tim is down to Earth and approachable."[20]

*Pick Up a Few Ideas by Observing a Role Model.* A direct way of developing and improving executive presence is to observe a person you think has strong executive presence and then model a few of that person's actions. The role model you choose could be a manager or leader where you work, a public figure, or a friend or family member. An advantage of finding a role model on YouTube is that you can watch the person several times to pick up a few hints.

Here are a few of many possible observation points in studying your role model:

- How frequently does he or she smile?
- How forceful is his or her communication?
- Any use of humor in general?
- Does the person make any use of self-deprecating humor?

- How much eye contact does the person make?
- How much does the person fidget?
- Does the person make any use of analogies and metaphors?
- How fashionably does the person dress?
- Is the person friendly enough that you would want to work with him or her?

# Guidelines for Action

1. Executive presence helps you inspire subordinates, peers, and senior leaders.

2. With executive presence you are better able to mobilize others in the direction of accomplishing something worthwhile.

3. A foundational component of executive presence is awareness of who you are, including your strengths and weaknesses and the impact you make on others.

4. Executive presence is highly dependent on projecting self-confidence. If you are self-assured without being bombastic or overbearing, you will create a positive impression.

5. Taking ownership of your ideas and decisions is another manifestation of self-confidence.

6. Superior speaking skills are an obvious contributor to executive presence.

7. A component of executive presence geared to the modern world is inclusivity or welcoming everybody.

8. A superficial, yet vital, component of executive presence is your physical appearance, including demeanor and clothing. Appearance has a heavy impact on first impressions, and making a positive first impression is a component of executive presence.

9. As with other forms of personal development, developing and improving executive presence requires considerable self-discipline. Self-discipline plays an important role in the continuous monitoring of your behavior to ensure that the needed self-development occurs.

10. Having a work-related vision and expressing it to others will enhance your executive presence.

11. How rapidly you get people to comprehend the potential contribution of your idea is a powerful part of executive presence.

12. To be perceived as having a strong executive presence, it is necessary to perform well in stressful situations. A field-tested, specific approach for dealing with such situations is rehearsal. You think in advance of the challenges you will be facing and then visualize how you will respond.

13.  Communicating assertively and directly is a notable way of displaying executive presence.

14.  A deep-level way of developing and improving executive presence is to purposely be passionate about your work.

15.  Setting hard standards for others, if not arbitrary and outlandish, will enhance your executive presence.

16.  Going out of your way to be kind to people will enhance your executive presence.

17.  Taking sensible risks will add to your executive presence.

18.  Taking steps to inspire others is an elegant way of enhancing your executive presence.

19.  A direct way of developing and improving executive presence is to observe a person who you think has executive presence and then model a few of that person's actions.

# 8

# Developing the Internal
# Attributes of Gravitas

An encouraging note about developing your gravitas is that many of its vital components are capable of being improved. We are not referring to an overhaul of your personality but instead honing and refining internal attributes you already possess. The fundamental idea is that human attributes are not binary but instead laid out on a continuum like height. Whether an adult is 3'6" or 7'1" tall, both possess height. Similarly, people have varying levels of self-confidence, rather than being accurately classified as "not self-confident" or "self-confident." We are making a technical point about human behavior, not expecting people to specify the exact degree of the attribute such as when stating that a person is "self-confident."

A reminder about the utility of enhancing gravitas comes from Antoinette Dale Henderson. She says that during her career as a communications coach and facilitator she and her colleagues referred to gravitas as though it were a "passport to senior positions."[1]

Before embarking on a journey to develop internal attributes it is helpful to obtain feedback as to where development is needed. The feedback can be combined with your observations and intuition about where you need development. Two potentially useful sources of feedback are coworkers and close friends—but do not rule out the value of exaggerated feedback from a couple of enemies. After you receive the feedback, it is best to work on one attribute at a time, such as emotional control.[2] For a leader, it is important to seek feedback on which specific attribute is creating a favorable (or unfavorable) impression.[3] For example, a leader might want to know if he or she is offering useful insights into business conditions to the group.

## Articulate Your Goals and Values

Articulating your goals and values helps other people take you seriously and is therefore a foundation for developing gravitas. J.K.

# Gravitas for Leadership

Symancyk, the CEO of PetSmart, is a high-gravitas leader. He regularly articulates his goal and mission for the company: "Every day with every connection, PetSmart's passionate associates help bring pet parents close to their pets so they can live more fulfilled lives." Here are three more examples of a CEO or other manager articulating a goal that enhances his or her gravitas:

*Manager of an athletic club:* "My goal is to make West End Athletic Club a third place for our members. The first two places are their job and their home, but our club also plays a major role in their life."

*Owner of Olé Mexican Restaurant:* "When people in this town crave Mexican food, I want them to think first of Olé."

*Real estate development manager:* "We must have an average of 75 percent occupancy rate in our office buildings by the end of this year. If we pull together as the strong team that I know we are, we can hit that target."

Values are the driving force behind goals. A value is a strongly held personal standard or conviction. It is a belief about something important to the individual such as dignity of work or honesty. Our values create within us a desire to behave consistently with them. If an executive values honesty, he or she will establish a goal of trying to hire only honest employees. The executive would therefore make extensive use of reference checks, background investigations, and honesty testing.

A major part of a top leader's role is to help promote values and principles that contribute to the welfare of individuals and the organization. Leaders who believe in good causes will then espouse principles and values that lead people toward good deeds in the workplace. Expressing these values sincerely enhances the leader's gravitas.

Another value that often helps an enterprise is a strong focus on the welfare of employees. A notable example is the leadership of Rich Snyder, CEO of the successful fast-food chain In-N-Out Burger. Wages and benefits are relatively high, and managers who meet their goals are eligible for company-paid luxury vacations. The Snyder family was committed to viewing employees as if they were family members. As a result, In-N-Out Burger boasts one of the lowest turnover rates in the industry. Snyder met an early death at age 49, but the family kept the business operating based on the same values.[4]

Hundreds of possibilities exist of values that could contribute to a leader's gravitas. The values expressed by executives at Juniper Networks, Inc., the network infrastructure company, provide useful examples of values that many people would take seriously. The three values are contained in The Juniper Way, a commitment to every worker that the culture and company will inspire their best work:

## Be Bold

We pursue simplicity. We challenge the status quo, including challenging ourselves. We embrace diverse ideas and the change they bring. That's what being bold is all about.

## Build Trust

Our success is determined by our customers' success. We say what we mean and take the initiative, so you can count on us to get things done.

## Deliver Excellence

We're obsessed with exceptional quality. Even when we've achieved it, we're always looking for ways to improve. And when we haven't, we act fast to fix the problem.[5]

## *Acquire Knowledge and Sharpen Your Insight*

A bedrock strategy for projecting gravitas is to develop a base of knowledge that enables you to provide sensible alternative solutions to problems. Intuition is very important, but working from a base of facts helps you project a serious, confident image. Displaying knowledge has become more impressive in the age of the Internet and AI because so many people rely on these sources rather than memory to access information. A reflex response when asked a question for so many people is "I don't know, but I will google it."

Formal education is an obvious and important source of information for your knowledge base. Day-by-day absorption of information directly and indirectly related to your career is equally important. A major purpose of formal education is to get you in the right frame of mind to continue your quest for knowledge.

In your quest for developing a solid knowledge base to project gravitas and self-confidence, be sensitive to abusing this technique. If you bombard people with quotes, facts, and figures, you are likely to be perceived as an annoying know-it-all.

Closely related to acquiring knowledge is knowing what to do with it, particularly having insight. The term refers to a depth of understanding that requires considerable intuition and common sense. Intuition is often the mental process used to provide the understanding of a problem. Insight helps speed decision-making. Jeff Bezos, the founder of **Amazon.com,** and Tim Cook, the CEO of Apple, Inc., believe that the bigger the decision, such as whether to enter a particular business, the greater the role of insight and intuition.

Having insight, including connecting facts, enhances a person's gravitas. Here is a basic example: Imagine that Amanda, a home-building executive, reads frequently that the population is aging rapidly. Her response is to build more one-floor housing because many older people are either unable or unwilling to ascend stairs. Amanda's insight pays big dividends because the demand for one-level housing soon outstrips supply.

You can gauge your insight by charting the accuracy of your hunches and predictions about people and business situations. For example, size up a new coworker or manager as best you can. Record your observations and test them against how that person performs or behaves many months later. The feedback from this type of exercise will help sharpen your insights.

## *Hone Your Emotional Intelligence*

Emotional intelligence was described in Chapter 2 as a component of gravitas. Many people believe that emotional intelligence can be acquired and developed, much as a person can learn to become more extraverted or learn to control his or her temper. Many consultants offer training programs to help employees develop emotional intelligence. Elkhonon Goldberg, a clinical professor of neurology at New York University School of Medicine, explains that emotional intelligence can be learned to a degree, much as musical talent or numerical ability can be developed. Having the right natural talent, however, is an important starting point. The combination of biological endowment (such as being aware of your emotions) and training will enable most people to enhance their emotional intelligence.[6]

Given that emotional intelligence has different components, to acquire and develop such ability would usually require working on one component at a time. For example, if a person had difficulty in self-management, he or she would study and be coached in an aspect of self-management, such as anger control. Training in anger management is widespread today because so many people have difficulty in managing their anger.

Monitoring one's behavior to exert emotional control will help many people enhance their emotional intelligence. Leadership coach Ian McKechnie posts that you should try to give other people a sense that your mind and body are calm and that you are under control both in your speech and actions. Avoid both positive and negative emotional outbursts because they might view you as being inconsistent. It is helpful to be more reflective and less reactive in most situations involving people. Be attentive to your steady breathing and surfacing emotions that might threaten your poise. Deeper breathing allows your voice to take on a deeper, more resonant tone, helping you sound more trustworthy.[7]

The accompanying exercise provides a step-by-step approach to the development of emotional intelligence.

---

## Enhancing Your Emotional Intelligence

A realistic starting point in improving your emotional intelligence is to work with one of its four components at a time, such as the empathy aspect of social awareness. A complex behavior pattern or trait such as emotional intelligence takes considerable time to improve, but the time will most likely be a good investment. Follow these steps:

1. Begin by obtaining as much feedback as you can from people who know you. Ask them if they think you understand their emotional reactions and how well they think you understand them. It is helpful to ask someone from another culture or someone who has a severe disability how well you communicate with him or her. (A higher level of empathy is required to communicate well with somebody much different from you.) If you work with customers, ask them how well you appear to understand their position. Empathy is part of the social awareness dimension of emotional intelligence.

2. If you find any area of deficiency, work on that deficiency steadily. For example, perhaps you are not perceived as taking the time to understand a point of view quite different from your own. Attempt to understand other points of view. Suppose you believe strongly that only people with lots of money can be happy. Speak to a person with a different opinion and listen carefully until you understand that person's perspective.

3. At a minimum of a few weeks later, obtain more feedback

about your ability to empathize. If you are making progress, continue to practice.

4. Prepare a document about your skill development. Describe the steps you took to enhance your empathy, the progress you made, and how people react differently to you now. For example, you might find that people talk more openly and freely with you now that you are more empathetic.

5. Then repeat these steps for another facet of emotional intelligence. As a result, you will have developed another valuable interpersonal skill that might enhance your gravitas. In review, the three other major dimensions of emotional intelligence are self-awareness, self-management, and relationship management.

---

The late Carl Wang is an example of a leader whose development of his cognitive knowledge and emotional intelligence contributed to his gravitas. The aspect of emotional intelligence Wang emphasized was humility. In 1981, he founded MID Labs (Medical Instrument Development Laboratories, Inc.) of San Leandro, California. The company soon became a global leader in the manufacture of ophthalmic surgical devices. Under the leadership and creativity of Wang, MID Labs pioneered the tools for modern vitrectomy. A vitrectomy is an eye surgery that cuts and removes the gel-like vitreous fluid from the eyeball without damaging the retina. The branded product line of MID Labs is supplied to more than 30 countries globally. The company was acquired by HOYA Surgical Optics in 2019.

One of Carl Wang's early goals was to develop a disposable cutter design that would be affordable in developing countries. Since its inception, MID Labs has made enough disposable cutters to keep more than five million people worldwide from going blind due to injuries and diseases like diabetes. Almost 100 percent of all cutters sold by competitors today are descendants of Wang's original design.

Andrew Wang, the son of Carl Wang, is an electrical engineer who began working at ML (a favored employee abbreviation for MID Labs) in 1992 when there were only five employees. The younger Wang stayed with the company until 2019 and has provided the firsthand facts and insights into the company and its founder that are reported here. His last position with the company was director of project management. He has stayed in touch with many ML employees. Carl Wang passed away in 2011, and the company shifted to a more formal, corporate-like identity.

## 8. Developing the Internal Attributes of Gravitas

MID employees are still strongly influenced by Carl Wang's mantra: "We can achieve anything working together." Company employees strongly believe that product quality and helping one another are key values, and the older Wang emphasized that employees were responsible for the company's success.

In 2008, the office manager at MID created a patent wall that listed company patents that were attributed both to Carl Wang and company employees. Yet Wang never talked much about the wall. He perceived the primary value of the patents to help in making alliances and friendships with ophthalmology surgeons. He gave credit to many ophthalmologists for developing new surgical procedures needed to maximize the benefits to the patient.

Carl Wang was a leader with humility in a multitude of ways, such as being on a first-name basis with work associates instead of being called "Dr. Wang." The senior Wang enjoyed having lunch with employees, most frequently with the lowest-paid assembly line employees. These employees were the heart of MID because the tiny and complex surgical tools, with a hollow tube-inside-a-tube and an embedded cutter, are mostly handmade. Quality is dependent on assembler patience and care and working with one another and with engineers and quality control when problems surfaced.

The younger Wang explained that his father's humility facilitated creating a company of dedicated and loyal employees who innovated new surgical tools for better patient outcomes. They worked as a team to launch better products and achieve the sharpest cutter in the industry.

The service-to-others aspect of humility of Wang surfaced when he set out to create a company where people would enjoy working hard as a team, accomplish something meaningful, and make money. He decided to start a company that would help keep people from going blind. As an engineer, Wang was often on the production floor working with assemblers to solve problems. But this problem-solving really started in the lunchroom, where open discussion allowed for trust and camaraderie.

MID employees understood implicitly that their leader took their ideas seriously. An outstanding example is that they independently came up with this mission statement: "To excel at providing quality and innovative ophthalmic products that benefit patients around the world." They had a banner made that contained the mission statement and placed it in the conference room. Wang believed so strongly that employees were the backbone of the company's success that he accepted the mission statement with enthusiasm.

Despite the contribution and acceptance of MID's products, the company went through two difficult financial periods. Twice when the company was about to go bankrupt, many employees banded together and worked harder without a paycheck to save the company. Andrew Wang contends the unusual employee effort could be attributed to the workforce believing in the mission of the company, and loyalty to his father. Many employees stayed with the company for decades, up until retiring.

When Wang was dying of an incurable illness, he told people not to fuss over him. This is the only time employees, surgeons, and friends actively disobeyed. Three hundred people showed up for Wang's memorial. Many people spoke of his genius but would also emphasize that he was a friend.

Carl Wang supported himself through college as an immigrant working as a waiter in a Chinese restaurant. Wang studied electrical engineering at Taida University in China for two years. After moving to the United States, he received a bachelor's degree and then a PhD in electrical engineering from the University of Illinois Urbana-Champaign, graduating near the top of his class.[8]

## Develop Your Self-Confidence

Self-confidence contributes strongly to gravitas. Improving your level of self-confidence therefore strengthens your gravitas. Self-confidence is generally achieved by succeeding in a variety of situations. A confident team leader may not be generally self-confident unless he or she also achieves success in activities such as forming good personal relationships, navigating complex software, writing a letter, learning a second language, and displaying athletic skills. Following are nine specific strategies and tactics for building and elevating self-confidence. They will generally work unless the person has deep-rooted feelings of inferiority. The nine tactics and strategies described here are arranged approximately in the order in which they should be tried to achieve good results.

*Take an Inventory of Personal Assets and Accomplishments.* Many people suffer from low self-confidence because they do not appreciate their own good points. Therefore, a starting point in increasing your self-confidence is to take an inventory of personal assets and accomplishments. Personal assets should be related to characteristics and behaviors rather than tangible assets, such as the value of investments.

The acquisition of knowledge and sharpening your insights described above is a major asset for developing self-confidence.

Accomplishments can be anything significant in which you played a key role in achieving the results. Try not to be modest in preparing your list of assets and accomplishments. You are looking for any confidence booster you can find. The value of these asset lists is that they add to your self-appreciation. Most people who lay out their good points on a list come away from the activity with at least a temporary boost in self-confidence. Two examples of assets are listening skills and technology skills. The temporary boost, combined with a few successful experiences, may lead to a long-term gain in self-confidence.

An important supplement to listing your own assets is hearing the opinion of others on your good points. For many people, positive feedback from others does more for building self-confidence than self-reflection. The reason is that self-confidence depends heavily on what people think others think about them. Consequently, if other people—whose judgment you trust—think highly of you, your self-image will be positive.

*Use Positive Self-Talk.* A basic method of building self-confidence is to engage in *positive self-talk.* The first step in using positive self-talk is to objectively state the incident that is casting doubt about your self-worth.[9] The key word here is **objectively.** Terry, who is fearful of poorly executing a report-writing assignment, might say, "I've been asked to write a summary of our team's activities, and I'm not a good writer."

The next step is to objectively interpret what the incident *does not* mean. Terry might say, "Not being a skilled writer doesn't mean that I can't figure out a way to write a good report or that I'm an ineffective employee." Next, you should objectively state what the incident *does* mean. Terry could state: "I have a problem with one small aspect of this job." The fourth step is to objectively account for the cause of the incident. Terry would say, "I'm really worried about writing a good report because I have very little experience in writing along these lines."

The fifth step is to identify some positive ways to prevent the incident from happening again. Terry might say, "I will look for some information online to help me write reports." Or, "Maybe I could get part of the report written by AI." The final step is to use positive self-talk. Terry imagines his boss saying, "This report is really good. I'm proud of my decision to select you to prepare this important report."

Positive self-talk builds self-confidence and self-esteem because it programs the mind with positive messages. Making frequent positive statements, or affirmations about the self, creates a more confident person. An example would be "I know I can learn this new software rapidly enough to increase my productivity within five days."

*Avoid Negative Self-Talk.* In addition to making positive statements, you should minimize negative statements about yourself to bolster self-confidence. A lack of self-confidence is reflected in statements such as, "I may be stupid, but...," "Nobody asked my opinion," "I know I'm usually wrong, but...," "I know I don't have as much education as some people, but...." Self-effacing statements such as these serve to reinforce low self-confidence.

It is also important not to attribute to yourself negative, irreversible traits, such as "verbally challenged." Instead, look on your weak points as areas for possible self-improvement. Negative self-labeling can do long-term damage to your confidence. If a person stops that practice today, his or her self-confidence may begin to increase.

*Use Positive Visual Imagery.* Suppose you have a situation in mind in which you would like to appear confident and in control. An example would be a meeting with a major customer who has told you by email that he is considering switching suppliers. Your intuitive reaction is that if you cannot handle his concerns without fumbling or appearing desperate, you will lose the account. An important technique in this situation is *positive visual imagery.* To apply this technique in this situation, imagine yourself engaging in a convincing argument about why your customer should retain your company as the primary supplier. Imagine yourself talking in positive terms about the good service your company offers and how you can rectify any problems.

Visualize yourself listening patiently to your customer's concerns and then talking confidently about how your company can handle these concerns. As you rehearse this moment of truth, create a mental picture of you and the customer shaking hands over the fact that the account is still yours.

Positive visual imagery helps you appear confident because your mental rehearsal of the situation has helped you prepare for battle. If imagery works for you once, you will be even more effective in subsequent uses of the technique.

*Set High Expectations for Yourself (the Galatea Effect).* If you set high expectations for yourself, and you succeed, you are likely to experience a temporary or permanent boost in self-confidence. The **Galatea Effect** is a type of self-fulfilling prophecy in which high self-expectations lead to high performance. The term *Galatea effect* stems from Greek mythology. Galatea was a maiden who was originally a statue carved by Pygmalion. She was later brought to life by Aphrodite in response to the sculptor's pleas. Similar to positive self-talk, if you believe in yourself, you are more likely to succeed. You expect to win, so you do. The Galatea effect does not work all the time, but it does work some of the time for many people.

*Behave as If You Feel Confident.* A principle of psychology developed over 110 years ago states that your behavior leads to attitudes. As you change your behavior, your attitudes will begin to change. This same idea can be used to project confidence. A useful example is the often-feared situation of making a presentation. Executive coach Gail Golden says that you should enter the room purposefully, holding your back straight. Look up and out at the audience instead of looking down at your notes or at the screen of your computer graphic presentation. Speak in a loud, clear voice and look the audience in the eye or on their foreheads.[10] Behaving in this manner will often make you feel more confident within several minutes.

*Bounce Back from Setbacks and Embarrassments.* Resilience is a major contributor to personal effectiveness. Overcoming setbacks also builds self-confidence. An effective self-confidence builder is convincing yourself that you can conquer adversity, such as setbacks and embarrassments. The majority of successful leaders have dealt successfully with at least one significant setback in their careers, such as being fired or demoted. In contrast, crumbling after a setback or series of setbacks will usually lower self-confidence.

Adversity has enormous emotional consequences. The emotional impact of severe job adversity can rival the loss of a personal relationship. The stress from adversity leads to a cycle of adversity followed by stress, followed by more adversity. A starting point in dealing with the emotional aspects of adversity is to *accept the reality of your problem.* Admit that your problems are real and that you are hurting inside. The next step is *not to take the setback personally.* Remember that setbacks are inevitable if you are taking some risks in your career. Not personalizing setbacks helps reduce some of the emotional sting. If possible, *do not panic.* Recognize that you are in difficult circumstances under which many others panic. Convince yourself to remain calm enough to deal with the severe problem or crisis. Also, *get help from your support network.* Getting emotional support from family members and friends helps overcome the emotional turmoil associated with adversity.

An inescapable part of planning a comeback is to solve your problem. You often need to search for creative solutions. Jason, a business student in Chicago, ran a sub shop to earn a living and support himself through college. Layoffs at nearby companies had driven his sales way down below the point at which it paid to keep the sub shop open. In the process of exploring all the possibilities of what he could do in a hurry to earn a living, Jason observed that loads of old buildings in downtown Chicago were being rebuilt and turned into apartments and retail space. Jason then thought of starting an "interior demolition" company, combining efforts with two relatives in the home repair business. Jason's creative solution accomplished what needed to be done to regain his financial equilibrium. His self-confidence continues to surge as his interior demolition business has prospered.

*Strive to Develop Positive Psychological Capital.* A comprehensive way of becoming more self-confident is to develop *positive psychological capital*, a positive psychological state of development in which you have hope, self-efficacy, optimism, and resilience. In more detail, the components of positive psychological capital are as follows:

- *Hope* refers to persevering toward goals and, when necessary, redirecting paths to a goal in order to succeed. In everyday language, don't give up when pursuing your goals.
- *Self-efficacy* refers to having the confidence to take on and invest the necessary effort to succeed at challenging tasks. Experience is a big help here, because if you have successfully completed the same task, or a similar one, previously you will be more confident that you can succeed.
- *Optimism* refers to making a positive attribution about succeeding now and in the future. If you are a natural pessimist, you will have to work harder at looking for the positive aspects of a given situation.
- *Resiliency* refers to dealing with problems and adversity by sustaining effort and bouncing back to attain success. Conquering a major setback would be an enormous contributor to your self-confidence.[11]

*Avoid Overconfidence.* As with most human qualities, self-confidence can be a negative factor if carried to the extreme. The overly self-confident individual might become intimidating and unwilling to listen to the advice of others. As a result, the individual might suffer a gravitas loss. During a group meeting, the highly self-confident person might typically make a comment before giving others their fair turn to speak. Overconfident individuals are so self-centered that they do not even notice eyes rolling when they hog the meeting. The excessively self-confident person also runs the risk of being perceived as a narcissist and can therefore be annoying.

## *Strengthen Your Authenticity and Integrity*

Developing authenticity and integrity are two robust approaches to enhancing your gravitas. *Authenticity* is about being genuine and honest about your personality, values, and beliefs as well as having integrity. Organizational psychologist Rebecca Newton notes that the best kind of gravitas stems from authenticity.[12] To become an authentic leader and demonstrate authenticity, be yourself rather than attempting to be a replica of someone else. Others respond to your leadership, partly because you are genuine rather than phony.

The authentic leader can emphasize different values and characteristics to different people without being inauthentic. The word *emphasize* is meaningful. To emphasize is to focus on one aspect of behavior without changing your expressed values to suit an audience. For example, a corporate-level manager at a chain of automotive service centers might engage in more banter when he visits a service center than when meeting with financial analysts. The manager is therefore being politically astute without being phony.

A helpful way of developing authenticity is to note specific behaviors and attitudes of authentic leaders and then work toward incorporating a feasible number of these behaviors and attitudes into your repertoire. The accompanying checklist is a good starting point.

---

## A Checklist of Authentic Leadership Behaviors and Attitudes[13]

1. I gather feedback to help me get along better with work associates.
2. I state clearly what I really mean.
3. I speak with the same type of voice to almost all people.
4. I am consistent with what I believe and how I act.
5. I display just about the same personality to most people I interact with.

6. I admit to my mistakes.
7. I base my decisions on what I believe.
8. Before I reach a conclusion, I listen carefully to other perspectives.
9. I have a clear understanding of my strengths and weaknesses.
10. On and off the job, my personality is about the same.
11. I frequently share information with people I work with.
12. I pronounce words the same no matter whom I am talking with.
13. I stick to my beliefs despite outside pressures.
14. I usually look at relevant data before making a decision.
15. I do not express different opinions on the same subject depending on whom I am talking with.
16. The saying "what you see is what you get" applies to me.
17. I am aware of the impact I make on others.
18. I express my ideas and thoughts clearly to others.
19. I have moral standards that guide my actions.
20. I am not a phony.

**Interpretation:** The more of these 20 statements you checked, the more likely it is that you are authentic and perceived to be authentic.

---

An ethical leader is honest and trustworthy and therefore has integrity. According to ethics researcher Thomas E. Becker, this quality goes beyond honesty and conscientiousness. *Integrity* refers to loyalty to rational principles; it means practicing what one preaches regardless of emotional or social pressure.[14] For example, a leader with integrity would believe that employees should be treated fairly, and the pressure to cut costs would not prompt the leader to renege on a commitment to reimburse an employee for relocation expenses.

Integrity is related to trust because it refers to consistency in the values a person possesses and the person's behavior. For example, a leader who says that feedback to employees is essential will show integrity when he or she provides feedback to employees regularly.

Ron Wallace began his 38-year career at UPS International as a delivery driver and eventually became CEO. He said that survey after survey indicates that the number one thing people want in a leader is integrity. "It's doing the right thing when no one else is looking."[15]

Developing and improving integrity is akin to becoming more moral and ethical, but the following nine suggestions might serve as a useful guide.

- Follow through on your promises. The heart of integrity is doing what you promised such as making bonus payments by the date you specified.
- Provide honest, open, and timely communication to group members. Keeping people informed helps team members trust you.
- Lead by example. If you serve as a model of how you want others to act, you will display the type of consistency necessary for integrity.
- Keep appointments. Leaders who break appointments not only frustrate work associates, but they are perceived as being low on integrity.
- Distance yourself from people who lack integrity. Associating with people who lack integrity will often make you appear to have equally low integrity. Your character will be judged by the character of your associates.
- Take responsibility for your mistakes. Explaining the nature of your mistake and taking responsibility for it will enhance your integrity as well as your authenticity.
- Minimize secrecy and be transparent. Minimize telling some work associates you have secret information to share with them. Instead, share as much information with others as feasible and allowable from the organization's perspective.
- Accept feedback and be receptive to learning from others. If you are willing to change your behavior or attitude on a topic based on constructive feedback from others, you will be perceived as having integrity (and usually gravitas).
- Minimize favoritism. It is difficult to avoid giving any preferential treatment to people in the workplace with whom you get along best. Basing assignments and other employee decisions on merit, however, will enhance your integrity.[16]

## Guidelines for Action

1. Gravitas is thought to be a "passport to senior positions."
2. Two potentially useful sources of feedback about where you need to develop are coworkers and close friends.
3. Articulating your goals and values helps other people take you seriously and is therefore a foundation for developing gravitas.

4. A major part of a top leader's role is to help promote values and principles that contribute to the welfare of individuals and the organization.

5. A bedrock strategy for projecting gravitas is to develop a base of knowledge that enables you to provide sensible alternative solutions to problems.

6. Having insight, including connecting facts, enhances a person's gravitas.

7. You can gauge your insight by charting the accuracy of your hunches and predictions about people and business situations.

8. Monitoring one's behavior to exert emotional control will help many people enhance their emotional intelligence. Try to give other people a sense that your mind and body are under control in both your speech and actions.

9. Improving your level of self-confidence strengthens your gravitas. Self-confidence is generally achieved by succeeding in a variety of situations.

10. A starting point in increasing your self-confidence is to take an inventory of personal assets and accomplishments.

11. A basic method of building self-confidence is to engage in positive self-talk. In addition to making positive statements, you should minimize negative statements about yourself to bolster your self-confidence.

12. Positive visual imagery helps you appear self-confident because your mental rehearsal of the situation has helped you prepare for the battle.

13. If you set high self-expectations and you succeed, you are likely to experience a temporary or permanent boost in self-confidence.

14. An effective self-confidence builder is to convince yourself that you can conquer adversity, such as setbacks and embarrassments.

15. Self-confidence can become a negative factor if carried to the extreme. The overly self-confident individual might become intimidating and unwilling to listen to the advice of others, thereby detracting from gravitas.

16. Developing authenticity and integrity are two robust approaches to enhancing your gravitas.

17. A helpful way of developing authenticity is to observe specific behaviors and attitudes of authentic leaders and then work toward incorporating a feasible number of these behaviors and attitudes into your repertoire.

18. The heart of integrity is doing what you promised such as making bonus payments by the date you specified.

19. Explaining the nature of your mistake and taking responsibility for it with enhance your integrity as well as your authenticity.

# Developing the Interpersonal Attributes of Gravitas

Gravitas is dependent on the perception of others about your seriousness of purpose and other positive characteristics. At the same time, these observations about you are strongly influenced by your interactions with people. To be perceived as having gravitas you therefore need to hone your attributes and skills that emphasize interpersonal relationships. For example, one of the subjects in this chapter is political skill because it is essential to interacting with people in an impressive way.

## *Gather Feedback About Your Gravitas*

A useful starting point in developing the interpersonal attributes of gravitas is to understand how you are currently perceived with respect to these attributes. Feedback is usually the most effective way to obtain information on your current level of gravitas. A group of executive coaches suggest that you ask for this feedback casually after a meeting or presentation. It would be revealing to ask coworkers, superiors, and subordinates one or more of the following questions:

- Did I sound like a professional and someone who had relevant facts at hand?
- Did you find me boring?
- Did I speak too quickly?
- How well organized were my ideas?
- Did I appear confident, in control of myself, and comfortable with the material I was presenting?[1]
- Did I interact with others in a way that demonstrated that I am self-confident and knowledgeable?

Job candidates for high-level leadership and management positions are often passed over because one or more interviewers said that candidate "lacked gravitas" or "didn't have enough gravitas." If a rejected candidate learns that this perceived lack cost him or her the job, the candidate might express appreciation for having gone so far in the candidate screening but ask what specifically the interviewer or interviewers meant by "lacking gravitas." The rejected interviewee might say, "I am not upset, and I am not objecting to your conclusions. I am just looking for ways to boost my personal qualifications for the future." With a help-seeking orientation like this, the candid interviewer might make statements such as, "You were vague in answering questions," "You didn't look us straight in the eye," "You did not dress well enough for the position," or "You mumbled a lot during the interview," or "You did not explain carefully enough a few of your biggest on-the-job accomplishments."

## *Build Rapport with Subordinates and Coworkers*

For other people to respect you, have confidence in you, and take you seriously, it is enormously helpful to build rapport with them. Rapport involves creating trust, inspiring confidence, and displaying a positive attitude. How to establish rapport with others might be considered the subject of the entire field of human relations, and many of the principles are common sense. Developing political skill, as described later in this chapter, is also part of rapport building. Here we highlight 12 key points for establishing rapport with subordinates and coworkers that even experienced leaders might sometimes overlook. The first six points involve relationships with subordinates and the next six with coworkers.

1. *Solicit opinions before taking action.* In the spirit of participative leadership, find out what group members think of your potential action, even on relatively small matters such as selecting a restaurant for a department banquet. Subordinates will be pleased that their input matters, and they will be more cooperative in implementing your decision. Listening to opinions is an essential tool of the participative leader or manager, and it is also an excellent way of cultivating subordinates. To be listened to is to be respected and considered important and facilitates respect of the leader.

2. *Ask how you can make their jobs better.* An excellent relationship builder with subordinates is playing an active role in facilitating the jobs of subordinates running more smoothly. Toward this end, ask such questions as "What drives you the craziest about the processes around here?" and "If you could have a fantasy tool that made your job easier, what would it be?"[2]

3. *Give recognition.* Most people are recognition-deprived, so being a boss who recognizes the contributions of subordinates goes a long way toward building positive relationships and establishing rapport with them. Effective forms of recognition include thank-you notes and face-to-face comments, such as "You really helped us out in a jam, and I appreciate it."

4. *Be courteous.* Many managers are rude to subordinates, so showing courtesy will help you build relationships with your direct reports. Being courteous to subordinates would include such acts as responding quickly to email messages, returning phone calls, not multitasking when subordinates are talking to you, not keeping people waiting for you, and not belittling them. Most high-gravitas leaders are courteous to group members.

5. *Look for opportunities to say yes to requests.* Repeated refusals on requests can be demoralizing and demotivating for employees, especially when the request is feasible. Some requests, such as asking for a cash bar in the lunchroom, must be refused. But look for opportunities to say yes. A useful guideline is when a group member makes a request, avoid automatically replying, "We cannot do that." Instead, ask yourself, "Can we do that?"[3]

6. *Provide leader political support.* A comprehensive way of establishing good relationships with subordinates is to use your influence to help the group accomplish its tasks, including getting the resources its needs. *Leader political support* refers to political acts and influence techniques by the leader to provide subordinates with the resources they need to accomplish individual, group, or organizational objectives.[4] Imagine that Cheryl is the manager of a distribution facility that badly needs a new mechanical system for moving goods through the warehouse, and that budgets are tight. Cheryl uses her contacts with the vice president of manufacturing to free up funds for the system, thereby exercising leader political support.

Another aspect of political support is to bring forth the demands of group members to higher management and then fight for these demands, such as needing new equipment. Carrying out this principle enhances your stature among group members and helps you win their support.

7. *Develop allies through being civil.* People who are courteous, kind, cooperative, and cheerful develop allies and friends in the workplace. Practicing basic good manners, such as being pleasant

and friendly, is also part of being civil. Being civil helps you stand out, because many people believe that crude, rude, and obnoxious behavior has become both the norm and a national problem. Uncivil behaviors characteristically involve rudeness and discourteousness.

Closely related to being civil is maintaining a positive outlook. Everyone knows that you gain more allies by being optimistic and positive than by being pessimistic and negative. Nevertheless, many people—including leaders—ignore this simple strategy for getting along well with others. Coworkers are more likely to solicit your opinion or offer you help when you are perceived as a cheerful person.

8. *Make other people feel important.* A fundamental principle of fostering good relationships with coworkers and others is to make them feel important. Making others feel important is honest because everybody in an organization has a contribution to make, including the CEO, payroll coordinator, and parking lot attendant. Although the leader has primary responsibility for satisfying this recognition need, coworkers also play a key role. One approach to making a coworker feel important would be to bring a notable accomplishment of the person to the attention of the group. Reciprocity enters the picture: if the leader makes other people feel important, they will perceive the leader as important.

9. *Be a team player.* An essential strategy for developing good relationships with coworkers is to be a team player. A team player is one who emphasizes group accomplishment and cooperation rather than individual achievement and not helping others. You will also have to be a team player if you reach the pinnacle of power in your organization. Executives are expected to be good team players as well as individual decision-makers. But team play is even more important on the way to becoming an executive, because impatience and making unilateral decisions is more tolerated in the executive suite. Being an effective team player is important because without such capability, collaborative effort is not possible.

A direct method of promoting team play is to share credit for good deeds with other team members. Instead of focusing on yourself as the person responsible for a work achievement, point out that the achievement was a team effort. You will make a poor team player if you try to grab all the glory for ideas that work and distance yourself from ideas that do not work. An effective team member wants all other members to succeed. You will stand out by praising the people you work with rather than hogging any praise for the team.

10. *Follow group standards of conduct.* The basic principle to follow in getting along with coworkers is to follow **group norms.** These refer to the unwritten set of expectations for group members— what people ought to do. Norms become a standard of what each person should do or not do within the group. Norms also provide general guidelines for reacting constructively to the behavior of coworkers. For example, sharing job-relevant information is a constructive group norm at all organizational levels.

11. *Express an interest in the work and personal lives of coworkers.* Almost everyone is self-centered to some extent. Thus, people favor topics closely related to themselves, such as their children, friends, hobbies, work, or possessions. Industrial sales representatives rely heavily on this fact in cultivating relationships with established customers. They routinely ask the customer about his or her hobbies, family members, and work activities. You can capitalize on this simple strategy by asking coworkers and friends questions such as these two: "How is your work going?" and "How does the company use the output from your department?"

12. *Provide emotional support to coworkers.* People at all organizational levels may need occasional emotional support, including the CEO who is under attack from activists who want to buy out the company. Such support can take the form of verbal encouragement for ideas expressed, listening to a group member's concerns, or complimenting achievement. An emotionally supportive comment to a coworker who appears to be stressed out might be, "This doesn't appear to be one of your better days. What can I do to help?"

## Develop Political Skill

Yet another way in which leaders and other professionals are taken seriously is to have political astuteness or skill. Such skill involves being socially astute and engaging in behaviors that lead to feelings of confidence, trust, and sincerity.[5] Leaders and managers use political skill to acquire the power necessary to reach objectives. Other political skills include establishing the right connections and impressing the right people. Furthermore, managers with strong political skills possess an astute understanding of people, along with a fundamental belief that they can control the outcomes of their interactions with people.

Political skill should be regarded as a supplement to job competence and the other basic skills. Managers who overemphasize political skill at the expense of doing work of substance focus too much on pleasing company insiders and advancing their own careers. Too much time invested in office politics takes time away from dealing with customer problems and improving productivity and often leads to mistrust from peers and subordinates. As a result, the person loses rather than enhances his or her gravitas.

Developing political skill is a long-term, complex process that involves developing the right strategies and tactics. The lion's share of organizational politics involves building positive relationships with network members who can be helpful now or later. The network includes superiors, subordinates, lower-ranking people, coworkers, external customers, and suppliers. Positive relationships, in turn, add to you being taken seriously.

Research suggests that political skill can be developed through careful observation and experience, coupled with improving one's emotional intelligence. A study conducted with 260 business graduate students showed that mentoring can be an effective way of developing political skill. Ninety percent of the students were employed, and those who had a mentor or mentors responded to a questionnaire about the quality of their mentoring. Results indicated that participants who had a mentor showed significantly better political skill than participants who did not have a mentor.[6]

A sampling of political strategies and tactics is described next that can be developed and refined to project gravitas. Developing these behaviors and attitudes requires self-awareness of where you already stand with these strategies and tactics, combined with the self-discipline to improve. For example, you might need to make a concentrated effort to flatter work associates sincerely.

1. *Develop power contacts through networking.* A fundamental principle of success is to identify powerful people and then establish alliances with them. Cultivating friendly, cooperative relationships with powerful organizational members and outsiders can make the managerial worker's cause much easier to advance. These contacts can support a person's ideas and recommend the person for promotions and visible temporary assignments. When other people are aware that you have powerful contacts, you will be taken more seriously.

A challenge in the era of digital communications is that face time, or in-person contact, is helpful for building contacts. It is important to converse with powerful people in person in addition to sending them electronic messages. Although not face to face, an occasional phone call is also a useful supplement to email or text messages for purposes of building a network.

2. *Manage your impression.* An example of an ethical impression management tactic would be to contribute outstanding performance and then make sure key people know of your accomplishments. Making others aware of what you accomplish is often referred to as *achieving visibility.* When tactics of impression management appear insincere, they are likely to create a negative impression and thus be self-defeating. A key person to impress is your immediate superior.

Managing your impression includes creating a positive image. Such an image can be cultivated by keeping your voice calm and well-modulated, dressing fashionably, and matching your humor to those around you. Speaking well is another critical factor. and being courteous, pleasant, and positive also contributes to a positive image.

A review of organizational psychology research about first impressions suggests that first impressions have long-term effects that extend beyond brief intervals of time. The first impression is lasting and underlies the adage that "one never gets a second chance to make a first impression." Yet with focused effort, it is possible to overcome the effects of a poor first impression.[7] For example, a person who made a bad first impression by showing up late for a meeting could change that impression by being prompt for a series of future meetings.

3. *Make your boss look good (managing up).* A bedrock principle of organizational politics is to help your boss perform well, which is probably one of the reasons you were hired. Positioning yourself as a supporting player for your boss will help your performance evaluation and therefore your career. Consultant Karl Bimshas suggests that a good starting point is to ask questions of this nature: "What do you think should be my highest priority right now?" Then turn in a good performance with respect to the priority.[8] As a result, your boss might even perceive you as having gravitas.

4. *Keep informed of internal developments.* It is politically important to keep informed. Successful managers and professionals develop a pipeline to help them keep abreast, or even ahead, of developments within the firm. For example, a politically astute individual might befriend a major executive's assistant.

147

5. *Be courteous, pleasant, and positive.* Courteous, pleasant, and positive people are the first to be hired and the last to be fired (assuming they are also technically qualified).[9] A key part of being courteous, pleasant, and positive is to socialize with coworkers, including having meals and drinks with them. Executive coach Leslie Williams observes: "Socialization has everything to do with influence. It's not enough to just be good at your job." In addition to doing a good job, you have to be somebody whom people know and know well enough to trust.[10] And, of course, being trusted is part of being taken seriously.

6. *Ask satisfied customers to contact your manager.* A favorable comment by a customer receives considerable weight because customer satisfaction is a corporate priority. If a customer says something nice, the comment will carry more weight than one from a coworker or subordinate. The reason is that insiders might praise you for political reasons, whereas a customer's motivation is thought to be pure.

7. *Bring forth solutions rather than problems.* A strongly meritorious political tactic is to focus on bringing solutions rather than problems to the attention of your direct manager. The basic approach is to say something to the effect of "Here is a problem I have identified, and here is what I would like to do about it with your approval." You will be taken quite seriously when you can identify and solve problems. According to business writer Matt Rosoff, managers hate to hear a direct report say, "Somebody should..." In other words, the subordinate is identifying a problem and thinks that the manager or somebody else should work on its resolution. The boss hears, "I'd like to add another task to your to-do list."[11]

8. *Reach out to your boss's boss.* Developing a working relationship with the manager of your immediate manager helps increase your power base at the same time. Your boss's boss is a key person in your network because that person can have considerable influence over your career. Several approaches for developing a good relationship with your manager's manager follow. First, connect with that individual on a personal level. Look for a common interest, such as both being a booster of the Paralympics. Second, if you receive a compliment for your good work from somewhere else in the organization or from a customer, pass that information along to your boss. The latter is likely to pass that information along to their boss. Third, volunteer for a cross-functional committee. Your boss's boss

is likely to quickly learn about this meritorious activity.[12] A simple verbal equation to keep in mind is that "meritorious = serious."

9. *Use sincere flattery.* A powerful tactic for ingratiating yourself to others is to flatter them honestly and sincerely. Although one meaning of the term *flattery* is insincere praise, another meaning refers to a legitimate compliment. High gravitas people use flattery regularly.

10. *Stay in touch with key people, even if performing remote or hybrid work.* A major reason that remote and hybrid workers are promoted less frequently is they have less face time and virtual contact with key members of the organization. Live Data Technologies found that people working from home were promoted 31 percent less frequently in 2023 than office-based workers. Close to 90 percent of CEOs indicated that they are more likely to select in-office employees for career-advancing projects, salary increases, or promotions.[13] A starting point for maintaining visibility is to ask your boss, and perhaps your boss's boss, how frequently he or she wants to hear from you. Being proactive by sending timely and useful messages to key people through the organization is effective. Suggesting an occasional videoconference is helpful, and so is greeting key people during the times when you are physically present in the company office. Share information about progress and results on projects of significance. Virtual work also provides the opportunity to communicate online with geographically dispersed members of the organization.

11. *Send thank-you notes to large numbers of people.* One of the most basic political tactics, sending thank-you notes profusely, is simply an application of sound human relations. Many successful people take the time to send handwritten notes to employees and customers. Handwritten notes are warmer than email messages and can help create bonds with their recipients. Text messages are more informal and are therefore a plausible substitute for handwritten notes.

## Send Out Power Signals

An advanced application of political skills is to emit signals that you are powerful in a pleasant, tactful way. If the power signals are interpreted as intended, your gravitas will be enhanced. A starting point in sending out power signals is to have a job title indicating that you have legitimate or formal power. If your job title is chief financial officer, you obviously have more formal power than an accounts receivable supervisor. If you have a job title indicating substantial power, it is helpful to mention your job title in a subtle way. The fading tradition of handing out a business card that includes an impressive job title is a power signal worth considering. Some people exchange business cards digitally.

What can you do if you do not have a power-laden job title? It is sometimes possible to negotiate an impressive new job title without a change in your job responsibilities or salary. Here are a few job-title possibilities for sending out at least a low power signal:

- *data wrangler* for the position of data analyst
- *head of people* for manager of human resources
- *growth hacker* for marketing manager
- *brand warrior* for marketing associate
- *customer happiness champion* for customer service manager
- *environmental sustainability manager* for manager of refuse disposal truck fleet
- *business controller* for senior accountant

My caveat is that while for some people these attractive job titles will emit a mild power signal, others might regard the titles as humorous.

A natural way to send out power signals is to develop expertise in a niche including logistics, artificial intelligence, cost cutting, and revenue enhancement. The power stemming from such specialized knowledge is referred to as *expert power*. To send out power signals via expert power, group members must value the expertise, and the leader must make others aware of his or her expertise.

Exercising expert power is the logical starting point for building one's power base. Having this power base is a key contributor to sending power signals. Powerful people in business, government, and education almost invariably launched their careers by developing expertise in a specialty of value to their employers. Mary Barra, the CEO of GM, began her career right out of college, as an electrical engineer at GM. Furthermore, expert power keeps a person in demand for executive positions. Another example is Michael Dell, who began Dell Computers (now Dell Technologies) by selling computers as a college student. His expert knowledge of how to sell computers directly to customers highlighted his credibility, and emitted power signals.

A low-key way of emitting power signals is to derive power from gossip, which is an important resource in many organizations. Most people know that an individual in possession of sought-after information can accrue a small degree of power, and a scientific analysis supports this idea. According to the analysis, a supplier of gossip will have a form of expert power. However, if the person provides mostly negative gossip, the person's power signals will weaken.[14]

Here is an example of the type of gossip that would emit positive power signals: "I heard from an inside source that one of the biggest seven tech companies is about to make an offer to buy out our company." Here is an example of the type of gossip that would decrease a person's power: "A reliable source told me that our chief marketing officer might soon be facing child pornography charges."

One of the strongest ways to send out power signals is to be well connected, as follows directly from the political tactic of "develop power contacts through networking." If other organizational members know that you are well connected, you will be perceived as powerful. Among the popular phrases acknowledging the utility of having a network with strong members are "Knowing the right people in the right places," "It's not what you know, it's who you know," and "Having a friend upstairs."

For a strong network to be useful for sending out power signals, you must make others aware of your powerful contacts. Name-dropping is the standard approach if carried out with a touch of finesse. Here is a plausible approach to name-dropping: "Our governor and I exchanged a few ideas over X on how we might increase tourism in our state." Here is an example of name-dropping that might seem exaggerated: "Mary Barra at GM and I were just chatting about when autonomous driving flying cars might be available to the public."

Carol Tomé, the CEO of UPS, and the former CFO of Home Depot, is a strong example of a leader who sends out power signals and has developed the interpersonal attributes of gravitas. In 2021 she was named the CEO of United Parcel Service (UPS). She became the first woman CEO of UPS, the twelfth CEO in the company's 113-year history, and the first outsider to hold the post. Tomé's journey to UPS was not part of her career planning. She retired from Home Depot after 24 years with the company and was once a contender for the CEO position. She felt it was the right time to leave Home Depot and had been on the UPS board since 2003.

An executive search firm approached Tomé for the UPS position. The position was intriguing to Tomé because she knew that UPS needed to unleash revenue and profits. Tomé said she told the recruiter, "You know I like to make money. I have a pretty good track record at it. I thought I could really move the needle here and that would be fun." Tomé was also enthralled about the opportunity to develop people. She knew that UPS has 540,000 full- and part-time employees, and she wanted to help them reach their highest potential. Tomé added also that she was bored being retired, and that she was driving her husband crazy by being around all day. She thought that becoming the CEO of UPS was her calling.

Tomé brought along some of her Home Depot ideas to UPS, such as the inverted pyramid (workers at the bottom of the organization hold most of the power). A key change she made at UPS was to post jobs internally so that seniority was not weighted so heavily for promotions. She also elevated the importance of diversity and inclusion, where UPS was already strong. The company relaxed its policy regarding facial hair and Black hairstyles to make all races feel comfortable and included. A new slogan at UPS is pointedly inclusive: "You belong at UPS." Other priorities of the company include preserving the planet and limiting climate change. UPS drivers log 2 billion miles per year, and it has hundreds of airplane flights every day to destinations around the world. In recognition of all this fuel consumption, UPS has established carbon reduction goals.

Tomé began her CEO position at the height of the pandemic, which created a surge in demand for package delivery. In the second quarter of 2019, UPS had to hire 40,000 people just to get the packages delivered. One of the major problems Tomé tackled along with her logistics specialists was increasing the speed of package deliveries, a phase of the business in which UPS lagged behind competitors.

Another skill set Tomé developed at Home Depot that she applied to her CEO role at UPS was finding the answer to strategic questions by listening. At Home Depot this meant listening to customers at the stores, including working as a store associate and wearing an orange apron. Furthermore, Tomé believes that the answer to everything can be found inside the facility, talking to associates and customers.

At UPS Tomé took on three big challenges during her first year. Job number one was helping employees attain their highest potential. Job number two was increasing the stock price, and job number three was preparing potential successors to take her place upon retirement. In terms of improving operations, Tomé approved the use of technology to automate some of the processes in company facilities. Robotic labeling of packages was a prime example. In addition to these challenges,

Tomé spearheaded a move to make UPS more profitable. The company became more selective about which packages it shipped. Sales leaders were instructed to evaluate customers less by volume than by profitability. Another move toward increased profitability was to selectively increase prices.

Tomé's stature as a leader to be taken seriously was solidified further in 2023, when she was instrumental in reaching a collective bargaining agreement with the Teamsters union. Tomé emphasizes that a CFO must understand the business in addition to being a financial expert. She notes, "When I started working, I had to put on an apron and work in the store. You need to be able to speak the language of the business, not the language of finance."

Tomé's personal purpose statement is "Lead to inspire. Serve to create. Give to remain." She says by following her purpose she can motivate workers and improve their morale. Tomé is a native of Jackson, Wyoming, and holds a bachelor's degree in communication from the University of Wyoming and a master's degree in finance from the University of Denver.[15]

## *Work on Making Inspirational Appeals*

Making inspirational appeals to work associates, particularly subordinates, is yet another tactic that enhances your gravitas. An inspirational appeal usually involves displaying emotion and appealing to group members' emotions. Making inspirational appeals is facilitated if you have *personal magnetism*, the quality of being captivating, charming, and charismatic.

A starting point in developing your skill in making inspirational appeals is to try appealing to an emotion, feeling, purpose, or cause people care about. Among these are money, improving the lives of others, saving lives, and having fun. Here are a few examples of how a leader might make appeals to a feeling, purpose, or cause group members might find inspirational:

- "If we can stretch ourselves to beat quota by 10 percent this fiscal year, we will all get a fat bonus."
- "Let's make these car windows 15 percent more shatterproof and save hundreds of lives."
- "Think of the thousands of people with arthritis who will have a much better day if we can make our jar tops a little easier to open."

- "If we could recruit only 10 more volunteers to drive our vans around the city on subfreezing days, we will prevent dozens of homeless people from freezing to death."

Another useful component of an inspirational appeal is for a leader to provide meaning to work, showing that it has significance to the entire organization or to the entire world. Most people like to be involved with projects that matter, and sometimes the leader must explain why the work matters. For example, the leader of a company that specializes in subprime mortgages might have to explain, "Without our type of work, loads of people with modest incomes could not become homeowners."

An advanced approach to inspiring workers is to create a vision that surpasses the wants and needs of most people.[16] One of the ways in which leaders at both Apple and Google have inspired workers is to involve them in a vision of "changing the world" with their product and services.

Here are two examples of how a leader is perceived to be making an inspirational appeal:

- Says a proposed activity or change is an opportunity to do something truly exciting and worthwhile.
- Makes an emotional, strongly worded presentation to arouse enthusiasm for a proposed activity or change. Uses phrases such as "We have hit a turning point," "Our time is now," and "We are building a better future for our team."

Developing the skill to make inspirational appeals often requires careful preparation. Before making the appeal, attempt to figure out what matters the most to your constituents, such as team, group, or subordinates. As described above, you need to know what people really care about. You might reflect on past observations, such as conversations with the group about the importance of hybrid work or the opportunity to interact with end users of your product or service. A stronger approach would be to informally collect fresh data about what matters to the group. You might ask a few group members, "What is really important to you in terms of the workplace?" Or, to use a phrase that might be dated for some people, "What are the hot-button issues around here?"

## *Enhance Your Spontaneous Communication*

Developing your skills in speaking spontaneously or "off the cuff" is a strong gravitas enhancer. When many leaders think of enhancing their communication skills, they think of improving their public speaking skills. Yet a much more frequent demand for communication skills is to speak well in impromptu situations such as answering a problem question from a customer or boss or giving on-the-spot feedback to a subordinate. Matt Abrahams, a lecturer in organizational behavior at the Stanford Graduate School of Business, offers several suggestions for "how to shine when you're put on the spot."[17]

- *Avoid the default response.* A person with gravitas minimizes giving a standard response when asked a question, and instead says something thoughtful and useful. Suppose that the CEO passes you in the lobby and asks, "How are you?" A standard response would be, "Very good, thanks." A more useful and impressive response would be to respond with a specific mood booster: "Feeling great today because our team completed a project 10 days ahead of schedule."
- *Deliver your message concisely but effectively.* When asked a question it is usually not necessary to repeat the question and provide lengthy backup information to your response. Explain in detail what went right or wrong such as, "Yes, we are already two weeks late with our deliverable. A key supplier had a strike that delayed delivering us a vital component to our system."
- *Listen as well as you talk.* Most people worry too much about what to say during impromptu encounters. It is preferable to instead focus on listening so you can better understand the immediate needs of your conversation partners and respond more effectively. For example, a division manager might listen carefully to find out why the HR manager is asking him if the division had reached its diversity hiring goals.
- *Organize your thoughts.* Developing a careful structure for your thoughts is not strictly for formal presentations. When talking on the fly you can still quickly craft a story with a beginning, middle, and end. Suppose that during a plant visit, vice president Steve asks plant manager Nina how she reduced accidents by 25 percent during the last fiscal year. Nina responds, "The data told us we had too many serious accidents [beginning of story]. We then collected data from supervisory observations and interviews with workers about what was going wrong [middle of story]. We concluded that production workers were peeking at their phones too frequently and were

therefore distracted. We discouraged frequent phone use, and accidents plunged [end of story]." Nina earned a few gravitas points.

---

# Guidelines for Action

1. Perceptions of your gravitas are highly influenced by your interactions with people.
2. A useful starting point in developing the interpersonal attributes of gravitas is to understand how you are currently perceived with respect to these attributes.
3. For other people to respect you, have confidence in you, and take you seriously, it is enormously helpful to build rapport with them.
4. An excellent relationship builder with subordinates is to play an active role in facilitating their jobs running more smoothly.
5. Showing courtesy will help you build rapport with your direct reports.
6. A comprehensive way of establishing good relations with subordinates is to use your influence to help the group accomplish its tasks, including getting the resources it needs.
7. Being civil helps you stand out because many people believe that crude, rude, and obnoxious behavior has become both the norm and a national problem.
8. A fundamental principle of fostering good relationships with coworkers and others is to make them feel important.
9. An essential strategy for developing good relationships with coworkers is to be a team player.
10. Political astuteness or skill is another way of being taken seriously.
11. The lion's share of organizational politics involves building positive relationships with network members who can be helpful now or later.
12. Political strategies and tactics can be developed and refined to project gravitas.
13. A bedrock principle of organizational politics is to help your boss perform well, which is probably one of the reasons you were hired.
14. An example of an ethical impression management tactic would be to contribute outstanding performance and then make sure key people know of your accomplishments.
15. A powerful tactic for ingratiating yourself to others is to flatter them honestly and sincerely.
16. An advanced application of political skills is to emit signals that you are powerful and pleasant.

17.  A natural way to send out power signals is to develop expertise in a job-relevant niche.

18.  Making inspirational appeals to work associates, particularly to subordinates, is yet another tactic that enhances your gravitas.

19.  An advanced approach to inspiring workers is to create a vision that surpasses the wants and needs of most people.

20.  Developing your skills in speaking spontaneously or "off the cuff" is a strong gravitas enhancer.

21.  When talking on the fly, you can still quickly craft a story with a beginning, middle, and end.

# 10

# Actions and Attributes
# That Detract from Gravitas

To display gravitas, and therefore be taken seriously, a positive (playing offense) approach is to follow the suggestions in the nine previous chapters. A defensive approach would be to avoid actions and attributes that detract from gravitas. One strategy would be to avoid doing the opposite of every positive suggestion made so far, such as appearing low in self-confidence, speaking poorly, or ignoring political skill. The chapter at hand supplements this strategy by describing actions and attributes that prevent many people from acquiring the gravitas they need to advance their career. Few people can avoid all these potential pitfalls, but with self-restraint and planning most of them can be sidestepped.

## Being a Difficult Person

A special type of leader, manager, or employee may perform adequately yet be annoying and waste other people's time. At times their performance slips below standard because they divert their energy from accomplishing work. A person in this category is often referred to as a *difficult person*, an individual whose personal characteristics disturb other people. Difficult people are such a drain on productivity and personal well-being that they are studied frequently in both the business press and in research journals. Approximately 10 percent of all employees can be classified as difficult, a statistic that highlights the importance of this topic.[1] Even if a person has advanced to a leadership position, it is still possible for that person to be a difficult person. Being perceived as a difficult person will often block that person from being classified as having gravitas.

Difficult people have been placed into many different categories or types. A common feature of difficult people is that they focus on their own needs and agenda, such as wanting to control and manipulate others. For example, the office bully who insults and intimidates others is attempting to control them. Here we focus on eight of the most frequently found types of difficult employees.

An *office jerk* is a person who makes life difficult for others, often by being obstinate, inflexible, and frequently insensitive to their needs. Office jerks are often a combination of other types of difficult people, and almost any difficult person might be classified as an office jerk. Tessa West, an associate professor of psychology at New York University, has studied office jerks extensively. A leading type of jerk she has observed is the free rider, a person who gets by on charm and social graces but passes off considerable work to others. Sometimes they split their work into small pieces. As a result, they ask team members for help "just this time," and no one person feels overloaded.[2]

*Workplace bullies* are people who try to control their victims through fear and intimidation. They frequently interrupt others, rant in a loud voice, excessively tease, make threats, and use hostile glances. A bullying boss will often mandate that things be done his or her way ("My way or the highway"). Bullying is often triggered by a person facing considerable pressure, such as a sales manager attempting to attain a difficult sales goal during a business downturn.

Workplace bullying can come from several directions, including upward—the bullying of managers by direct reports. Upward bullying often begins with hidden behaviors, such as withholding information, and subtle approaches to making the boss feel irrational and not credible, such as contradicting many of the facts he or she presents. (This form of manipulation is called *gaslighting.*) The upward bully might spread negative rumors about the manager, circumventing him or her—in other words, outright insubordination. The Workplace Bullying Institute has found that 14 percent of all workplace bullying is bullying of managers by subordinates.[3]

*Disgruntled workers* are angry and often see themselves as victims. They justify their feelings by blaming work associates, including supervisors, coworkers, and customers. Typically, they isolate themselves from those around them.[4] Extremely disgruntled employees with low emotional stability may engage in workplace violence. Few disgruntled workers become leaders, but it is conceivable for a person to become disgruntled while occupying a demanding leadership role.

The *passive-aggressive worker,* on the other hand, expresses anger and hostility by neglecting to take care of an emergency or sitting silently in a meeting without contributing. Neglecting to conduct performance appraisals on time might be passive-aggressive behavior on the part of a manager.

The presence of *uncivil workers* has grown rapidly as standards for civility in society continue to diminish. Representative examples of uncivil behavior include dealing with your request while talking on the phone with another person, processing email while talking to you, insulting you in public, and barging past you from the other direction as you exit a door. According to a Civility in America survey, 86 percent of respondents described their workplaces as civil and respectful. Despite this positive statistic, one-quarter of the 1,100 respondents said they quit a job because of an uncivil work environment.[5] Uncivil behavior can sometimes be triggered by mistreatment from customers. One study found that customer service employees tend to react negatively to customer incivility by being uncivil in return. Customer service quality can therefore suffer.[6]

*Change resisters* tend to live in the past and have difficulty learning new procedures and adjusting to new initiatives.[7] They will often cling to old technologies or processes when the rest of the unit or organization has adopted newer versions. Years ago, change resisters might have been the last to accept direct deposit of their paychecks. In the present, they might resist communicating with work associates through social platforms, instead clinging to email and the telephone.

*Destructive heroes or heroines* are high-performing people whose contributions to the organization make it difficult to fire them even when they are egotists, prima donnas, and/or poor team players. A destructive hero or heroine can also be characterized as a brilliant jerk. Destructive heroes and heroines intimidate coworkers and lower morale.[8] Brilliant jerks regularly belittle coworkers and teams when they do not see the brilliance of or agree with his or her ideas.[9]

*Workplace cynics* are employees who carry extremely negative attitudes toward their employers, and these negative attitudes often take the form of cynicism. Much of the cynicism appears to be a reaction to top-level management actions, such as boosting their own compensation substantially while laying off lower-ranking workers to save money. Hiring so many contract and temporary workers at the expense of offering full-time employment also leads to cynicism. Global outsourcing creates cynicism because executive positions are rarely sent overseas. Cynics are classified as difficult people because they express their cynicism more negatively and persistently than others.

Cynicism is usually expressed by finding something negative about even the best intentions of others. An investigation into the topic concludes that workplace cynicism is shown on any of three dimensions:

- *A belief that the organization lacks integrity*: The cynic might say, "Our advertising is a pack of lies."
- *A negative affect toward the organization*: Cynics frequently make such comments as "This company is the pits" or "Who in his right mind would join this company today?"
- Tendencies toward *disparaging and critical behaviors* directed at the organization that are consistent with these beliefs (the cynic might use a competitor's consumer product and brag about it).[10]

Whatever form being a difficult person takes, a frequent result is that the individual is likely to be perceived as lacking a seriousness of purpose.

## Committing Excessive Blunders

If you commit too many political blunders, your gravitas will suffer because many people will question whether you have good judgment. A pattern of committing political blunders could reflect low emotional intelligence, and even worse, self-defeating behavior. In addition to being perceived as being low on gravitas, a serious blunder can be a swift path to derailing a person's career. Take the accompanying self-assessment quiz to examine your tendencies toward making blunders. Several leading blunders are described next.

---

### The Blunder Quiz

**Directions:** Indicate whether you agree or disagree with the following statements.

| | AGREE | DISAGREE |
|---|---|---|
| 1. It is acceptable to criticize your manager in a meeting if the criticism is valid. | | |
| 2. If your boss criticizes you, an effective way of getting revenge is to post a tweet making fun of him or her. | | |
| 3. If my boss showed me a photo of his or her dog, and I thought the dog was ugly, I would say so. | | |

## Gravitas for Leadership

| | AGREE | DISAGREE |
|---|---|---|
| 4. If I worked for Microsoft, I would still use whatever search engine was best instead of using Microsoft Bing (the Microsoft search engine). | | |
| 5. If I thought my company's product or service was not worth the price, I would openly express my opinion on the job. | | |
| 6. If I objected to a decision made by top management, I would send a company-wide message explaining my objection. | | |
| 7. I am willing to insult any coworker if the insult is deserved. | | |
| 8. If I am at a meeting, and the content becomes boring, I will take out my smartphone and check my messages or surf the Internet. | | |
| 9. If I thought that my company's stock was a poor investment, I would freely share my opinion with work associates. | | |
| 10. During a national election, I would place campaign banners for my favorite candidate outside my cubicle or office, or on my desk in an open work area. | | |
| 11. I see no problem in using competitors' products or services and letting my superiors know about it. | | |
| 12. If I thought the CEO of my company was way overpaid, I would send him or her an email making my opinion known. | | |
| 13. During a company picnic or garden party, I would go on at length about the effectiveness of a major political figure. | | |
| 14. I openly criticize (or would criticize) most new ventures my company or department is contemplating, pointing out that most new ventures fail. | | |
| 15. I avoid any deliberate attempt to please or impress coworkers or superiors. | | |
| Total: "Agree" _____ "Disagree" _____ | | |

*Scoring and Interpretation:* The greater the number of statements you agree with, the more prone you are to political blunders that can damage your career. You need to raise your awareness level of workplace blunders.

---

1. *Criticizing the boss in a public forum.* The oldest saw in human relations is to "praise in public and criticize in private." Yet in the passion of the moment, we may still surrender to an irresistible impulse to criticize the boss publicly. Also, hundreds of people have lost their jobs because they make a vindictive statement about their boss on a social media website, particularly Facebook or Twitter. Negative email or text messages about the company can be political suicide also. An example would be a professional at a pharmaceutical company posting a statement that the company was being unethical in way overpricing a new drug for lowering blood pressure.

A cartoon appeared in *The Wall Street Journal* depicting a man dressed in a business suit standing in front of a building. His hat was on the ground for collecting donations. A large sign hanging from his neck read, "Actually believed boss welcomed criticism."[11]

2. *Bypassing the boss.* Protocol is still highly valued in a hierarchical organization. Going around the boss to resolve a problem is therefore hazardous. You might be able to accomplish the bypass, but your career could be damaged and recourses limited. Except in cases of outrageous misconduct such as blatant sexual harassment or criminal misconduct, your boss's boss will probably side with your boss. This technique must be used with sensitivity to avoid the appearance of a boss bypass.

3. *Declining an offer from top management.* Turning down top management, especially more than once, is a political blunder. You thus must balance sensibly managing your time against the blunder of refusing a request from top management. Today, an increasing number of managers and corporate professionals decline opportunities for promotion when the new job requires geographic relocation. For these people, family and lifestyle preferences are more important than gaining political advantage on the job.

4. *Putting your foot in your mouth (being needlessly tactless).* To avoid hurting your career, it is important to avoid—or at least minimize—being blatantly tactless toward influential people. An example would be telling the CEO to delegate speech making to another person because he or she is such a poor speaker. When you feel you are on the verge of being critical, delay your response and perhaps reword it for later delivery. Use your emotional intelligence!

If you are needlessly tactless, compensate the best you can by offering a full apology later.

Putting your foot in your mouth can also take the form of making a public statement that many people interpret to have a negative meaning or to reflect callousness. The Deepwater Horizon oil rig explosion in 2010 spewed hundreds of millions of gallons of oil into the Gulf of Mexico and killed 11 workers. BP chief executive at the time, Tony Hayward, made a series of public appearances explaining the company's recovery efforts. During one appearance, Hayward said he wanted his "life back," which angered many people because they thought he had not suffered much in comparison to the many victims of the disaster. This gaffe contributed to his inability to elicit much empathy from the U.S. public, and he was dismissed shortly thereafter.[12]

5. *Not conforming to the company dress code.* Although some degree of independence and free thinking is welcome in many organizations, violating the dress code can block you from being perceived as having gravitas. Conforming to the dress code suggests that you are part of the team and understand what is expected. Dress codes can be violated by dressing too informally *or* formally or by wearing clothing that symbolizes a political position.

6. *Demonstrating out-of-control avarice.* Being too greedy is a political blunder because it leads to shame and humiliation for the greedy person and therefore detracts from the person's gravitas. Even if the executive can extract extraordinary sums of money from the organization legally, being publicly humiliated and never being invited to hold an executive position again are severe negative consequences. To maneuver to obtain excessive compensation when the organization is retrenching or performing poorly is a substantial blunder because many shareholders might protest.

Another form of avarice that can lead to shame, and even dismissal, for an executive is spending enormous sums of money on decorations and furnishings for almost the exclusive benefit of the executive. An example is when a CEO spends $35,000 to refurbish a private bathroom adjacent to his or her office.

7. **Behaving** *indiscreetly in private life.* Employees are representatives of the company, so their behavior off the job is considered to contribute to their performance—particularly in the case of managers. Embarrassing the company will often lead to dismissal, combined with a negative reputation that will be difficult

to shake for purposes of future employment. Indiscreet behavior in private life that can lead to dismissal includes being caught for shoplifting, being cited for driving under the influence of alcohol, being arrested for a drug offense, being charged with using the services of a prostitute, and committing assault and battery against another person. Although sports and entertainment celebrities are well known for such indiscreet behavior, business and government officials have engaged in similar behavior. When the person's indiscreet behavior becomes public, his or her gravitas sinks.

8. *Being politically incorrect or taking correctness to extremes.* Political correctness involves being careful not to offend or slight anyone and being extra civil and respectful.[13] In recent years the emphasis on political correctness has approached being a social movement, with an untold number of people concerned that almost any statement about another person might be offensive. Some people even hesitate to use the pronouns "he" or "she" out of fear of offending those who do not divide people into two genders or think in binary terms about sexual/gender status. For example, a middle manager who had lunch with the transgender woman VP of engineering might say "I had a great lunch with the VP of engineering" or "I had a great lunch with Clark" just to avoid using a politically incorrect pronoun.

The politically correct person therefore avoids creating some enemies who might erode the person's power. An effective use of political correctness would be to say, "We need a ladder in our department because we have workers of different heights who need access to the top shelves." It would be politically incorrect to say, "We need ladders because we have some short workers who cannot reach the top shelves."

Despite the virtues of political correctness, when the leader carries it too far, the leader might appear patronizing and therefore less than authentic. For example, it might appear unnatural to many people to avoid the terms "man" and "woman" just to prevent offending the small number of people who do not believe there is a biological difference between males and females. Another example is avoiding mention of a person's physical size or nationality even when it is job-relevant and true. A leader who is more authentic might be willing to say, "We have this Black guy on our team from Nigeria and he has given us a few useful insights into how to penetrate the Nigerian market." A less illuminating statement would be to say, "We have a person on our team who has given us a few useful insights into how to penetrate the Nigerian market." In this situation race is relevant because being Black adds credibility to the person giving advice about Nigeria.

9. *Being insensitive to cultural differences.* A specific form of political correctness deals with cultural differences. As organizations have become increasingly culturally diverse, the importance of being able to recognize and understand cultural differences has grown. To engage in culturally insensitive behavior is therefore a political blunder. An example would be asking a person to take off a head covering during a meeting when the head covering represents a cultural or religious tradition for the meeting participant.

Insensitivity to cultural differences can be a blunder in dealing with customers as well as with organizational members and subtracts gravitas points. Here is an extreme example: The chief marketing officer is dining at a restaurant with the CEO of an Indian company. To the CMO's shock, the Indian CEO begins to eat the entrée with his fingers. The CMO says, "What's the problem? Did the waitress forget to bring you a fork?" The CEO was unaware that some Indians follow their cultural tradition of eating food with their hands.

10. *Attacking sacred cows.* The stories passed on in many organizations include fond beliefs about what is positive and effective, such as certain products, services, and values. The person who attacks these sacred cows runs the risk of being perceived as disloyal. A sacred cow at Chipotle (a casual dining Mexican food chain) is that frontline experience in a company restaurant, including cleaning restrooms, is essential for promotion to a general manager position.

A sacred cow in most business organizations is that high-level leadership skill is worth more money than technical skill. As a result, in a major corporation, the CEO might receive $35 million in annual compensation, whereas the inventor who helped the company become successful might earn $175,000.

11. *Gossiping about taboo subjects and oversharing personal information.* Gossiping about off-limits subjects is a political blunder that can damage a worker's relationship with coworkers and the manager. A survey conducted by a consulting firm indicated the following topics to be off-limits, whether they be in reference to oneself or other workers: sexually transmitted disease, domestic

violence, mental illness, alcohol and drug abuse, and fertility problems. Topics to avoid were political beliefs and religious beliefs.[14]

Related to the blunder of gossiping about taboo subjects is oversharing personal information with coworkers. According to business writer Sue Shellenbarger. "Oversharers spew gritty details about their romantic exploits, marital woes, financial problems, recent surgeries or the latest moves by their mother-in-law—whether colleagues share interest or not."[15]

12. *Rejecting business social invitations.* The culture of many organizations emphasizes attendance at business social events including company activities such as picnics and attendance at sporting events, meals, and after work drinks with coworkers. Although these activities take time away from work and personal life, it is a political blunder to reject too many of them. When invitations are rejected, the rejection should be based on a solid excuse.

13. *Wearing overly sexy clothing.* Dressing fashionably but appropriately adds to gravitas. *Appropriately* is key. Part of the dress code in many organizations is for workers not to dress in a sexually provocative manner. Although many coworkers and managers might enjoy the sexy attire of the worker, dressing in such a manner can be a political blunder. Both men and women in high-status positions should avoid committing this type of political blunder.

14. *Being revengeful and hostile during an exit interview.* After a person resigns a position, many companies conduct an exit interview in which departing employees are asked to discuss the reason for quitting. Under the best of circumstances, the employee who quits would offer constructive suggestions that would improve the working conditions and work climate for present and future employees. This would enhance a person's reputation and perhaps lead to a more positive employment reference in the future. The exiting employee is invited to be frank, but frankness to the point of getting revenge by saying hostile things about the company and the manager is a career-retarding error. Often the employee will receive a negative, or at best neutral, employment reference.

A useful political skill is to be able to recover from blunders considering that such missteps can lead to embarrassment or even career retardation, as well as denting your gravitas. Considering that the other side is most likely to be offended, it is best to appease that person. Appeasing might work because the primary intent of the blunderer is to attain forgiveness, rather than gain advantage. Suppose that a person has been indiscreet in private life in the form of having spent one night in jail for drunken and disorderly conduct. An appeasement approach to higher-ups might be to apologize and then ask to take on a community task on behalf of the company without pay as a form of retribution. A community task could be something like delivering gifts to children hospitalized for a serious illness.

## Abuse of Power

When powerful leaders push the exercise of power too far, they run the risk of losing some of their gravitas. A frequent abuse of power is directing it more toward self-serving behavior than the good of others, including the organization and all stakeholders. A set of studies helps explain why some people who attain power act out of self-interest, whereas others with power act in the interest of others. The influential variable studied was *moral identity*—the extent to which an individual holds morality as part of their self-concept. Trait power was measured through a questionnaire about power, and subjective power was measured from study participants describing situations in which they experienced power. The study concluded that individuals with a strong moral identity were less likely to act in self-interest when they had strong trait power or subjective feelings of experiencing power. In contrast, individuals with a weak moral identity were more likely to act in self-interest under trait power or feelings of power.[16] If you are moral, you are less likely to use power for your own good. The message here is that being moral contributes to a leader's gravitas.

A subtle abuse of power is when a leader thinks he or she is too powerful to bother keeping promises, and therefore projects low integrity.[17] This type of low integrity will often manifest itself with respect to small commitments such as granting an addition to a travel allowance, approving the hiring of a gig worker, or recommending a team member's child for a summer internship. One such broken commitment may not do much damage to a leader's gravitas, but failing to keep two or three promises has a major negative impact.

## Indecisiveness

A swift route to lacking gravitas is indecisiveness because a leader who is hesitant to make important decisions will obviously not be perceived as a strong and confident person. Decisiveness is the extent to which a person makes up his or her mind promptly and prudently. Good decision-makers, by definition, are decisive. A major problem with indecisive leaders is a low propensity for taking risks. A cautious, conservative leader or manager opts for a low-risk solution, such as an HR manager recruiting at only a handful of elite colleges. An extremely cautious person may avoid making decisions for fear of being wrong.

Perfectionism is a contributor to indecisiveness. Leaders who seek the perfect solution to a problem are usually indecisive because they hesitate to accept the fact that a particular alternative is good enough. The perfectionistic leader will frequently ask for more and more data before making a decision, such as asking for bids from four suppliers before choosing one.

Flip-flopping is a frequent form of indecisiveness. It involves changing from one idea to another quickly or casually. Too much opinion changing detracts for a leader's seriousness of purpose. Politicians are frequently accused of flip-flopping on financial issues, but business executives are also known to change their position on matters of importance. For example, a CEO might insist several times that the company should grow organically. A few months later the executive insists that growth via acquisition is the most sensible course of action. A caveat about flipflopping is that it sometimes is a healthy adaptation to changing conditions. The executive in question might have recognized that the company's existing market has stabilized and that no new promising products are on the horizon.

## Excessive Humility

A dash of humility often adds to a leader's gravitas because it suggests the leader is not excessively self-confident and dismissive of the ideas of others. When the leader pushes humility to the point of lacking decisiveness and backing away from exercising authority, humility is a liability. As a result, the leader's positive impact on others is reduced. Subordinates welcome a reasonable degree of humility in their leader but do not expect the person to abdicate authority.

A leader's gravitas can also suffer when humility reaches the point of subservience. This is true because being a humble leader or professional also does not mean being subservient. Executive business coach Paulette Ashlin says that a humble leader needs to be assertive while depending on other people. Effective humble leaders collaborate with others. Humble leaders who get into trouble are those who are subservient and do whatever others ask them to do. True humility is not simply pleasing other people but holding oneself and the group accountable for results.[18]

False modesty is an inauthentic type of humility that can also detract from gravitas. A person with effective humility accepts praise and compliments yet can still share the praise with contributors to the effort. Suppose that team leader Jackson is told by his manager that he has done an outstanding job this last quarter. Ineffective humility would be to say, "I really didn't do anything. It was the team that produced the good results." A more positive form of humility would be to respond, "I appreciate the compliment. I am proud of what the team and I accomplished this previous quarter." The latter statement is likely to lead to respect for Jackson.

## *Excessive Narcissism*

Narcissism has a close relationship with gravitas because the optimum amount of narcissism enhances gravitas, yet too much is a diminishing factor. *Narcissism* refers to an extremely positive and inflated view of the self, combined with limited empathy for others. The narcissist is self-absorbed, self-adoring, and self-centered and has a grandiose preoccupation with his or her importance. Talking down to work associates is another symptom of an annoying level of narcissism.

With a reasonable dose of narcissism, a person can be productive in a high-level position, such as a charismatic leader being self-confident, self-promoting, and flamboyant.[19] A large proportion of successful business leaders have sufficient narcissistic tendencies to be flamboyant and self-promoting, yet subordinates respond positively to their leadership. Many entrepreneurs tend toward being narcissistic because their love for the product or service they are promoting is intertwined with self-admiration.

A starting point in thinking through the potential positive consequences of an optimum level of narcissism for enhancing gravitas is to take the accompanying self-quiz.

## The Positive Narcissist Checklist

| Item | Attitude or Behavior | Fits Me |
|------|----------------------|---------|
| 1. | I am quite proud of my appearance. | |
| 2. | I am quite proud of how I express myself. | |

## 10. Actions and Attributes That Detract from Gravitas

| Item | Attitude or Behavior | Fits Me |
|------|---------------------|---------|
| 3. | People are drawn to me at networking events. | |
| 4. | I smile frequently because I know people appreciate it. | |
| 5. | I frequently compliment others so they will like me. | |
| 6. | I feel quite comfortable being photographed. | |
| 7. | I dress much more carefully than most people in my network. | |
| 8. | I am quite confident that I can successfully complete almost all assignments given me. | |
| 9. | My mistakes are so few, I hardly make excuses for myself. | |
| 10. | Negative feedback just gives me another suggestion for being more successful. | |
| 11. | When I receive a compliment, I conclude that the giver of the compliment has good judgment. | |
| 12. | I often think that I am the smartest person in the room. | |
| 13. | People who know me well think highly of my potential for promotion. | |
| 14. | My talents are in demand. | |
| 15. | I make a wonderful first impression. | |

**Scoring and Interpretation:** If you believe that between nine and 13 of these statements fit you well, it could be that you have a level of narcissism that is an asset in a leadership role in terms of establishing relationships with people. Yet if you believe that 14 or 15 of these statements fit you well, your level of conceit and narcissism could create some interpersonal friction and detract from your gravitas. If you believe that only 8 or fewer of these statements fit you well, you might be experiencing a level of self-confidence too low to have much gravitas.

When leaders are highly narcissistic, organizational performance may suffer. One reason is that the highly narcissistic leader will be disliked and resented, and that will weaken their gravitas. An analysis of many studies revealed that a moderate amount of narcissism is associated with leadership effectiveness, but both low and high levels of the trait lowered leadership effectiveness.[20] (Leaders with too little narcissism may be perceived as bland and lacking much self-confidence.)

Additional evidence indicates that organizations led by narcissistic CEOs experience considerable downsides including high risk-taking and overpaying for acquisitions. One study using a sample of 32 firms found that those led by narcissistic CEOs are more likely to be involved in protracted lawsuits. Narcissism was measured with an online questionnaire completed by company employees who knew the CEO. The problem appeared to be that narcissists are less sensitive to objections when making decisions about whether to settle a lawsuit. The narcissistic CEOs were also less willing to listen to advice from legal experts.[21] Such stubbornness can reduce a leader's chances of being perceived as having gravitas.

An analysis by Dan Ciampa points to other negative consequences of a highly charismatic and narcissistic organizational leader. Two of these concerns follow. One is that because the narcissistic leader's views and actions are the only ones that matter, followers become less proactive. A group member might think, "Why should I suggest a new course of action when only his (or her) ideas count?" Another concern is that people still comply with what the narcissistic and charismatic leader wants, but the passion vanishes because the people do not feel they are contributing. Eventually, the subordinates stop listening and become cynical.[22]

---

# Guidelines for Action

1. A defensive approach to displaying gravitas is to avoid attitudes and actions that detract from gravitas.

2. Even if you have advanced to a leadership position, you could possibly be a difficult person, thereby detracting from your gravitas.

3. A major block to displaying gravitas is the office jerk, a person who makes life difficult for others, often by being obstinate, inflexible, or insensitive to their needs.

4. Highly capable professionals need to guard against being a destructive hero or heroine—high performing people whose contributions make it difficult to fire them even if they are egoists, prima donnas, and/or poor team players.

5. If you commit too many political blunders, your gravitas will suffer because many people will question whether you have good judgment.

6. A political blunder that is relatively easy to commit is to criticize the boss publicly.

7. To avoid hurting your gravitas, as well as your career, it is important to avoid—or at least minimize—being blatantly tactless toward influential people.

8. Being too greedy is a political blunder because it leads to shame and humiliation for the greedy person and therefore detracts from the person's gravitas.

9. Despite the virtues of political correctness, when the leader carries it too far the leader might appear patronizing and therefore less than authentic.

10. To engage in culturally insensitive behavior is a political blunder.

11. Gossiping about off-limits subjects is a political blunder that can damage your relationship with coworkers and your boss.

12. A useful political skill is to be able to recover from blunders considering that such missteps can lead to embarrassment or even career retardation, as well as denting your gravitas.

13. When powerful leaders push the exercise of power too far, they run the risk of losing some of their gravitas. A frequent abuse of power is directing it more toward self-serving behavior than the good of others.

14. A subtle abuse of power is when a leader thinks he or she is too powerful to bother keeping promises, and therefore projects low integrity.

15. A swift route to lacking gravitas is indecisiveness, because a leader who is hesitant to make important decisions will obviously not be perceived as a strong and confident person.

16. Leaders who seek the perfect solution to a problem are usually indecisive because they hesitate to accept the fact that a particular alternative is good enough.

17. A dash of humility often adds to a leader's gravitas because it suggests the leader is not excessively self-confident and dismissive of the ideas of others. Yet when the leader pushes humility to the point of lacking and backing away from exercising authority, humility is a liability.

18. A leader's gravitas can also suffer when humility reaches the point of subservience.

19. Narcissism has a close relationship with gravitas because the optimum amount of narcissism enhances gravitas, yet too much is a diminishing factor.

20. When leaders are highly narcissistic, organizational performance may suffer.

# Chapter Notes

## Chapter 1

1. E-Coach Associates, "Ignored by People You Want to Impress? Understand and Develop Gravitas!" *QWIK-COACH*, March 31, 2017, 1.

2. Amanda L. Golbeck, Ingram Olkin, and Yulia R. Gel, eds., *Leadership and Women in Statistics* (London: CRC Press, Taylor & Francis Group, July 15, 2015), 14.

3. Manfred F.R. Kets de Vries, "Finding Gravitas," INSEAD Knowledge, September 9, 2015, 1.

4. James Blair, "How's Your Presence? Prominence and Gravitas in Comms Explained," The Comms Guru, June 30, 2021, 1.

5. Kathleen Ward, "Unlocking the Power of Executive Gravitas: What It Is and How to Develop It," OATUU (oatuu.org), June 5, 2023, 1.

6. Chris Jackson, "Transformational Leadership and Gravitas: 2000 Years of No Development?" *Personality and Individual Differences*, April 1, 2020, 109760, 3.

7. Lida Citroën, "'Gravitas' in Leadership: What It Is, Why It Matters and How to Get It," Military.com, 2023, 1.

8. "How to Cultivate Gravitas," dorothydalton.com, March 20, 2016, 1.

9. "Gravitas Leadership Information," Gravitas Leadership (www.gravitas-leadership.com), 2021, 1.

10. Annie Palmer, "Amazon CEO Jassy's Cost Cuts Deliver Investors Biggest Profit Beat Since 2020," *CNBC*, August 3, 2023, 1–4; Alex Kantrowitz, "Running Amazon Became a Lot Less Fun Once Jeff Bezos Left," Slate, June

18, 2023, 1–3; "Andy Jassy, President and Chief Executive Officer," *Amazon Investor Relations* (www.ir.aboutamazon.com), 2023, 1.

11. Sylvia Ann Hewett, Center for Talent Innovation, 2013, as quoted in Jen Baggett, "Gravitas: The Heart of Executive Presence," Catchlight Consulting, LLC (www.wecatchlight.com), July 30, 2018, 1.

12. Rebecca Newton, "Leadership Gravitas Is a Quality You Can Develop," *Harvard Business Review*, September 24, 2020, 1.

13. Citroën, "'Gravitas' in Leadership," 2–3.

14. Antoinette Dale Henderson, "Gravitas: How to Command Respect and Get Promoted," *The Treasurer Magazine*, 2022, 1.

15. Laura Cooper, "Kardashian's Private-Equity Firm Hires Ex-Apple, Burberry Executive," *The Wall Street Journal*, August 8, 2023, B3; Dov Seidman, "Angela Ahrendts DBE," *The How Institute for Society*, 2023, 1–2; Thomas Barrabi, "Kim Kardashian Hires Ex-Apple Retail Boss Angela Ahrendts for Private Equity Firm," *New York Post*, August 7, 2023, 1–3; "Angela Ahrendts: SVP, Retail, Apple," *Forbes*, 2023, 1–3.

16. Kathleen Ward, "Unlocking the Power of Executive Gravitas: What It Is and How to Develop It," OATUU (www.oatuu.org), June 5, 2023, 8.

17. Ward, "Unlocking the Power of Executive Gravitas," 7–8.

18. Ward, "Unlocking the Power of Executive Gravitas," 8. The examples in this section, however, are originals.

19. P. Balkundi, M. Kilduff, and D.A.

Harrison, "Centrality and Charisma: Comparing How Leader Networks and Attributions Affect Team Performance," *Journal of Applied Psychology*, June 2011, 1209–22.

20. Gordon Tredgold, "What Leadership Style Is the Best in Motivating Your Employees During a Pandemic?" https://gordontredgold.com, 2021, 2.

21. Erika Hayes James and Lynn Perry Wooten, "How to Display Competence in Times of Crisis," *Organizational Dynamics*, Vol. 34, no. 2, 2005, 146.

22. Megan Sauer, "Airbnb CEO Shares the Best Advice He's Ever Received—It's Counterintuitive to Almost Everything Everyone Says," *CNBC*, May 24, 2023, 1–3; "Brian Chesky: CEO and Cofounder Airbnb," *Forbes*, 2023, 1–3; Nilay Patel, "Airbnb CEO Brian Chesky on Taking It Back to Basics," *The Verge*, May 9, 2023, 1–38.

23. "The Gravitas Trap," *Ariel Group* (www.arielgroup.com), 2023, 1–2.

## *Chapter 2*

1. Charles Garfield, *Peak Performers: The New Heroes of American Business* (New York: Avon Books, 1987), 22–52; Michael Rozek, "Can You Spot a Peak Performer?" *Personnel Journal*, June 1991, 77–78; Bill Cole, "Peak Performance in the Workplace: The New Corporate Ethic," www.mentalgamecoach.com, 2023, 1–9.

2. Paolo Confino, "New CNN CEO Mark Thompson Once Rescued the *New York Times* from the End of Newspapers. Can He Do the Same with CNN as Cable TV Dies?" *Yahoo! Finance*, August 30, 2023, 1–4; Jake Kanter, "Mark Thompson Named Chairman and CEO of CNN—Update," *DEADLINE*, September 1, 2023, 1–7.

3. "Is Your Executive Presence and Gravitas Preventing You from Getting Ahead?" www.businesscoaching.co.uk, 2009–2023, 1.

4. Sylvia Ann Hewlett, "Executive Presence," Thrive Street Advisors (www.thrivestreetadvisors.com), 2023, 1–2.

5. Rich Thomaselli, "Sara Nelson Re-Elected as Flight Attendant Union President," *Travel Pulse*, May 17, 2022, 1–3; Morgan Clendaniel, "The Ascent of Sara Nelson," *Fast Company*, Summer 2021, 44–45; "Gruber Distinguished Lecturer in Women's Rights: Sara Nelson," Yale Law School, 2023, 1–2; "Sara Nelson, International President, Association of Flight Attendants-CWA, AFL-CIO," afcacwa.org, 2023, 1–3.

6. Daniel Goleman, Richard Boyatzis, and Annie McKee, "Primal Leadership: The Hidden Driver of Great Performance," *Harvard Business Review*, December 2001, 52–61.

7. Thomas E. Becker, "Integrity in Organizations: Beyond Honesty and Conscientiousness," *Academy of Management Review*, January 1998, 154–161.

8. Manuel London, *Principled Leadership and Business Diplomacy: Value-Based Strategies for Management Development* (Westport, CT: Quorum Books, 1999).

9. Carmen W. Landrau, "Six Key Elements of Gravitas," drlandrau.com, 2023, 1–2.

10. David Lawder, "World Bank's New Chief Asks Staff to 'Double Down' on Development, Climate Efforts," *Reuters*, June 2, 2023, 1–4; Rachel Kytle, "Can this Former CEO Fix the World Bank?" *Fast Company*, May 5, 2023, 1–4; Clifton Leaf (interview), "The Conversation: Ajay Banga," *Fortune*, December 2020/January 2021, 10–14; Atlantic Council Experts, "The Big Questions (and Answers) About Ajay Banga's Nomination to Lead the World Bank," www.atlanticcouncil.org, February 23, 2023, 1–3; Robin Sidel, "Banga to Be MasterCard's Protector," *The Wall Street Journal*, May 29–30, 2010, B1.

11. Angela Duckworth, Christopher Peterson, Michael D. Matthews, and Dennis B. Kelly, "Grit, Perseverance and Passion for Long-Term Goals," *Journal of Personality and Social, Psychology*, No. 6, 2007, 1087–1101; Angela Duckworth, *Grit: The Power of Passion and Perseverance* (New York: Scribner, 2016).

12. "What Is Big-Picture Thinking in

Business?" http://study.com, February 18, 2022, 1.

13. "Seeing the Big Picture," posted in *Being in Business* (www.theparadigm shifts.com), April 15, 2012, 2–3.

14. Daniel P. Amos, "Aflac's CEO Explains Howe He Fell for the Duck," *Harvard Business Review*, January–February, 131–133.

15. Cited in David Brock, "Strategic Thinking: Getting the Big Picture," http://partnersinexcellenceblog.com, August 30, 2011, 1–2.

16. Based on Lisa A. Bing, "Big-Picture Mentality: How to Develop Strategic Leadership Skills," www.blackenterprise.com, July 26, 2013, 1.

## Chapter 3

1. Brent A. Scott and Timothy A. Judge, "The Popularity Contest at Work: Who Wins, Why, and What Do They Receive?" *Journal of Applied Psychology*, January 2009, 20–33.

2. Cited in Donna M. Owens, "Incivility Rising: Researchers Say Workers Might Not Have the Time to Be Civil," *Human Resource Management*, February 2012, 33; Christine M. Pearson and Christine L. Porath, "On the Nature, Consequences and Remedies of Workplace Incivility: No Time for 'Nice'? Think Again," *Academy of Management Executive*, February 2005, 7–18.

3. Cort W. Rudolph, Ian M. Katz, Regina Ruppel, and Hannes Zacher, "A Systematic and Critical Review of Research on Respect in Leadership," *The Leadership Quarterly*, February 2021, 1–15 (101492).

4. Rudolph, Katz, Ruppel, and Zacher, "A Systematic and Critical Review," 6.

5. Based on information in Pauline Ziegler, "How Leaders Earn Respect: 10 Proven Ways to Master in 2023," www.bestdiplomats.org, May 9, 2023, 1–7; "How Courageous Leaders Earn Respect from Their Team," www.geeknack.com, May 23, 2021, 1–20.

6. Based on observations and facts in the following sources: Shawn Tully, "Fortune Most Powerful Women: Karen Lynch, 58 CVS Health," October/November 2021, 60–61; "Most Powerful Women 2022: 1, Karen Lynch, President and CEO, CVS Health," *Fortune*, October/November 2022, 65–70; David Gelles, "The Chief of CVS Health Wants to Be Part of People's 'Everyday Life,'" *The New York Times*, January 12, 2022, 1–13; "Karen S. Lynch, President and Chief Executive Officer, CVS Health," www.cvshealth.com, 2023, 1–2.

7. Quoted in Rachel Feintzeig, "Want Power? Stop Saying Sorry So Much," *The Wall Street Journal*, October 24, 2022, A11.

8. Carol Kinsey Gorman, "Project a More Powerful Image at Work," American Management Association, March 25, 2019, 1–5; Malia Wollan, "How to Project Power," *New York Times Sunday Magazine*, August 9, 2015, 21.

9. Timothy DeGroot, Federico Aime, Scott G. Johnson, and Donald Kluemper, "Does Talking the Talk Help Walking the Walk? An Examination of the Effect of Global Attractiveness in Leader Effectiveness," *The Leadership Quarterly*, August 2011, 680–689.

10. Laura Mathis, "Five Strategies to Demonstrate Gravitas," *The Speech Improvement Company* (www.speechimprovement.com), 2023, 1.

11. "Which Buzzwords Would You Ban?" *The Wall Street Journal*, January 2, 2014, B4.

## Chapter 4

1. Based on Robert K. Greenleaf, *Servant Leadership: A Journey into the Nature of Legitimate Power and Greatness* (Mahwah, NJ: Paulist Press, 1997); Robert C. Liden, Sandy J. Wayne, Hao Zhao, and David Henderson, "Servant Leadership: Development of a Multidimensional Measure and Multi-Level Assessment," *The Leadership Quarterly*, April 2008, 161–177; Rik Kirkland, "Wharton's Adam Grant on the Key to Professional Success," McKinsey & Company, June 2014, 3.

# Chapter Notes

2. Cited and quoted in Eric Solomon, "Stop Talking about Empathy and Start Acting On It," *Entrepreneur*, September 2, 2020, 60.

3. Andrew J. DuBrin, "Personal Attributes and Behaviors of Effective Crisis Leaders," in DuBrin (ed.), *Handbook of Research on Crisis Leadership in Organizations* (Cheltenham, UK: Edward Elgar, 2013), 12–13.

4. Jane E. Dutton et al., "Leading in Times of Trauma," *Harvard Business Review*, Summer 2020, 38.

5. Lauren Weber, "One CEO's Hands-On Crisis Management," *The Wall Street Journal*, September 21, 2016, B8.

6. Original story created from facts and observations in the following sources: Akshay Om, "Satya Nadella, Microsoft, Compassion, and Goddess Kamakshi," *Medium* (www.medium.com), April 24, 2023, 1–10; Marco della Cava, "Nadella Counts on Culture Shock to Drive Microsoft Growth," *USA Today*, February 20, 2017, 4B; Shira Ovide, "The Quiet Evolution at Microsoft's Office," *The Wall Street Journal*, September 30, 2015, B6; Dina Bass, "Beyond Windows," *Bloomberg Businessweek*, February 23–March 1, 2015, 30–31; Richard Hay, "Satya Nadella Lays Out New Mission and Vision for Microsoft," *SuperSite Windows* (http://winsupersite.com), June 25, 2014, 1–4; Harry McCraken, "Satya Nadella Rewrites Microsoft's Code, *Fast Company*, September 18, 2017, 52–53.

7. Lauren R. Locklear, Shannon G. Taylor, and Maureen L. Ambrose, "How a Gratitude Intervention Influences Workplace Mistreatment: A Multiple Mediation Model," *Journal of Applied Psychology*, September 2021, 1315; Hun Whee Lee et al., "The Benefits of Receiving Gratitude for Helpers: A Daily Investigation of Proactive and Reactive Helping at Work," *Journal of Applied Psychology*, February 2019, 197–213.

8. Quoted in Jennifer Thomas, "Motivating Workers," *HR Magazine*, Summer 2020, 82.

9. Erica Boothby, Xuan Zhao, and Vanessa K. Bohns, "A Simple Compliment Can Make a Big Difference," *Harvard Business Review*, February 24, 2021, 1–5.

10. Kerry Roberts Gibson, Kate O'Leary, and Joseph Weintraub, "The Little Things That Make Employees Feel Appreciated," *Harvard Business Review*, July 23, 2020, 1–7.

11. Hun Whee Lee et al., "The Benefits of Receiving Gratitude for Helpers: A Daily Investigation of Proactive and Reactive Helping at Work," *Journal of Applied Psychology*, February 2019, 197–213.

12. Robert Hogan as cited in Neal Burgis, "Importance of Humility in Your Leadership," www.successful-solutions.com, February 29, 2019, 1.

13. Justin Flunder, "How Important Is Humility in Leadership?" *Country Sunrise News*, April 24, 2014, 2.

14. Matt Norman, "5 Ways Humble Leaders Put Others in the Spotlight," www.mattnorman.com, June 20, 2018, 1–3.

15. Cited in Brian O'Connell, "Lead with Humility," *HR Magazine*, Winter 2021, 83.

16. Bradley P. Owens and David R. Hekman, "Modeling How to Grow: An Inductive Examination of Humble Leader Behaviors, Contingencies, and Outcomes," *Academy of Management Journal*, August 2012, 787–818.

17. Jeff Kirschner, "Humility and Leadership," RHR International, October 30, 2018, 1–2.

18. Jess Johnson, "Humility in Leadership: Battling the Vices of Pride," www.crowdstaffing.com, May 1, 2018, 3.

19. Christopher Lochhead, "3 Lessons in Humble Leadership from Four-Star General Stanley McChrystal," growwire.com, October 10, 2018, 1–2.

20. Darren K. Bharanitharan et al., "Seeing Is Not Believing: Leader Humility, Hypocrisy, and the Impact on Followers' Behaviors," *The Leadership Quarterly*, April 2021, 1–16 (101440).

21. Xin Qin et al., "The Double-Edge Sword of Lader Humility: Investigating When and Why Leader Humility Promotes Versus Inhibits Subordinate Deviance," *Journal of Applied Psychology*, July 2020, 693–712.

22. Joann Ellison Rodgers, "Go Forth in Anger," *Psychology Today*, April 2014, 72–79.

23. Deanna Geddes, Ronda Roberts Callister, and Donald E. Gibson, "A Message in Madness: Functions of Workplace Anger in Organizational Life," *Academy of Management Perspectives*, February 2020, 28–47.

## Chapter 5

1. Original story created from facts and observations in the following sources: Joseph F. Kovar, "Accenture CEO Julie Sweet: IT Growth to Exceed Macro Impacts," *CRN*, December 16, 2022, 1–5; "The 50 Most Powerful Women: 2, Julie Sweet. Chair and CEO, Accenture," *Fortune*, October/November 2022, 67; "How Fortune's Most Powerful Woman in Business Is Helping Shape the World for the Better," Accenture, November 5, 2020, 1–2; Rich Karlgaard, "'Let There Be Change' Says Accenture's Trail-Blazing Chief Executive, Julie Sweet," *Forbes*, October 20, 2020, 1–13; David Gelles, "Julie Sweet of Accenture Could See Her Future, So She Quit Her Job," *The New York Times*, January 2, 2019, 1–6; "Julie Sweet, Chief Executive Officer," Accenture, 2021, 1.

2. Andrew Razeghi, "Innovation: Vehicle to Greatness," *Executive Leadership*, December 2011, 3.

3. David J. Hughes et al., "Leadership, Creativity, and Innovation: A Critical Review and Practical Recommendations," *The Leadership Quarterly*, October 2018, 549–569.

4. Maria Bartiromo, "Entrepreneur Lives the Dream: Chobani's Ulukaya Created Greek Yogurt Craze," *USA Today*, June 18, 2013.

5. Emma Hinchliffe, "In Focus: Laura Alber," *Fortune*, December 2023/January 2024, 14–17; Sheryl Estrada, "The Longest-Tenured Woman CEO in the Fortune 500 Makes the Case for Sticking Around for 10+ Years at a Brand You Love," *Fortune*, October 11, 2023, 1–6

6. Quoted in John D. Stoll, "Feel the Force: Gut Instinct, Not Data Is the Thing," *The Wall Street Journal*, October 19–20, 2019, B4.

7. Ian Combe and David J. Carrington, "Leaders' Sensemaking Under Crises: Emerging Cognitive Consensus Over Time within Management Teams," *The Leadership Quarterly*, June 2015, 307–322.

8. Brent Adamson, "Sensemaking for Sales," *Harvard Business Review*, January–February 2022, 122–129.

9. Hermina Ibarra and Anne Scoular, "The Leader as Coach," *Harvard Business Review*, November–December 2019, 110–119.

10. Tina Smagala, "Giving Effective Feedback on the Fly," *Democrat and Chronicle*, May 28, 2013, 5B.

11. Craig Chappelow and Cindy McCauley, "What Good Feedback Really Looks Like," *Harvard Business Review*, May 13, 2019, 1–3.

12. Karen Wright, "A Chic Critique," *Psychology Today*, March/April 2011, 59.

13. Marcus Buckingham and Ashley Goodall, "The Feedback Fallacy," *Harvard Business Review*, March–April 2019, 92–101.

14. Lolly Daskal, "How to Coach a Struggling Employee," www.lollydaskal.com, January 23, 2020, 1.

15. Andrew Neitlich, "Coaching vs. Consulting: Find the Right Balance to Get Buy-in and Results," www.clomedia.com, August 4, 2016, 2.

16. John Baldoni, "Why I Cheerlead for Those I Coach," *SmartBrief*, June 12, 2024, 1–3.

17. Ginka Toegel and Jean-Louis Barsoux, "How to Preempt Team Conflict," *Harvard Business Review*, June 2016, 78–83.

18. Deb Levine, "Solutions: Advice from HR Knowledge Advisors," *HR Magazine*, October 2013, 18.

19. Patrick S. Nugent, "Managing Conflict: Third-Party Interventions for Managers," *Academy of Management Executive*, February 2002, 152.

20. Personal communication with Lindsay Collier in years past.

## Chapter 6

1. Jay A. Conger and Rabindra Kanungo, *Charismatic Leadership in Organizations* (Thousand Oaks, CA: SAGE Publications, 1998).
2. Thomas Sy, Calen Horton, and Ronald Riggio, "Charismatic Leadership: Eliciting and Channeling Follower Emotion," *The Leadership Quarterly*, February 2018, 58–69.
3. Amir Erez, Vilmost Misangyi, Diane E. Johnson, Marcie A. LePine, and Kent C. Halverson, "Stirring the Hearts of Followers: Charismatic Leadership as the Transferal of Affect," *Journal of Applied Psychology*, May 2008, 602–613.
4. Phil Wahba, "Walmart's Mr. Fix-It," *Fortune*, June/July 2024, 74–79; Dan Craft, "Leadership Insights: Lessons from Walmart CEO Doug McMillon," *Doing Business in Bentonville* (www.dbbnwa.com), July 11, 2023, 1–2; "Doug McMillon, President and CEO Walmart," Business Roundtable, 2024, 1–2; "The Success Story of C. Douglas McMillon, the President and Chief Executive Officer of Walmart," www.primeinsights.com, October 5, 2023, 1–8.
5. Research cited in Nicole Torres, "Defend Your Research: Fast Thinkers Are More Charismatic," *Harvard Business Review*, March 2016, 28–29.
6. Warren Bennis, "Acting the Part of a Leader," *Business Week*, September 19, 2009, 80.
7. Manfred F.R. Kets de Vries, "Beyond Narcissism: How Leaders Can Avoid the Hubris Trap," INSEAD Knowledge, March 12, 2024, 1–3.
8. Dennis A. Romig, *Side by Side Leadership: Achieving Outstanding Results Together* (Marietta, GA: Bard Press, 2001), 157.
9. Research cited in Mark Greer, "The Science of Savoir Faire," *Psychology Today*, January 25, 2005, 28–39.
10. Thomas Smale, "5 Steps to Build Your Personal Brand," *Entrepreneur*, September 25, 2015, 1.
11. Research synthesized in Ray A. Smith, "How to Boost Your E-Charisma," *The Wall Street Journal*, November 30, 2020, A11.
12. Jeff Gothelf, "Storytelling Can Make or Break Your Leadership," *Harvard Business Review*, October 19, 2020, 4.

## Chapter 7

1. Gerry Valentine, "Executive Presence: What It Is, and Why You Need It," *Forbes*, December 10, 2021, 1.
2. Suzanne Bates, "The Wow Factor," May 2019, 1. Website no longer available.
3. "Your 'Executive Presence' Needs a Second Look," www.recovertolead.com, May 20, 2012, 1.
4. Rose O. Sherman, "The Importance of Executive Presence," *American Nurse Today*, May 2015, 1–2.
5. Sofia Calheiros, "Executive Presence: The Elements of Leadership Material." *Best of Us* (www.blog.sofiacalheiros), March 4, 2017, 1.
6. Kathleen Ward, "Unlocking the Power of Executive Gravitas: What It Is and How to Develop It," OATUU (www.oatuu.org), June 25, 2023, 5.
7. Ward, "Unlocking the Power of Executive Gravitas," 27.
8. Sylvia Ann Hewlett, "The New Rules of Executive Presence," *Harvard Business Review*, January–February 2024, 134–139.
9. Noah Zandan and Lisa Shalett, "What Inclusive Leaders Sound Like," *Harvard Business Review*, November 19, 2020, 1–7.
10. Juliet Bourke and Andrea Titus, "The Key to Inclusive Leadership," *Harvard Business Review*, March 8, 2020, 1–5.
11. Original story based on facts and observations in the following sources: Douglas A. Wilson, "CEOs in Action: Manny Roman of PIMCO on How He Leads," (www.douglaswilson.com), March 1, 2022, 1–3; Justin Baer, "Bond Star Pimco Tries to Change Its Culture," *The Wall Street Journal*, April 19, 2021, B1, B9; Ankita Dixit, "Bond Giant Pimco Attempts to Change Its Culture," *Postin-Trend* (https://postintrend.com), April 17, 2021, 1–3; "Emmanuel Roman, '87:

Chief Executive Officer PIMCO," Chicago Booth, 2021, 1–2.

12. Hewlett, "The New Rules of Executive Presence," 135.

13. Yingyi Chang and Jose M. Cortina, "What Should I Wear to Work? An Integrative Review of the Impact of Clothing in the Workplace," *Journal of Applied Psychology*, May 2024, 755–778.

14. Valentine, "What Is It, Why You Need It and How to Get It," 2.

15. Anwesha Barari, "What Is Executive Presence: The Leadership Quality No One Told You About," *Emeritus* (www.emeritus.org), July 15, 2022, 6.

16. "Rehearse for Stressful Events," www.healthylifestyle.com, 2019, 1.

17. Yasmina Khelifi and Irina Cozma, "How to Be Direct Without Being Rude," *Harvard Business Review*, July 31, 2023, 3.

18. Cited in interview by Arianne Cohen, "What I Wear to Work: Sonja Lyubomirsky," *Bloomberg Businessweek*, January 12–18, 2015, 71.

19. Quoted in Sonja D. Mack, "Sara Mensah: Chief Operating Officer & Chief Marketing Officer, Portland Trailblazers," *Black Enterprise*, February 2011, 106.

20. Quoted in Jefferson and Jon Swartz, "After 5 Years of Cook, More Cash, Less Splash," *USA Today*, August 24, 2015, 4B.

## Chapter 8

1. Antoinette Dale Henderson, "Leading with Gravitas: Unlock the Six Keys to Impact and Influence," www.antionettehenderson.com, 2024, 1.

2. "Gravitas Leadership, Discovering this Little Known but Very Important Quality," *Share* (www.share-coach.com), 2024, 2.

3. Justin Standfield, "Stop Telling People They Need More Gravitas," *Incendo* (www.incendo-uk-com), 2024, 2.

4. Stacy Perlman, "The Secret Sauce at In-N-Out Burger" (Book Excerpt), *Business Week*, April 20, 2009, 68–69; Peter Romeo, "Employees Say In-N-Out is the Best Workplace in the Restaurant Business," www.restaurant-business online.com, January 12, 2021, 1.

5. "Juniper Values," Juniper Networks (www.juniper.net), 2024, 1.

6. Cited in "Leading by Feel: Train the Gifted," *Harvard Business Review*, January 2004, 31.

7. Ian McKechnie, "Six Tips to Develop Your 'Gravitas,'" www.linkedin.com, November 11, 2019, 2.

8. Original story based on facts and observations in a personal communication from Andrew Wang, July 17, 2023; "MiD-LABS (Medical Instrument Development Laboratories, Inc.)," July 29, 2016, 1–3.

9. Jay T. Knippen and Thad B. Green, "Building Self-Confidence," Supervisory Management, August 1989, 22–27.

10. Cited in "Present with Panache," *Manager's Edge*, June 2007, 8.

11. Fred Luthans, James R. Avey, and Jaime L. Patera, "Experimental Analysis of a Web-Based Training Intervention to Develop Positive Psychological Capital," *Academy of Management Learning & Education*, June 2008, 209–221.

12. Rebecca Newton, "Leadership Gravitas Is a Quality You Can Develop," *Harvard Business Review*, September 24, 2020, 4.

13. Linda L. Neider and Chester A. Schriesheim, "The Authentic Leadership Inventory (ALI): Development and Empirical Tests," *The Leadership Quarterly*, December 2011, 1149.

14. Thomas E. Becker, "Integrity in Organizations: Beyond Honesty and Conscientiousness," *Academy of Management Review*, January 1998, 154–161.

15. "A Conversation with Ron Wallace: From UPS Driver to President," *Executive Leadership*, September 2016, 3.

16. Robin Amster, "9 Tips to Help You Strengthen Your Integrity," *Success* (www.success.com), updated March 1, 2021, 3–4; Mark Schinkel, "9 Tips for Leading with Integrity," *Achieve Centre for Leadership* (www.achievecentre.com), 2024, 1–3; "6 Tips to Ensure You're Leading with Integrity," *Delphinium* (www.delphiniumcc.co.uk), October 10, 2022, 1–4.

# Chapter Notes

## Chapter 9

1. Adapted but not quoted from E-Coach Associates, "Why Is 'Having Gravitas' Often Difficult for Certain Strong and Capable to Achieve, and Too Easy for Others to Fake?" *QWIKCOACH* (www.quickcoach.com), March 3, 2017, 2.

2. "Improve Your Gravitas and Perception," www.growcfo.net, April 11, 2023, 2.

3. "Motivate by Telling Staffers Yes," *Manager's Edge*, May 2007, 4.

4. B. Parker Ellen III, Gerald R. Ferris, and M. Ronald Buckley, "Leader Political Support: Reconsidering Leader political Behavior," *The Leadership Quarterly*, December 2013, 842–857.

5. Pamela L. Perrewé et al., "Political Skill: An Antidote to Workplace Stressors," *Academy of Management Executive*, August 2000, 115.

6. Suzzette M. Chopin, Steven J. Danish, Anson Seers, and Joshua N. Hook, "Effects of Mentoring on the Development of Leadership Self-Efficacy and Political Skill," *Journal of Leadership Studies*, Issue 3, 2013, 17–32.

7. Brian W. Swider, T. Brad Harris, and Qing Gong, "First Impression Effects in Organizational Psychology," *Journal of Applied Psychology*, March 2022, 346–369.

8. Cited in Susan Ricker, "Make Your Boss, Yourself Look Good," CareerBuilder.com, October 26, 2014, 1.

9. "Personalize Your Management Style," *Manager's Edge*, June 2007, 3.

10. Quoted in Amy Joyce, "Schmoozing on the Job Pays Dividends," *The Washington Post*, November 13, 2005.

11. Matt Rosoff, "The Two Words Your Boss Never Wants to Hear from You," *CNBC*, May 27, 2013, 1.

12. Rebecca Knight, "To Boost Your Career, Get to Know Your Boss's Boss," *Harvard Business Review*, September 15, 2016, 1.

13. Jack Kelly, "Remote Workers Are Overlooked for Promotion and Raises—Here's How You Can Get Noticed," *Forbes*, January 17, 2024, 1–4.

14. Nancy B. Kurland and Lisa Hope Pelled, "Passing the Word: Toward a Model of Gossip and Power in the Workplace," *Academy of Management Review*, April 2000, 429.

15. Original story based on the following sources: Chris Morris, "UPS Strike Update: 7 Things to Know About CEO Carol Tomé," *Fast Company*, July 25, 2023, 1–5; Maria Saporta, "Carol Tomé on Becoming CEO of UPS: 'This Was My Calling,'" *Saporta Report* (https://saportareport.com), March 8, 2021, 1–6; Aaron Pressman, "New UPS CEO Carol Tomé on Coming Out of Retirement and What It Takes to Handle 21.1 Million Packages a Day—During a Pandemic," *Fortune*, October 19, 2020, 1–7; "Carol B. Tomé: UPS Chief Executive Officer," UPS Stories (https://stories.ups.com), 2021, 1; Paul Ziobro, "This UPS CEO Preaches the Power of No," *The Wall Street Journal*, February 27–28, 2021, B1, B8; Tatyana Shumsky, "Home Depot CFO to Retire After 18-Year Tenure," *The Wall Street Journal*, April 30, 2019.

16. Carlin Flora, "The Art of Influence," *Psychology Today*, September/October 2011, 68–69.

17. Matt Abrahams, "How to Shine When You're Put on the Spot," *Harvard Business Review*, September–October 2023, 139–143.

## Chapter 10

1. Tim McClintock, "Dealing with Difficult People," *Projects@Work* (www.projectsatwork.com), November 17, 2008, 1.

2. Tessa West, "How to Deal with the Office Jerk," *The Wall Street Journal*, February 22, 2022, R8.

3. Ludmila N. Praslova, Ron Carucci, and Caroline Stokes, "What to Do When a Direct Report Is Bullying You," *Harvard Business Review*, December 8, 2022, 1–10.

4. Paul Falcone, "Welcome Back Disgruntled Workers," *HR Magazine*, February 2001, 133.

5. Leslie Gaines-Ross, "Offices Can Be Bastions of Civility in an Uncivil Time," *Harvard Business Review*, July 14, 2017,

2; "Why We Need to Kick Incivility Out of the Office," (Interview with Christine Porath, *Knowledge@Wharton* (https://knowledgewharton.upenn.edu), June 20, 2017, 1–3.

6. David D. Walker, Danielle D. van Jaarsveld, and Daniel P. Skarlicki, "Sticks and Stones Can Break My Bones but Words Can Also Hurt Me: The Relationship Between Customer Verbal Aggression and Employee Incivility," *Journal of Applied Psychology*, February 2017, 163–179.

7. "Tame Team Tigers: How to Handle Difficult Personalities," *Manager's Edge*, Special Issue 2008, 8.

8. John Grossman, "The Long Odds of Reforming an Employee Who Is a 'Destructive Hero,'" *The New York Times*, October 29, 2014, 1–4.

9. Art Petty, "The 'Brilliant Jerk' Dilemma and Why So Many Managers Get It Wrong," *SmartBrief*, May 27, 2021, 1.

10. James W. Dean Jr., Pamela Brandes, and Ravi Dharwadkar, "Organizational Cynicism," *Academy of Management Review*, April 1998, 341–352.

11. "Pepper ... and Salt," *The Wall Street Journal*, April 5, 2016, B10.

12. Paul Sonne, "Hayward Fell Short of Modern CEO Demands," *The Wall Street Journal*, July 26, 2010, A7.

13. Robin J. Ely, Debra Meyerson, and Martin N. Davidson, "Rethinking Political Correctness," *Harvard Business Review*, September 2006, 80.

14. Cited in Sue Shellenbarger, "Ovulating? Depressed? The Latest Rules on What Not to Talk About at Work," *The Wall Street Journal*, July 21, 2005, D1.

15. Sue Shellenbarger, "Office Oversharers: Don't Tell Us about Last Night," *The Wall Street Journal*, June 25, 2014, D2.

16. Katherine A. DeCelles et al., "Does Power Corrupt or Enable? When and Why Power Facilitates Self-Interested Behavior," *Journal of Applied Psychology*, May 2012, 681–689.

17. "Executive Presence's Key Building Block, Gravitas," *Origin Bluy* (www.originbluy), 2023, 2.

18. "Leaders as Learners: Humility Is at the Heart of Great Leadership," (Interview with Paulette Ashlin), www.globalgirlproject.org, October 28, 2014, 2.

19. Emily Grijalva et al., "Narcissism and Leadership: A Meta-Analytic Review of Linear and Nonlinear Relationships," *Personnel Psychology*, no. 1, 2015, 1–47.

20. Charles A. O'Reilly III, Bernadette Doerr, and Jennifer A. Chatman, "'See You in Court': How CEO Narcissism Increases Firms' Vulnerability to Lawsuits," *The Leadership Quarterly*, June 2018, 365–378.

21. Charles A. O'Reilly III et al., "Narcissistic CEOs and Executive Compensation," *The Leadership Quarterly*, April 2014, 219.

22. Dan Ciampa, "When Charismatic Leadership Goes Too Far," *Harvard Business Review*, November 21, 2016, 4.

# Bibliography

Abrahams, Matt. "How to Shine When You're Put on the Spot." *Harvard Business Review*, September–October 2023, 139–143.

Adamson, Brent. "Sensemaking for Sales." *Harvard Business Review*, January–February 2022, 122–129.

Ahrendts, Angela. "SVP, Retail, Apple." *Forbes*, 2023.

Amos, Daniel P. "Aflac's CEO Explains How He Fell for the Duck." *Harvard Business Review*, January–February 2010, 131–133.

Amster, Robin. "9 Tips to Help You Strengthen Your Integrity." *Success*, updated March 1, 2021, 3–4.

"Andy Jassy, President and Chief Executive Officer." Amazon Investor Relations. www.ir.aboutamazon.com. 2023.

Atlantic Council Experts, "The Big Questions (and Answers) About Ajay Banga's Nomination to Lead the World Bank." Atlantic Council, February 23, 2023, 1–3.

Baer, Justin. "Bond Star Pimco Tries to Change Its Culture." *The Wall Street Journal*, April 19, 2021, B1, B9.

Baldoni, John. "Why I Cheerlead for Those I Coach." *SmartBrief*, June 12, 2024, 1–3.

Balkundi, P., M. Kilduff, and D.A. Harrison. "Centrality and Charisma: Comparing How Leader Networks and Attributions Affect Team Performance." *Journal of Applied Psychology*, June 2011, 1209–1222.

Barari, Anwesha. "What Is Executive Presence: The Leadership Quality No One Told You About." *Emeritus*, July 15, 2022, 6.

Barrabi, Thomas. "Kim Kardashian Hires Ex-Apple Retail Boss Angela Ahrendts for Private Equity Firm." *New York Post*, August 7, 2023.

Bartiromo, Maria. "Entrepreneur Lives the Dream: Chobani's Ulukaya Created Greek Yogurt Craze." *USA Today*, June 18, 2013.

Bass, Dina. "Beyond Windows." *Bloomberg Businessweek*, February 23–March 1, 2015, 30–31.

Bates, Suzanne. "The Wow Factor." May 2019. Website no longer available.

Becker, Thomas E. "Integrity in Organizations: Beyond Honesty and Conscientiousness." *Academy of Management Review*, January 1998, 154–161.

Bennis, Warren. "Acting the Part of a Leader." *Business Week*, September 19, 2009, 80.

Bharanitharan, Darren K., et al. "Seeing Is Not Believing: Leader Humility, Hypocrisy, and the Impact on Followers' Behaviors." *The Leadership Quarterly*, April 2021, 1–16 (101440).

Bing, Lisa. "Big-Picture Mentality: How to Develop Strategic Leadership Skills." www.blackenterprise.com, July 26, 2013.

Blair, James. "How's Your Presence? Prominence and Gravitas in Comms Explained." The Comms Guru, June 30, 2021.

Boothby, Erica. "A Simple Compliment Can Make a Big Difference." *Harvard Business Review*, February 24, 2021, 1–5.

Bourke, Juliet, and Andrea Titus. "The Key to Inclusive Leadership." *Harvard Business Review*, March 8, 2020, 1–5.

"Brian Chesky: CEO and Cofounder Airbnb." *Forbes*, 2023.

Brock, David. "Strategic Thinking: Getting the Big Picture." http://partners inexcellenceblog.com, August 30, 2011, 1–2.

Buckingham, Marcus, and Ashley Goodall. "The Feedback Fallacy." *Harvard Business Review*, March–April 2019, 92–101.

Burgis, Neal. "Importance of Humility in Your Leadership." www.successful-solutions.com, February 29, 2019, 1.

Calheiros, Sofia. "Executive Presence: The Elements of Leadership Material." *Best of Us* (www.blog.sofiacalheiros), March 4, 2017, 1.

"Carol B. Tomé: UPS Chief Executive Officer." UPS Stories (https://stories.ups.com), 2021, 1.

Chang, Yingyi, and Jose M. Cortina. "What Should I Wear to Work? An Integrative Review of the Impact of Clothing in the Workplace." *Journal of Applied Psychology*, May 2024, 755–778.

Chappelow, Craig, and Cindy McCauley. "What Good Feedback Really Looks Like." *Harvard Business Review*, May 13, 2019, 1–3.

Chopin, Suzzette M., Steven J. Danish, Anson Seers, and Joshua N. Hook. "Effects of Mentoring on the Development of Leadership Self-Efficacy and Political Skill." *Journal of Leadership Studies*, Issue 3, 2013, 17–32.

Ciampa, Dan. "When Charismatic Leadership Goes Too Far." *Harvard Business Review*, November 21, 2016, 4.

Citroën, Lida. "'Gravitas' in Leadership: What It Is, Why It Matters and How to Get It." Military.com, 2023.

Clendaniel, Morgan. "The Ascent of Sara Nelson." *Fast Company*, Summer 2021, 44–45.

Cohen, Arianne. "What I Wear to Work: Sonja Lyubomirsky." *Bloomberg Businessweek*, January 12–18, 2015, 71.

Cole, Bill. "Peak Performance in the Workplace: The New Corporate Ethic." www.mentalgamecoach.com, 2023, 1–9.

Collier, Lindsay. Personal communication in years past.

Combe, Ian, and David J. Carrington, "Leaders' Sensemaking Under Crises: Emerging Cognitive Consensus Over Time Within Management Teams." *The Leadership Quarterly*, June 2015, 307–322.

Confino, Paolo. "New CNN CEO Mark Thompson Once Rescued the New York Times from the End of Newspapers. Can He Do the Same with CNN as Cable TV Dies?" *Yahoo! Finance*, August 30, 2023, 1–4.

Conger, Jay A., and Rabindra Kanungo. *Charismatic Leadership in Organizations.* Thousand Oaks, CA: SAGE Publications, 1998.

"A Conversation with Ron Wallace: From UPS Driver to President." *Executive Leadership*, September 2016, 3.

Cooper, Laura. "Kardashian's Private-Equity Firm Hires Ex-Apple, Burberry Executive." *The Wall Street Journal*, August 8, 2023.

Craft, Dan. "Leadership Insights: Lessons from Walmart CEO Doug McMillon." *Doing Business in Bentonville* (www.dbbnwa.com), July 11, 2023, 1–2.

Daskal, Lolly. "How to Coach a Struggling Employee." www.lollydaskal.com, January 23, 2020, 1.

Dean, James W., Jr., Pamela Brandes, and Ravi Dharwadkar, "Organizational Cynicism." *Academy of Management Review*, April 1998, 341–352.

DeCelles, Katherine, et al. "Does Power Corrupt or Enable? When and Why Power Facilitates Self-Interested Behavior." *Journal of Applied Psychology*, May 2012, 681–689.

DeGroot, Timothy, et al., Federico Aime, Scott G. Johnson, and Donald Kluemper. "Does Talking the Talk Help Walking the Walk? An Examination of the Effect of Global Attractiveness in Leader Effectiveness." *The Leadership Quarterly*, August 2011, 680–689.

della Cava, Marco. "Nadella Counts on Culture Shock to Drive Microsoft Growth." *USA Today*, February 20, 2017, 4B.

Dixit, Ankita. "Bond Giant Pimco Attempts to Change Its Culture." *Postin-Trend* (https://postintrend.com), April 17, 2021, 1–3.

# Bibliography

"Doug McMillon, President and CEO Walmart." *Business Roundtable*, 2024.

DuBrin, Andrew J. "Personal Attributes and Behaviors of Effective Crisis Leaders." In *Handbook of Research on Crisis Leadership in Organizations*, edited by Andrew J. DuBrin. Cheltenham, UK: Edward Elgar, 2013.

Duckworth, Angela. *Grit: The Power of Passion and Perseverance.* New York: Scribner's, 2016.

Duckworth, Angela, et al. "Grit, Perseverance and Passion for Long-Term Goals." *Journal of Personality and Social Psychology*, No. 6, 2007, 1087–1101.

Dutton, Jane, et al. "Leading in Times of Trauma." *Harvard Business Review*, Summer 2020, 38.

E-Coach Associates, "Ignored by People You Want to Impress? Understand and Develop Gravitas!" *QWIKCOACH* (www.quikcoach.com), March 31, 2017.

E-Coach Associates, "Why Is 'Having Gravitas' Often Difficult for Certain Strong and Capable to Achieve, and Too Easy for Others to Fake?" *QWIK-COACH* (www.quickcoach.com), March 3, 2017, 2.

Ellen, B. Parker, III, Gerald R. Ferris, and M. Ronald Buckley. "Leader Political Support: Reconsidering Leader Political Behavior." *The Leadership Quarterly*, December 2013, 842–857.

Ely, Robin J., Debra Meyerson, and Martin N. Davidson. "Rethinking Political Correctness." *Harvard Business Review*, September 2006, 80.

"Emmanuel Roman, '87: Chief Executive Officer PIMCO." Chicago Booth (www.chicagobooth.edu), 2021, 1–2.

Erez, Amir, Vilmost Misangyi, Diane E. Johnson, Marcie A. LePine, and Kent C. Halverson, "Stirring the Hearts of Followers: Charismatic Leadership as the Transferal of Affect." *Journal of Applied Psychology*, May 2008, 602–613.

Estrada, Sheryl. "The Longest-Tenured Woman CEO in the Fortune 500 Makes the Case for Sticking Around for 10+ Years at a Brand You Love." *Fortune*, October 11, 2023, 1–6.

"Executive Presence's Key Building Block, Gravitas." *Origin Bluy* (www.originbluy), 2023, 2.

Falcone, Paul. "Welcome Back Disgruntled Workers." *HR Magazine*, February 2001, 133.

Feintzeig, Rachel. "Want Power? Stop Saying Sorry So Much." *The Wall Street Journal*, October 24, 2022, A11.

"The 50 Most Powerful Women: 2, Julie Sweet. Chair and CEO, Accenture." *Fortune*, October/November 2022, 67.

Flora, Carlin. "The Art of Influence." *Psychology Today*, September/October 2011, 68–69.

Flunder, Justin. "How Important Is Humility in Leadership?" *Country Sunrise News*, April 24, 2014, 2.

"Functions of Workplace Anger in Organizational Life." *Academy of Management Perspectives*, February 2020, 28–47.

Gaines-Ross, Leslie. "Offices Can Be Bastions of Civility in an Uncivil Time." *Harvard Business Review*, July 14, 2017, 2.

Garfield, Charles. *Peak Performers: The New Heroes of American Business.* New York: Avon Books, 1987.

Geddes, Deanna, Ronda Roberts Callister, and Donald E. Gibson. "A Message in Madness: Functions of Workplace Anger in Organizational Life." *Academy of Management Perspectives*, February 2020, 28–47.

Gelles, David. "The Chief of CVS Health Wants to Be Part of People's 'Everyday Life.'" *The New York Times*, January 12, 2022, 1–13.

Gelles, David. "Julie Sweet of Accenture Could See Her Future, So She Quit Her Job." *The New York Times*, January 2, 2019, 1–6.

Gibson, Kerry Roberts. "The Little Things That Make Employees Feel Appreciated." *Harvard Business Review*, July 23, 2020, 1–7.

Golbeck, Amanda L., Ingram Olkin, and Yulia R. Gel, eds. *Leadership and Women in Statistics.* London: CRC Press, 2015.

Goleman, Daniel, Richard Boyatzis, and Annie McKee. "Primal Leadership:

The Hidden Driver of Great Performance." *Harvard Business Review*, December 2001, 52–61.

Gorman, Carol Kinsey. "Project a More Powerful Image at Work." American Management Association, March 25, 2019, 1–5.

Gothelf, Jeff. "Storytelling Can Make or Break Your Leadership." *Harvard Business Review*, October 19, 2020, 4.

"Gravitas Leadership, Discovering this Little Known but Very Important Quality." *Share* (www.share-coach.com), 2024, 2.

"Gravitas Leadership Information." Gravitas Leadership. www.gravitas-leadership.com. 2021.

"The Gravitas Trap." Ariel Group. www.arielgroup.com. 2023.

Greenleaf, Robert K. *Servant Leadership: A Journey into the Nature of Legitimate Power and Greatness*. Mahwah, NJ: Paulist Press, 1997.

Greer, Mark. "The Science of Savoir Faire." *Psychology Today*, January 25, 2005, 28–39.

Grijalva, Emily, et al. "Narcissism and Leadership: A Meta-Analytic Review of Linear and Nonlinear Relationships." *Personnel Psychology*, no. 1, 2015, 1–47.

Grossman, John. "The Long Odds of Reforming an Employee Who Is a 'Destructive Hero.'" *The New York Times*, October 29, 2014, 1–4.

"Gruber Distinguished Lecturer in Women's Right: Sara Nelson." Yale Law School, 2023, 1–2.

Hay, Richard. "Satya Nadella Lays Out New Mission and Vision for Microsoft." *SuperSite Windows* (http://winsupersite.com), June 25, 2014, 1–4.

Henderson, Antoinette Dale. "Gravitas: How to Command Respect and Get Promoted." *The Treasurer Magazine*, 2022.

Henderson, Antoinette Dale. "Leading with Gravitas: Unlock the Six Keys to Impact and Influence." www.antionettehenderson.com, 2024, 1.

Hewlett, Sylvia Ann. "Center for Talent Innovation, 2013." In Jen Baggett, "Gravitas: The Heart of Executive Presence." Catchlight Consulting, LLC. www.wecatchlight.com. July 30, 2018.

Hewlett, Sylvia Ann. "Executive Presence." Thrive Street Advisors (www.thrivestreetzdvisors.com), 2023, 1–2.

Hewlett, Sylvia Ann. "The New Rules of Executive Presence." *Harvard Business Review*, January–February 2024, 134–139.

Hinchliffe, Emma. "In Focus: Laura Alber." *Fortune*, December 2023/January 2024, 14–17.

Hogan, Robert. Cited in Neal Burgis, "Importance of Humility in Your Leadership." www.successful-solutions.com, February 29, 2019, 1.

"How Fortune's Most Powerful Woman in Business Is Helping Shape the World for the Better." Accenture, November 5, 2020, 1–2.

"How to Cultivate Gravitas." dorothydalton.com, March 20, 2016.

Hughes, David J., et al. "Leadership, Creativity, and Innovation: A Critical Review and Practical Recommendations." *The Leadership Quarterly*, October 2018, 549–569.

"Improve Your Gravitas and Perception." Grow CFO (www.growcfo.net), April 11, 2023, 2.

"Is Your Executive Presence and Gravitas Preventing You from Getting Ahead?" www.businesscoaching.co.uk, 2009–2023, 1.

Jackson, Chris. "Transformational Leadership and Gravitas: 2000 Years of No Development?" *Personality and Individual Differences*, April 1, 2020.

James, Erika Hayes, and Lynn Perry Wooten. "How to Display Competence in Times of Crisis." *Organizational Dynamics*, Vol. 34, no. 2, 2005.

Johnson, Jess. "Humility in Leadership: Battling the Vices of Pride." *Crowdstaffing* (www.crowdstaffing.com), May 1, 2018, 3.

Joyce, Amy. "Schmoozing on the Job Pays Dividends." *The Washington Post*, November 13, 2005.

"Julie Sweet." *Forbes*, October 20, 2020, 1–13.

"Julie Sweet, Chief Executive Officer." Accenture, 2021, 1.

# Bibliography

"Juniper Values." Juniper Networks (www.juniper.net), 2024, 1.

Kanter, Jake. "Mark Thompson Named Chairman and CEO of CNN—Update." *DEADLINE*, September 1, 2023, 1–7.

Kantrowitz, Alex. "Running Amazon Became a Lot Less Fun Once Jeff Bezos Left." *Slate*, June 18, 2023.

"Karen S. Lynch, President and Chief Executive Officer." CVS Health, 2023, 1–2.

Karlgaard, Rich. "'Let There Be Change' Says Accenture's Trail-Blazing Chief Executive." *Forbes*, October 20, 2020, 1–13.

Kelly, Jack. "Remote Workers Are Overlooked for Promotion and Raises—Here's How You Can Get Noticed." *Forbes*, January 17, 2024, 1–4.

Kets de Vries, Manfred F.R. "Beyond Narcissism: How Leaders Can Avoid the Hubris Trap." INSEAD Knowledge. March 12, 2024, 1–3.

Kets de Vries, Manfred F.R. "Finding Gravitas." INSEAD Knowledge. September 9, 2015.

Khelifi, Yasmina, and Irina Cozma. "How to Be Direct Without Being Rude." *Harvard Business Review*, July 31, 2023, 3.

Kirkland, Rik. "Wharton's Adam Grant on the Key to Professional Success." McKinsey & Company, June 2014, 3.

Kirschner, Jeff. "Humility and Leadership." RHR International (www.rhrinternational), October 30, 2018, 1–2.

Knight, Rebecca. "To Boost Your Career, Get to Know Your Boss's Boss." *Harvard Business Review*, September 15, 2016, 1.

Knippen, Jay T., and Thad B. Green. "Building Self-Confidence." *Supervisory Management*, August 1989, 22–27.

Kovar, Joseph F. "Accenture C EO Julie Sweet: IT Growth to Exceed Macro Impacts." *CRN*, December 16, 2022, 1–5.

Kurland, Nancy B., and Lisa Hope Pelled. "Passing the Word: Toward a Model of Gossip and Power in the Workplace." *Academy of Management Review*, April 2000, 429.

Kytle, Rachel. "Can this Former CEO Fix the World Bank?" *Fast Company*, May 5, 2023, 1–4.

Landrau, Carmen W. "Six Key Elements of Gravitas." drlandrau.com. 2023, 1–2.

Lawder, David. "World Bank's New Chief Asks Staff to 'Double Down' on Development, Climate Efforts." *Reuters*, June 2, 2023, 1–4.

"Leaders as Learners: Humility Is at the Heart of Great Leadership." (Interview with Paulette Ashlin), www.globalgirldproject.org. October 28, 2014, 2.

Leaf, Clifton (interview). "The Conversation: Ajay Banga." *Fortune*, December 2020/January 2021, 10–14.

Lee, Hun Whee, et al. "The Benefits of Receiving Gratitude for Helpers: A Daily Investigation of Proactive and Reactive Helping at Work." *Journal of Applied Psychology*, February 2019, 197–213.

Levine, Deb. "Solutions: Advice from HR Knowledge Advisors." *HR Magazine*, October 2013, 18.

Liden, Robert C., et. al. "Servant Leadership: Development of a Multidimensional Measure and Multi-Level Assessment." *The Leadership Quarterly*, April 2008, 161–177.

Lochhead, Christopher. "3 Lessons in Humble Leadership from Four-Star General Stanley McChrystal." growwire.com, October 10, 2018, 1–2.

Locklear, Lauren R. "How a Gratitude Intervention Influences Workplace Mistreatment: A Multiple Mediation Model." *Journal of Applied Psychology*, September 2021, 1314–1331.

London, Manuel. *Principled Leadership and Business Diplomacy: Value-Based Strategies for Management Development*. Westport, CT: Quorum Books, 1999.

Luthans, Fred, James R. Avey, and Jaime L. Patera. "Experimental Analysis of a Web Based Training Intervention to Develop Positive Psychological Capital." *Academy of Management Learning & Education*, June 2008, 209–221.

Mack, Sonja D. "Sara Mensah: Chief

# Bibliography

Operating Officer & Chief Marketing Officer, Portland Trailblazers." *Black Enterprise*, February 2011, 106.

Mathis, Laura. "Five Strategies to Demonstrate Gravitas." The Speech Improvement Company, 2023.

Mayer, John D. "Leading by Feel: Train the Gifted." *Harvard Business Review*, January 2004, 31.

McClintock, Tim. "Dealing with Difficult People." *Projects@Work* (www.projectsatwork.com). November 17, 2008, 1.

McCraken, Harry. "Satya Nadella Rewrites Microsoft's Code." *Fast Company*, September 18, 2017, 52–53.

McKechnie, Ian. "Six Tips to Develop your 'Gravitas.'" www.linkedin.com. November 11, 2019, 2.

"MiDLABS (Medical Instrument Development Laboratories, Inc.)." July 29, 2016.

Morris, Chris. "UPS Strike Update: 7 Things to Know About CEO Carol Tomé." *Fast Company*, July 25, 2023, 1–5.

"Most Powerful Women 2022: 1, Karen Lynch, President and CEO, CVS Health." *Fortune*, October/November 2022, 65–7.

"Motivate by Telling Staffers Yes." *Manager's Edge*, May 2007, 4.

Neitlich, Andrew. "Coaching vs. Consulting: Find the Right Balance to Get Buy-in and Results." www.clomedia.com. August 4, 2016, 2.

Newton, Rebecca. "Leadership Gravitas Is a Quality You Can Develop." *Harvard Business Review*, September 24, 2020, 4.

Norman, Matt. "5 Ways Humble Leaders Put Others in the Spotlight." www.mattnorman.com. June 20, 2018, 1–3.

Nugent, Patrick S. "Managing Conflict: Third-Party Interventions for Managers." *Academy of Management Executive*, February 2002, 152.

O'Connell, Brian. "Lead with Humility." *HR Magazine*, Winter 2021, 83.

O'Leary, Kate, and Joseph Weintraub. "The Little Things That Make Employees Feel Appreciated." *Harvard Business Review*, July 23, 2020, 1–7.

Om, Akshay. "Satya Nadella, Microsoft, Compassion, and Goddess Kamakshi." *Medium*, April 24, 2023, 1–10.

O'Reilly, Charles A., III, Bernadette Doerr, and Jennifer A. Chatman. "'See You in Court': How CEO Narcissism Increases Firms' Vulnerability to Lawsuits." *The Leadership Quarterly*, June 2018, 365–378.

Ovide, Shira. "The Quiet Evolution at Microsoft's Office." *The Wall Street Journal*, September 30, 2015, B6.

Owens, Bradley P., and David R. Hekman. "Modeling How to Grow: An Inductive Examination of Humble Leader Behaviors, Contingencies, and Outcomes." *Academy of Management Journal*, August 2012, 787–818.

Owens, Donna M. "Incivility Rising: Researchers Say Workers Might Not Have the Time to Be Civil." *Human Resource Management*, February 2012, 33.

Palmer, Annie. "Amazon CEO Jassy's Cost Cuts Deliver Investors Biggest Profit Beat Since 2020." *CNBC*, August 3, 2023.

Patel, Nilay. "Airbnb CEO Brian Chesky on Taking It Back to Basics." *The Verge*, May 9, 2023.

Pearson, Christine M., and Christine Porath. "On the Nature, Consequences and Remedies of Workplace Incivility: No Time for 'Nice'? Think Again." *Academy of Management Executive*, February 2005, 7–18.

"Pepper ... and Salt." *The Wall Street Journal*, April 5, 2016, B10.

Perlman, Stacy. "The Secret Sauce at In-N-Out Burger" (Book Excerpt). *Business Week*, April 20, 2009, 68–69.

Perrewé, Pamela, et al. "Political Skill: An Antidote to Workplace Stressors." *Academy of Management Executive*, August 2000, 115.

"Personalize Your Management Style." *Manager's Edge*, June 2007, 3.

Petty, Art. "The 'Brilliant Jerk' Dilemma and Why So Many Managers Get It Wrong." *SmartBrief*, May 27, 2021, 1.

Praslova, Ludmila N., Ron Carucci, and Caroline Stokes. "What to Do When a Direct Report Is Bullying You." *Harvard*

# Bibliography

*Business Review*, December 8, 2022, 1–10.

"Present with Panache." *Manager's Edge*, June 2007, 8.

Pressman, Aaron. "New UPS CEO Carol Tomé on Coming Out of Retirement and What It Takes to Handle 21.1 Million Packages a Day—During a Pandemic." *Fortune*, October 19, 2020, 1–7.

Qin, Xin, et al. "The Double-Edge Sword of Lader Humility: Investigating When and Why Leader Humility Promotes Versus Inhibits Subordinate Deviance." *Journal of Applied Psychology*, July 2020, 693–712.

Razeghi, Andrew. "Innovation: Vehicle to Greatness." *Executive Leadership*, December 2011, 3.

"Rehearse for Stressful Events." www.healthylifestyle.com, 2019, 1.

Ricker, Susan. "Make Your Boss, Yourself Look Good." www.CareerBuilder.com, October 26, 2014.

Rodgers, Ellison Joann. "Go Forth in Anger." *Psychology Today*, April 2014, 72–79.

Romeo, Peter. "Employees Say In-N-Out is the Best Workplace in the Restaurant Business." Restaurant Business (www.restaurant-businessonline.com), January 12, 2021.

Romig, Dennis A. *Side by Side Leadership: Achieving Outstanding Results Together.* Marietta GA: Bard Press, 2001.

Rosoff, Matt. "The Two Words Your Boss Never Wants to Hear from You." *CNBC*, May 27, 2013.

Rozek, Michael. "Can You Spot a Peak Performer?" *Personnel Journal*, June 1991, 77–78.

Rudolph, Cort. W., et al. "A Systematic and Critical Review of Research on Respect in Leadership." *The Leadership Quarterly*, February 2021, 1–15 (101492).

Saporta, Maria. "Carol Tomé on Becoming CEO of UPS: 'This Was My Calling.'" *Saporta Report*, March 8, 2021, 1–6.

"Sara Nelson, International President, Association of Flight Attendants-CWA, AFL-CIO." afcacwa.org, 2023.

Sauer, Megan. "Airbnb CEO Shares the Best Advice He's Ever Received—It's Counterintuitive to Almost Everything Everyone Says." *CNBC*, May 24, 2023.

Schinkel, Mark. "9 Tips for Leading with Integrity." Achieve Centre for Leadership, 2024.

Scott, Brent A., and Timothy A. Judge. "The Popularity Contest at Work: Who Wins, Why, and What Do They Receive?" *Journal of Applied Psychology*, January 2009, 20–33.

"Seeing the Big Picture." Posted in *Being in Business* (www.theparadigmshifts.com), April 15, 2012, 2–3.

Seidman, Dov. "Angela Ahrendts DBE." The How Institute for Society, 2023.

Shellenbarger, Sue. "Office Oversharers: Don't Tell Us About Last Night." *The Wall Street Journal*, June 25, 2014, D2.

Shellenbarger, Sue. "Ovulating? Depressed? The Latest Rules on What Not to Talk About at Work." *The Wall Street Journal*, July 21, 2005, D1.

Sherman, Rose O. "The Importance of Executive Presence." *American Nurse Today*, May 2015, 1–2.

Shumsky, Tatyana. "Home Depot CFO to Retire After 18-Year Tenure." *The Wall Street Journal*, April 30, 2019.

Sidel, Robin. "Banga to Be MasterCard's Protector." *The Wall Street Journal*, May 29–30, 2010, B1.

"6 Tips to Ensure You're Leading with Integrity." *Delphinium* (www.delphiniumcc.co.uk), October 10, 2022, 1–4.

Smagala, Tina. "Giving Effective Feedback on the Fl." *Democrat and Chronicle*, May 28, 2013, 5B.

Smale, Thomas. "5 Steps to Build Your Personal Brand." *Entrepreneur*, September 25, 2015.

Smith, Ray A. "How to Boost Your E-Charisma." *The Wall Street Journal*, November 30, 2020, A11.

Solomon, Eric. "Stop Talking about Empathy and Start Acting on It." *Entrepreneur*, September 2020, 60.

Sonne, Paul. "Hayward Fell Short of Modern CEO Demands." *The Wall Street Journal*, July 26, 2010, A7.

Standfield, Justin. "Stop Telling People

They Need More Gravitas." *Incendo* (www.incendo-uk-com), 2024, 2.

Stoll, John D. "Feel the Force: Gut Instinct, Not Data Is the Thing." *The Wall Street Journal*, October 19–20, 2019, B4.

"The Success Story of C. Douglas McMillon, the President and Chief Executive Officer of Walmart." Prime Insights (www.primeinsights.com), October 5, 2023, 1–8.

Swartz, Jefferson, and Jon Swartz. "After 5 Years of Cook, More Cash, Less Splash." *USA Today*, August 24, 2015, 4B.

Swider, Brian W., T. Brad Harris, and Qing Gong. "First Impression Effects in Organizational Psychology." *Journal of Applied Psychology*, March 2022, 346–369.

Sy, Thomas, Calen Horton, and Ronald Riggio. "Charismatic Leadership: Eliciting and Channeling Follower Emotion." *The Leadership Quarterly*, February 2018, 58–69.

"Tame Team Tigers: How to Handle Difficult Personalities." *Manager's Edge*, Special Issue 2008, 8.

Taylor, Shannon G., and Maureen L. Ambrose. "How a Gratitude Intervention Influences Workplace Mistreatment: A Multiple Mediation Model." *Journal of Applied Psychology*, September 2021, 1314–1331.

Thomas, Jennifer. "Motivating Workers." *HR Magazine*, Summer 2020, 82.

Thomaselli, Rich. "Sara Nelson Re-Elected as Flight Attendant Union President." *Travel Pulse*, May 17, 2022.

Toegel, Ginka, and Jean-Louis Barsoux. "How to Preempt Team Conflict." *Harvard Business Review*, June 2016, 78–83.

Torres, Nicole. "Defend Your Research: Fast Thinkers Are More Charismatic." *Harvard Business Review*, March 2016, 28–29.

Tredgold, Gordon. "What Leadership Style Is the Best in Motivating Your Employees During a Pandemic?" gordontredgold.com, 2021.

Tully, Shawn. "Fortune Most Powerful Women: Karen Lynch, 58." CVS Health, October/November 2021, 60–66.

Valentine, Gerry. "Executive Presence: What It Is, and Why You Need It." *Forbes*, December 10, 2021, 1.

Wahba, Phil, "Walmart's Mr. Fix-It." *Fortune*, June/July 2024, 74–79.

Walker, David W., Danielle D. van Jaarsveld, and Daniel P. Skarlicki. "Sticks and Stones Can Break My Bones but Words Can Also Hurt Me: The Relationship Between Customer Verbal Aggression and Employee Incivility." *Journal of Applied Psychology*, February 2017, 163–179.

Ward, Kathleen. "Unlocking the Power of Executive Gravitas: What It Is and How to Develop It." OATUU, June 5, 2023, 5.

Weber, Lauren. "One CEO's Hands-On Crisis Management." *The Wall Street Journal*, September 21, 2016, B8.

West, Tessa. "How to Deal with the Office Jerk." *The Wall Street Journal*, February 22, 2022, R8.

"What Is Big-Picture Thinking in Business?" Study.com, February 18, 2022.

"Which Buzzwords Would You Ban?" *The Wall Street Journal*, January 2, 2014, B4.

"Why We Need to Kick Incivility Out of the Office." (Interview with Christine Porath). knowledgewharton.upenn.edu, June 20, 2017, 1–3.

Wilson, Douglas A. "CEOs In Action: Manny Roman of PIMCO on How He Leads." www.douglaswilson.com, March 1, 2022.

Wollan, Malia. "How to Project Power." *New York Times Sunday Magazine*, August 9, 2015, 21.

"Workplace Mistreatment: A Multiple Mediation Model." *Journal of Applied Psychology*, September 2021, 1315.

Wright, Karen. "A Chic Critique." *Psychology Today*, March/April 2011, 59.

"Your 'Executive Presence' Needs a Second Look." Recover to Lead (www.recovertolead.com), May 20, 2012, 1.

Zandan, Noah, and Lisa Shalett. "What Inclusive Leaders Sound Like." *Harvard Business Review*, November 19, 2020, 1–7.

# Bibliography

Zhao, Xuan, and Vanessa K. Bohns. "A Simple Compliment Can Make a Big Difference." *Harvard Business Review*, February 24, 2021, 1–5.

Ziegler, Pauline. "How Leaders Earn Respect: 10 Proven Ways to Master in 2023." Best Diplomats (www.best diplomats.org), May 9, 2023, 1–7.

Ziobro, Paul. "This UPS CEO Preaches the Power of No." *The Wall Street Journal*, February 27–28, 2021, B1, B8.

# Index

**193**

# Index

hubris 95; humanism 101–103; meaning of 90; name remembering 98; persistence 97–98; personal brand for 97–98; propensity for risk taking 100; qualities developable 96–104; risk taking, sensible 99–101; romanticizing risk 94; storytelling 101; synchrony 98; trust and confidence inspiring 103–104; trust inspiring 93; vision creation 97; visionary characteristic 93

Chesky, Brian 16–17, 62

Ciampa, Dan 172

Citroën, Lida 7

civility 39, 143–144

Clairborne, Liz 8

clothing impact 113–114

CNN 22

coaching 45–46, 79–83; emotional support and empathy 82; feedback for improvement 81, 82; gentle advice and guidance 83; GROW model 79–80; obstacle removing 82; on-the-spot feedback 82; progress cheering 83; relationship building 80; working on solution together 82–83

cognitive skills 74–75

Collier, Lindsay 87

communications network center 38

communication skills: for charisma 93; for executive presence 109; for gravitas 50–53 (anecdotes to communicate meaning 51; business jargon 52; clear speaking 50; deep listening 50; language errors 52–53; vocal attractiveness 50)

components of gravitas (interpersonal) 2, 38–54; civility to develop allies 2; climate of respect 44; coaching and mentoring 45–46; communication network center 38–39; complaint minimizing 41; compliment giving 42; engaging communication skills 50–53; giving respect 44; high self-esteem 38; importance feelings form others 39–40; leading by example 44; listening 46; making people feel important quiz 40–41; nonverbal communication for 48–49; ownership of mistakes and failures 45; positive interaction with work associates 38–42; projecting power 47–50; respect earning 44; respectful negative feedback and criticism 44–45; self-esteem and 38–39

components of gravitas (self-related) 19–37; big-picture questions 34–35; big-picture thinking 32–34; courage 24–25; defined set of values 26–28; displaying through work 19–23; emotional intelligence 26; fixit person 22–23; grit 30–31; high-level skills and abilities 23; self-confidence and decisiveness 23–26; speaking truth to power 24; strategic thinking 32–34; tendencies toward big-picture thinking quiz 35–36; value clarification exercise 28; work attitudes quiz 19–20; work for displaying gravitas 19–23

conclusion backup 51

conflict resolution 84–85

Cook, Tom 122, 128

courage 24–25

courtesy 143, 148

Craft, Dan 92

creative and innovative thinking 74–77; cognitive skills 74–75; intuition 75–77

crisis leadership 14–15

cultural difference insensitivity 166

CVS Health 46–47

default response 155

Dell, Michael 48, 150

dependability 44

depth of personality 5

destructive hero or heroine 160

detractions from gravitas 158–173; blunder quiz 161–163; difficult person 158–161; flip flopping 169; gaslighting 159; humility overdoing 169–170; indecisiveness 168–169; narcissism excess 170–172; perfectionism 169; political blunders 161–167; positive narcissism checklist 170–171; power abusing 168

development of people 61

difficult persons 158–161; change resistors 160; destructive hero or heroine 160; disgruntled worker 159; office jerk 159; passive-aggressive worker 159–160; uncivil workers 160; workplace bully 159; workplace cynic 160

disgruntled worker 159

downside of gravitas 17–18

drama and uniqueness for charisma 94

dress code nonconformance 164

Duckworth, Angela, L. 30

e-charisma projection 99

Ellison, Larry 94

**194**

# Index

www.ingramcontent.com/pod-product-compliance
Lightning Source LLC
Chambersburg PA
CBHW022102210326
41518CB00039B/387